Praise for
Money Well Spent
by PAUL BREST AND HAL HARVEY

"Brest and Harvey have distilled the essence of strategic philanthropy into a highly accessible book. Their work will be an invaluable resource for those new to philanthropy and those seeking to achieve a greater social impact with their giving."

—BILL GATES
Cochair, Bill & Melinda Gates Foundation

"*Money Well Spent* is far and away the best 'handbook plus' for those who believe that philanthropic dollars are a sacred trust that should be administered according to the highest standards of stewardship. Many give fervent allegiance to the imperative of being focused, strategic, and attuned to measuring results in deploying such funds, but no other authors have produced so readable, sensible, and balanced a guide to the practice of strategy in solving real-world problems, informed by solid theory and illuminated by easy-to-understand examples. It's no surprise that this unique book is both so valuable and so likely to be useful; its coauthors have many years of rich experience in guiding the giving of one of America's great private foundations."

—JOEL L. FLEISHMAN
Author, *The Foundation: A Great American Secret*
Professor of Law and Public Policy Sciences, Terry
Sanford Institute of Public Policy, Duke University

"In philanthropy, as in investing, you need a solid strategy to understand what works, what fails, and why. *Money Well Spent* provides the tools philanthropists need to create an effective strategy and achieve success."

—GEORGE SOROS

"This is not a how-to-do-it book; rather, this book helps the reader *think* about how to do it. A rich combination of analytical power, excellent examples (including many of failed initiatives), and just plain common sense provide a wide variety of models of how to have an impact as a philanthropist. This is an ever-so-practical and yet ever-so-thoughtful contribution to our understanding of how philanthropy should work."

—WILLIAM G. BOWEN
Former President, The Andrew W. Mellon
Foundation and Princeton University

"For donors who want to think clearly about how to achieve their charitable objectives, reading this excellent guide to philanthropic strategy will be time well spent."

—ADAM MEYERSON
President, The Philanthropy Roundtable

"*Money Well Spent* is critical reading for anyone who wants to ensure that philanthropy is having a real and lasting impact on the most urgent challenges facing our world. Paul Brest and Hal Harvey present a clear and powerful roadmap for grantmakers committed to setting clear goals and achieving measurable results. In the process, they demonstrate that a clear strategy is one of the most important elements of effective philanthropy."

—LUIS UBIÑAS
President, Ford Foundation

MONEY
WELL
SPENT

MONEY WELL SPENT

A STRATEGIC PLAN *for* SMART PHILANTHROPY

Paul Brest

Hal Harvey

BLOOMBERG PRESS
NEW YORK

This publication contains the authors' opinions and is designed to provide accurate and authoritative information. It is sold with the understanding that the authors, publisher, and Bloomberg L.P. are not engaged in rendering legal, accounting, investment-planning, or other professional advice. The reader should seek the services of a qualified professional for such advice; the authors, publisher, and Bloomberg L.P. cannot be held responsible for any loss incurred as a result of specific investments or planning decisions made by the reader.

First edition published 2008

1 3 5 7 9 10 8 6 4 2

Library of Congress Cataloging-in-Publication Data

Brest, Paul.
    Money well spent : a strategic plan for smart philanthropy / Paul Brest, Hal Harvey.
       p. cm.
    Includes bibliographical references and index.
    Summary: "Starting with the premise that strategy makes all the difference in effective giving, the book shows foundations and individual philanthropists the best way to design a strategy to achieve their stated philanthropic goals. Drawing on examples from many different foundations, the authors give philanthropists the framework necessary to harness expert knowledge in various sectors"—Provided by publisher.
    ISBN 978-1-57660-312-3 (alk. paper)
   1. Nonprofit organizations—United States. 2. Philanthropists—Charitable contributions—United States. 3. Charities—United States. I. Harvey, Hal. II. Title.

HD2769.2.U6B74 2008
658.4'012—dc22

2008032637

*We dedicate this book (and its royalties) to
The William and Flora Hewlett Foundation, with
whose board and staff we have collaborated in
learning and practicing strategic philanthropy.*

Contents

Part I

The Framework of Strategic Philanthropy

Preface

EVEN BEFORE WARREN Buffett's $31 billion gift to the Bill & Melinda Gates Foundation garnered huge media attention, the twenty-first century was on its way to being the century of philanthropy. There are at least fifty U.S. foundations with assets over $1 billion; one hundred with assets over $500 million; and myriad foundations with assets over $1 million. Transfers of wealth by gift and bequest in the coming decades are forecast to increase greatly, with significant portions of this money going to philanthropy.

The recent growth of interest in philanthropy has been manifest in the creation of new organizations—including the Bridgespan Group, the Center for Effective Philanthropy, Grantmakers for Effective Organizations, and FSG Social Impact Advisors—to serve the sector. Duke, Harvard, Indiana University, Stanford, USC, and other institutions are building interdisciplinary research centers focusing on philanthropy and the not-for-profit sector. At the same time, several new books, most notably Joel Fleishman's *The Foundation: A Great American Secret; How Private Wealth Is Changing the World* (2007) and Peter Frumkin's *Strategic Giving: The Art and Science of Philanthropy* (2006), have explored different aspects of the topic.

Although these books provide rich historical, philosophical, and sociological perspectives, they are essentially about philanthropy rather than guides on how to design strategies to bring about results.

Money Well Spent is written for individual philanthropists as well as the program officers of the foundations they have created, for the staffs of not-for-profit organizations that seek gifts and grants, and for the attorneys, the financial planners, and the increasing number of other professionals who advise wealthy clients on philanthropy. This book arises out of our belief that philanthropy can make a great difference in the world but that much of its potential is unrealized. The book is intended to do for philanthropists what the best books on business strategy do for business entrepreneurs and executives: provide readers with the concepts necessary to design a strategy to achieve their goals—in this case, their charitable goals.

Although we draw on varied examples, the book is not about the substance of any particular domain. For a philanthropist interested in combating global warming, this book is not a substitute for understanding the science and politics of greenhouse-gas emissions. Rather, we provide the philanthropist with the framework for mustering expert knowledge in environmental sciences and policy making toward the end of affecting policies in the area. By the same token, we focus on strategy rather than tactics. There is a substantial literature on how to incorporate a foundation, choose a board of directors, maintain good relationships with grantees, and the like. There is no equivalent literature about the very essence of the philanthropic enterprise.

The Website: Smartphilanthropy.org

Although the book's focus is unique, we hardly think that we have the last word in this rapidly developing field. Quite the contrary. There are many areas where we just touch the surface, where examples from a broader range of practice would illuminate our basic points or modify or contradict them. For these reasons, we hope that the book will stimulate conversation and argument, and we have created a website, *http://www .smartphilanthropy.org*, to invite dialogue.

References throughout the book point to relevant pages of the website.

Sources

Although Hal was the founding president of the Energy Foundation and is a director of a family foundation, much of our own experience in philanthropy has been at The William and Flora Hewlett Foundation, which has given us intimate knowledge of its grant-making strategies and procedures. Our experience at the Hewlett Foundation also provides a particularly rich source of examples, because the inner workings of most philanthropies tend to be private. At the same time, we recognize that the work of one of the largest foundations in the world—albeit with a relatively small staff—is not typical of philanthropy in general. Taking this into account, we use examples from the Hewlett Foundation where they illuminate general points about strategic philanthropy, but we also use many examples from other foundations of various sizes and scopes.

Acknowledgments

OUR WORK ON this book has been aided by a number of excellent research assistants: Alyssa Battistoni, Casia Freitas, Emily Gerth, Kelvin Low, Kari Mah, Tony Wang, and Em Warren. We are particularly grateful to Kelvin Low for undertaking a first draft of the portion of Chapter 10 dealing with social return on investment.

We received helpful feedback from a number of colleagues at the Hewlett Foundation, including Danielle Deane, Tamara Fox, Julie Fry, Jacob Harold, Laurance Hoagland, Jennifer Ratay, Dana Schmidt, Mike Smith, and Sara Seims. We are particularly grateful to Danielle Deane, the program officer responsible for the New Constituencies for the Environment initiative, who wrote the case study of that initiative that appears in Chapter 4.

We also received assistance and helpful comments from colleagues outside the foundation: Demmy Adesina, Thomas Backer, Matthew Bannick, Ivan Barkhorn, Lucy Bernholz, Jeremy Brest, Phil Buchanan, Kevin Bolduc, Jeff Bradach, Alexa Culwell, Chris DeCardy, Jim Fishkin, Joel Fleishman, Bettina Forbes, Lawrence Friedman, Peter Frumkin, Cynthia Gair, Eleanor Clement Glass, Joe Grundfest, Jacqueline Khor, Mark Kramer, Carla Javits, Cynthia Esposito Lamy, Carol Larson, Amy Luckey, Barbara Merz, Adam Meyerson, Debra Meyerson, Lisa Monzón, Jeremy Nicholls, Rachel Odell, Sally Osberg, Julie Petersen, James Piereson, Mary Anne Rodgers, Nancy Roob, Ed Skloot, Steve Toben, Melinda Tuan, Brian Trelsdad, Michael Weinstein, Lowell Weiss, Mark Wolfson, and Simon Zadek. We are particularly grateful to Ivan Barkhorn for his suggestions for reorganizing the book.

We got helpful feedback from a dinner group of Bay Area foundation presidents (including Jim Canales, Susan Clark, Alexa Culwell, Crystal Hayling, Sandra Hernandez, Ira Hirschfield, Carol Larson, Tom Layton, Cate Muther, and Drummond Pike), a group of alumni of The Philanthropy Workshop West (including Simone Coxe, Russ Hall, Tom Perkins, Margaret Raffin, Peggy Rawls, and Steve Zuckerman), a faculty seminar at Stanford Law School, and a seminar of graduate students at the Stanford Center on Philanthropy and Civil Society, led by Malka Kopell, Debra Meyerson, and Woody Powell.

Donald Lamm and his colleagues Emma Parry and Christy Fletcher of Fletcher & Parry LLC helped find the ideal publisher for our manuscript. Finally, our sincere thanks to Iris Brest, who commented on, edited, and argued about successive drafts of the manuscript.

Introduction

PEOPLE CHOOSE TO engage in philanthropy for any number of reasons: to solve pressing social problems, to act on religious or philosophic beliefs that privilege entails responsibility toward the less fortunate, to instill altruistic values in their children, to achieve recognition, or to give meaning to their lives.[1]

Regardless of motive, philanthropists want to use their money to best effect. Yet the history of philanthropic efforts to improve the world—from reducing drug addiction and high-school dropout rates to protecting ecosystems to ameliorating global disease and poverty—demonstrates how difficult it is to actually make a difference.

There are three basic requirements for having real impact as a philanthropist: money, motivation, and a winning strategy. You need to bring the first two to the table; this book serves up the third. Strategy matters in philanthropy, just as it does in investing, running businesses, and conducting wars. Although it cannot ensure success, it improves the odds, and its absence virtually ensures failure.

Effective grantmaking requires strategies based on clear goals, sound evidence, diligent care in selecting which organizations to fund, and provisions for assessing the results—good or bad. Whether you are giving away $100,000 or $1 billion a year, your funds are not unlimited, and a good strategy can multiply their impact many times over.

Our goal is to help you make the world a better place according to your own lights. We do not presume to tell you either how much to give or what passions to pursue.[2] Those are personal choices. A philanthropist's conception of what is good for society determines his or her philanthropic goals, and these values can vary greatly. You may wish to promote the arts, religion, social services, education, health and medicine, or world peace; or protect the environment; or support the search for extraterrestrial life. You may want to stimulate social change, preserve the status quo, or return to halcyon days gone by. Your choice of goals—commissioning symphonies versus supporting the destitute—can be debated from a moral point of view, but such issues are outside the scope of this book. The subjects considered here are relevant to *all* philanthropic goals. They are as useful for advocates of gun control as for those who want to protect Americans' right to bear arms; for opponents of abortion as for proponents of a woman's right to choose.

Philanthropy can be conducted in many different ways, ranging from writing checks at your kitchen table to supporting a fully staffed foundation. We'll touch on these alternatives later in the book, after you have a better sense of both the possibilities and the demands of strategic philanthropy. But we should disclose at the outset that it requires a great deal of focus, time, energy, and consultation.

As individual philanthropists come to see what's required to make a real difference, they often conclude that high-impact philanthropy is not a one-person, part-time operation. It usually requires at least some professional staff. That's why most of our examples are drawn from foundations with several program officers. If, as you read the following pages, you decide that you can't or don't want to do it on your own, but don't have the resources or interest to establish a staffed foundation, there are other options. For example, you can follow Warren Buffett's lead and place your assets in a trusted private foundation, or put them in a strategically oriented community foundation or in one of the increasing number of funds that manage portfolios of grants domestically and in developing countries.

In any event, our book is intended not only for those who amass or inherit the fortunes that make large-scale philanthropy possible but also for the many others who counsel them and help spend their money. It should also be useful to the directors and staff members of the myriad not-for-profit organizations that seek support from individual donors and foundations.

Endnotes

1. See Peter Frumkin, *Strategic Giving: The Art and Science of Philanthropy* (Chicago: University of Chicago Press, 2006).

2. Peter Singer, "What Should a Billionaire Give—and What Should You?" *New York Times Magazine*, December 17, 2006.

The Framework
of Strategic Philanthropy

The basic imperative of strategic philanthropy is to deploy your resources to achieve your goals most effectively. This calls for approaching the work with a clear-eyed appreciation of the inevitable risks of failure as well as the potential for great success. In the first part of the book, we walk through the essential processes of smart philanthropy—from choosing goals to designing and implementing strategies to monitoring performance and measuring impact.

Your chances of success are greatly increased by having well-defined goals and a sound strategic plan to achieve them. The goals should describe what success would look like, and the strategic plan should detail every step necessary to achieve the goals, including indicators that you are on the right path—or that you've strayed or lost your way. Because a philanthropic strategy is essentially a plan for making some aspect of the world a better place, it must be premised on a valid empirical understanding of how the world works.

Although knowledge, reputation, and relationships can add value to your work, the core activity of philanthropy is grantmaking. Your choice among different modes of funding depends on how closely a grantee's activities are aligned with your own goals and strategies. And you can sometimes complement grants with financial investments that combine social impact with the possibility of a financial return. Just like your own effectiveness, the effectiveness of your grantees depends on the clarity and soundness of their goals, strategies, and indicators of progress.

Proper feedback is necessary to make corrections to your strategies and grants, and collecting that feedback is an essential part of strategic philanthropy. Gathering the necessary information involves monitoring grantees' performance, tracking progress toward shared goals, and evaluating actual impact.

C h a p t e r   O n e

The Promise of Strategic Philanthropy

PHILANTHROPIC DOLLARS ARE often said to be society's "risk capital." This implies that in addition to producing great results, some promising philanthropic investments do not succeed and should not succeed if philanthropy is taking appropriate risks.

Philanthropists can fail stupidly by not grounding their grantmaking in sound premises and by being careless in the design and implementation of strategies. Or they can fail wisely—the inevitable flip side of succeeding brilliantly. This book has as many examples of failure as it does of success, because acknowledging and learning from one's failures is among the core tenets of strategic philanthropy. To get into the spirit of this, let's begin with two cases of failure, one smart and the other not.

The Robert Wood Johnson Foundation's (RWJF's) Fighting Back initiative, in which it invested $87.9 million between 1988 and 2003, provides an example of a well-planned program that failed.[1] Before undertaking the program, RWJF undertook an extensive two-year analysis of past community efforts to address alcohol and drug abuse, which had centered around decreasing the supply of drugs and hence around increased law enforcement. None had succeeded. The foundation discovered an absence of community leadership and a lack of coordination among programs, communities, and local and state governments.

Consistent with the best thinking in the field of community change, Fighting Back was premised on the belief that a local community could address its drug problems by coordinating the work of government agencies, schools, and not-for-profit organizations with community efforts

3

and individual treatment programs. The initiative specified measurable outcome indicators, including sustained reductions in new cases of drug and alcohol abuse among children and adolescents, in drug- and alcohol-related deaths and injuries, in health problems related to alcohol and drug abuse, and in drug-related crimes.

From over three hundred applications, RWJF chose fifteen communities whose proposals linked strategies for prevention, early intervention, treatment, and relapse prevention. In each community, a lead organization was chosen on the basis of its demonstrated ability to pull together health-care and other community resources. Each community pursued three complementary strategies:

> Increasing the physical and social conditions that deter alcohol and drug use through community policing, street lighting, and cleaning up housing projects
> Strengthening individuals' abilities to resist and recover from alcohol and drug use through parenting classes, youth programs, academic assistance, and case management for alcohol- and drug-abuse clients
> Diminishing the availability and accessibility of alcohol and drugs by closing crack houses, demolishing abandoned buildings, and closing liquor outlets in high-risk areas

Yet, as a comprehensive evaluation concluded, "a sustained, 10-year community-based coalition approach with ample technical assistance and direction, top-notch people, and sites that were pre-selected, did not produce robust results in terms of decreasing substance abuse."[2] Among the explanations for the initiative's failure were distrust and competition for funding among organizations and agencies, which distracted from the project's main goal.

RWJF's evaluation contributed to the growing body of information about what works and doesn't work in community change. (The RWJF's practice of evaluating its projects and publishing the outcomes is, unfortunately, a rarity in philanthropy—a subject that we shall return to later in the book.)

If RWJF's Fighting Back initiative is an example of a thoughtful failure, the Annenberg Challenge provides a contrasting example.[3] In 1993, the publishing magnate and former ambassador Walter Annenberg committed $500 million, to be matched by local philanthropists and corporations, to improve American public education. Over half of this amount was directed toward transforming urban school districts, including those of New York, Chicago, Philadelphia, and San Francisco. The strategies in all the districts were responsive to a particular theory of change—the belief that not-for-profit organizations, acting as intermediaries outside the system, could work with administrators and teachers to catalyze change within schools.[4] Although some schools had modest successes, the overall results were unimpressive. The problems encountered in implementing the Annenberg Challenge included the following:

> The intermediary not-for-profit organizations vied with each other for funding at the expense of collaboration.
> In their haste to get grants out the door, funders did not hold the organizations to high standards of accountability, and grant funds were committed to schools before they had made commitments to reform. As a result, funds were used to cover existing operating expenses rather than being deployed incrementally for reform.
> In some cases, changes of district leadership undermined the initiative's reform efforts, or rendered them irrelevant.

Not all of these problems could have been anticipated, any more than could analogous problems in RWJF's Fighting Back initiative. The fundamental flaw, however, lay in the Annenberg Challenge's premises and assumptions.[5] Raymond Domanico, a veteran educator and researcher who studied the program, commented on its naive assumption that external agencies could "negotiate change with the existing power structure of public education—the teachers' unions, board of education, and politicians," and its reliance "upon much the same set of relationships and processes that had yielded the status quo in large public school systems."[6]

Chester Finn and Marci Kanstoroom wrote that the Annenberg Challenge "picked an unpromising, even archaic, theory, one that by 1993 had largely been discarded by other educational reformers."[7] Together with Domanico, they concluded that the Annenberg Challenge placed less importance on the validity of its theory of change than on being nonconfrontational and "secur[ing] the middle ground."

Of course, hindsight is 20/20. Had the Annenberg Challenge been a great success, we might have different views of how well thought out its plans were.[8] But Finn and Kanstoroom are surely right in their admonition, which applies well beyond educational reform: "One's theory of change should be clear before one embarks on educational reform, and the theory itself must be sound. It is essential that the actual strategies one then embraces are faithful to one's carefully chosen theory of change. That includes putting one's money on the right change agents."[9]

You can't know in advance whether your philanthropy will have world-changing consequences or turn out in retrospect to be money down the drain. But you do know in advance that because social change is complex, and causal chains are often murky, strategic philanthropy requires real clarity of goals, sound analysis, follow-through, and continuous feedback. And this means that you can change the odds in your favor through strategies that are based on evidence (rather than hope) and through careful planning and execution.

Strategic leverage is essential because the philanthropic sector is tiny compared with the issues it confronts. Its grant dollars are minuscule compared with spending by the government and transactions in the private sector. Consider, for example, that American consumers alone spend approximately $1 trillion per year on energy—and that energy is probably the largest source of environmental damage. By contrast, philanthropic spending directed to this trillion-dollar problem is about $100 million—that is, only 1/10,000 of the amount that supports the vast and well-established energy market is available for trying to change it.[10] This is the challenge for donors and foundation trustees and staff who seek to reduce global warming. To succeed, they need to build the incentives to achieve a fundamental transition to lower-carbon energy sources.

Similar challenges confront donors concerned with eradicating hunger, curing diseases, or reforming education. This is difficult work not just because social change is the product of a large variety of forces that are hard to identify, much less affect with any certainty, but also because, unlike the financial returns of a business or even electoral returns in politics, philanthropy has no common measures of success. Philanthropy is a field with poor feedback and messy signals—and those signals are often distorted by the pervasive flattery that colors many transactions in the money-giving business.

What Strategic Philanthropy Is

All of this means that accomplishing philanthropic goals requires having great clarity about what those goals are and specifying indicators of success before beginning a philanthropic project. It requires designing and then implementing a plan commensurate with the resources committed to it. This, in turn, requires an empirical, evidence-based understanding of the external world in which the plan will operate. And it requires attending carefully to milestones to determine whether you are on the path to success, with a keen eye for signals that call for midcourse corrections. These factors are the necessary parts of what we regard as the essential core of strategic philanthropy—the concern with *impact.*

"Impact" is obviously not the same as good intentions. Nor is it the same as engaging in the activities called for by your strategic plan. Given the complexities of the world, even well-thought-out activities do not always achieve their goals. Impact is not even the same as seeing the outcome you intended come about—at least not if the outcome would have happened anyway. Simply put, impact is *making a difference*—not in some universal sense, but in terms of your own philanthropic goals.

"My question is: Are we making an impact?"

We'll say more shortly about the theoretical framework for asking whether you're making a difference. But first, a big practical question: Given the complexities of solving society's big problems, is the philanthropic effort foolhardy or quixotic? Or can philanthropists find the right levers and a place to stand, and actually move the world? The answer: it depends.

It depends in large measure on how well you understand the social, political, and economic forces that shape your chosen field, and whether you can use your understanding to find the levers for change. It depends on whether you can build programs that effectively work those levers. It depends on staying power, on focus, and perhaps most important, on supplementing passion with analysis. With the right choices, smart philanthropy can have enormous impact. Consider the following example.[11]

Harlem Children's Zone (HCZ) is a not-for-profit, community-based organization that works to improve outcomes for poor children and families in some of New York City's most devastated neighborhoods. Today, HCZ serves more than 12,600 children and adults, including over 7,500 at-risk children. It provides after-school education, social services, recreation, and other services. HCZ's mission is to create significant, positive opportunities for all children living in a sixty-block area of central Harlem by helping parents, residents, teachers, and other stakeholders create a safe learning environment for youths. HCZ grew to achieve this scale beginning in the late 1990s, with the support of the Edna McConnell Clark Foundation (EMCF) and others.

After a period of self-evaluation in the mid-1990s, EMCF, whose $25 million grants budget then supported five distinct programs, decided to focus its grantmaking solely on youth development. HCZ was part of a pilot effort by the foundation to test a new approach to grantmaking by supporting organizational growth. Seeing the great potential in HCZ, EMCF made a grant to help the organization expand beyond a one-block neighborhood building project and underwrote the costs of engaging the Bridgespan Group, a not-for-profit consulting firm, to help HCZ develop a business plan. With EMCF's support, HCZ also developed standards for assessing outcomes and began a continuous evaluation process to measure its impact on youth and families served. Nancy Roob, president of EMCF, remarked:

The business planning process at HCZ helped executive director Geoff Canada and Harlem Children's Zone take a careful, thoughtful look at its programs and operations. In doing so, HCZ realized that some of its efforts did not fit into its larger goal of helping youth and families. By realigning its services and programming (including spinning off some divisions) toward its larger mission, HCZ today is now able to more effectively help young people in Harlem make a successful transition to productive adulthood.[12]

After HCZ created a business plan that mapped out stages to scale up effectively, EMCF began providing the organization with general operating support; so did a number of other funders, including the Robin Hood and the Picower foundations. As we will discuss later in the book, such unrestricted support is the lifeblood of not-for-profit organizations, because it gives their boards and CEOs the autonomy to allocate resources as they deem most effective. Providing general operating support can be highly strategic—but *only* when you have determined that the organization's mission is aligned with your own goals. This in turn requires that you have done the necessary due diligence to ensure that the organization has the capacity to carry out its mission and that it has solid plans for assessing its progress and results.

EMCF's decision to focus its small staff and $25 million annual grants budget on one specific area was a signal act of strategic philanthropy. We don't mean to say that an individual philanthropist or a foundation cannot have multiple objectives. (After all, the Hewlett Foundation has six program areas.) The question is how much you can accomplish with whatever financial and human resources you have. EMCF's belief that it could be more effective by focusing all its resources on youth development made great sense in its circumstances, and the decision has paid off magnificently, not just in HCZ but also in other ventures that have followed.

EMCF's grants to HCZ have two noteworthy characteristics: First, they support the provision of direct services, helping one child at a time (though with the broader objective of improving the social environment of the children's neighborhoods). Second, the grants provide general operating support to help strengthen and increase the organization's reach. But these are only a few of the tools in the strategic philanthropist's toolkit. Which tools you use depends on your particular goals and on the external context in which you pursue them.

For example, the means for achieving the goal of curing a disease or reforming a government policy may involve research and advocacy rather than direct services. With respect to funding, it is sometimes more effective to support particular projects rather than an organization as a whole. If your goal is to help find a cure for breast cancer, you would more likely make a project grant to support a particular research team rather than make an unrestricted gift to the university or even to the medical school where the researchers work. (Though, as we emphasize in Chapter 11, there also is great strategic value in supporting institutions of higher education.)

Here are some examples of effective strategic philanthropy employing a wide variety of approaches. (Several of these and other examples in this book are based on the *Casebook for the Foundation: A Great American Secret* by Joel Fleishman and his colleagues.[13])

➤ Building on their history of working to de-escalate tensions between the United States and the Soviet Union during the cold war, the MacArthur Foundation and the Carnegie Corporation launched an initiative in the late 1980s to reduce the threat of nuclear war. The foundations supported grants for research; the dissemination of articles, books, and briefing papers; and seminars for members of Congress. This initiative likely contributed to Congress's adoption of the Soviet Nuclear Threat Reduction Act (commonly known as the Nunn-Lugar Act), which established a fund to pay for dismantling the Soviet nuclear arsenal.

➤ In the 1980s, the Lynde and Harry Bradley Foundation, with support from the Joyce Foundation, began a campaign to implement the vision of school vouchers proposed by the free-market economist Milton Friedman.[14] The Bradley Foundation funded an academic study that favored school choice, funded a private voucher program for low-income students to serve as a pilot for an eventual government program, and supported the legal defense of Milwaukee's experimental voucher program, which the U.S. Supreme Court upheld in 2002. Although the success of the school-voucher movement remains uncertain,[15] vouchers have become a prominent if still controversial idea for improving educational outcomes.

➤ In 2005, the Thomas & Stacey Siebel Foundation, founded by the software entrepreneur Thomas Siebel, decided to address methamphetamine abuse in Montana.[16] In addition to ruining the lives of many young people, meth was costing the state $100 million a year.[17] Traditional law enforcement efforts to try to reduce the supply of the drug were not succeeding. Using print media, radio, and television, the Siebel Foundation's "Not Even Once" campaign was targeted at teens who had not yet used meth. The ads were scary, vivid, and blunt, portraying the negative physical, psychological, and social effects of meth use—teeth falling out, attempted suicide, physical violence—through personal testimonials.[18] A preliminary report by Montana's attorney general indicates large declines in the use of meth in the workplace, in meth-related crimes, and in arrests where the suspects tested positive for meth use.[19] It is noteworthy that although the Siebel Foundation's Meth Project includes not-for-profit grantees, much of its work involves advertising through conventional for-profit and public media.

In contrast to the Edna McConnell Clark Foundation's grants to support an organization as a whole, most of the grants in these examples supported discrete projects involving research, litigation, advocacy, and the like. If EMCF was an investor, the foundations in these examples were more like general contractors who purchase a selection of products or services to build a house that none of the subcontractors could build themselves. Sometimes, as with the Pew Charitable Trusts' creation of the Pew Center on Global Climate Change, the strategy includes building a new organization.

We will return to these and other models of philanthropy later in the book. The point for now is that strategic philanthropy neither privileges nor excludes any of these different approaches in the abstract. On the contrary, it calls for choosing whatever mix of approaches will best achieve your philanthropic objectives.

What Strategic Philanthropy Is Not

Having seen some of the many forms that strategic philanthropy can take, you might wonder what it doesn't include. The answer, unfortunately, is that it doesn't include a considerable amount of philanthropy as it is actually practiced. If a strategy is a road map for achieving a goal, the goals of many philanthropic gifts and grants are not sufficiently specific to know if those goals have been achieved, let alone to draw the map to reach them.[20]

We do not suggest that such philanthropy is harmful. In our personal lives, we regularly make year-end gifts to organizations for which we have warm feelings. These gifts make us feel good, and doubtless they help good organizations. But this isn't the way to change the world, and it certainly is not a responsible way to give away someone else's money.

Why Grantee Organizations Don't Always Like Strategic Philanthropy

There are two potential sources of tension between strategic philanthropists and the organizations they support.

The first is that organizations do not necessarily enjoy being scrutinized by funders or like being accountable to them for achieving outcomes. Consider the Edna McConnell Clark Foundation's rigorous process of selecting and supporting youth service organizations:[21]

➤ Identify and prescreen organizations that meet specific foundation criteria, including enhancing educational opportunities, aiding youth in the transition to self-sustaining work at competitive wages, or avoiding high-risk behaviors such as crime and unprotected sex.
➤ Conduct due diligence on quality and efficacy of services, proven leadership, financial health, organizational strength and growth potential, interest in tracking performance, and compatibility with the foundation's values.
➤ Make a planning grant to the organization to help it develop a strategic business plan with respect to goals and benchmarks of performance.
➤ Make an unrestricted grant based on the milestones outlined in the organization's business plan.
➤ Execute ongoing performance tracking and evaluation of the organization's outcomes.

For high-performing organizations like Harlem Children's Zone, this is a constructive and invigorating process. But many organizations lack the clarity of goals, strategies, or measures of success to be accountable to themselves, let alone to a funder. And even those that have the capacity for accountability often prefer not to subject themselves to the due diligence and reporting processes required by strategic philanthropy. These tensions surfaced in the responses to the 2006 *Grantee Perception Report* commissioned from the Center for Effective Philanthropy by the Hewlett Foundation. One grantee commented: "The application is quite rigorous and thus we always stock up on our supply of chocolate to help inspire us as we move throughout the process! But it is actually quite instructive and it does require a level of preparation and thought that we might not ever get to if it was not required of us." And another commented that it "really has assisted our organization in strengthening our ability to articulate our project goals and objectives." But a third grantee, noting that "the interactions have strengthened our focus, our resolve, and our work," went on to say that "there's a very fine line between being an engaged funder and interference. At more than one point in this process the line has been crossed."[22]

The second tension arises from the fundamentally different perspectives of a strategic philanthropist and an operating not-for-profit organization. The strategic philanthropist funds an organization to further particular goals. The organization looks to philanthropy as a source of capital—the less restricted the better—to fund its operations. When funding takes the form of strengthening the organization's capacity and especially providing general operating support, as in the case of the Edna McConnell Clark Foundation's funding of the Harlem Children's Zone, this is the best of both worlds. But as some of the preceding examples suggest, the philanthropist may often be more interested in supporting a particular project. Many not-for-profit organizations understandably do not like to be viewed as subcontractors.

What About the Passion?

Philanthropy comes from the heart—from the love of humankind. It is love or passion that leads philanthropists to determine their missions and set ambitious goals.

But once you have determined these goals, the process becomes outcome-centered. At this point, mind and muscle come in to design and implement a strategy to achieve those goals. A strategy comprises the unromantic, nitty-gritty working out of the means to accomplish your goals. It is never an end in itself, only a tool to aid an organization in achieving its mission.

Consider a few examples of how philanthropists converted passion into action:[23]

> ➤ John Dorr, a wealthy engineer, was convinced that the absence of a white line separating a highway shoulder from the road caused accidents. He persuaded Connecticut officials to do a field test on a portion of the Merritt Parkway in Connecticut, which proved his hypothesis. The Dorr Foundation continued to engage in advocacy, research, and the dissemination of information; as a result, such lines—often supplemented by textured shoulders—are now standard on highways throughout the United States.
> ➤ David Levin's and Michael Feinberg's experiences as Teach for America volunteers in Houston public schools led them to create a charter school that provided disadvantaged children with long, disciplined, and structured school days. With funding from Don and Doris Fisher, the founders of the Gap, the amazing success of this venture has led to an increasing number of KIPP (Knowledge is Power Program) Academies throughout the country. (Teach for America itself grew out of the passion of Wendy Kopp, then a recent Princeton graduate, and the program has gained the support of both individual philanthropists and foundations.)
> ➤ When his wife was treated heartlessly by hospital staff, Dr. Harvey Picker, a pioneer in X-ray technology, used the resources of his family foundation in collaboration with the Commonwealth Fund to support research and advocacy that established the concept of patient-centered care.

A sense of mission, commitment, and passion are essential to every aspect of the work of philanthropists and the not-for-profit organizations they support. But for every one of the preceding examples where passion was translated into impact, there probably are hundreds of cases where other philanthropists acted as if passion alone sufficed. In any event, strategy is not a substitute for good values and passion, but rather the vehicle for realizing them. Without the capacity to move beyond passion to effective planning and execution, the sector would be left largely with well-meaning efforts that confuse good intentions with real effects.

The Attitude of Strategic Philanthropy: Maximizing Social Return on Investment and Expected Return

It's not just effective planning and execution but also effective allocation of resources that lie at the core of strategic philanthropy, and we would like to propose an attitude that captures these ideas and just about everything that follows in the book: maximizing the social return on your investment. This is not about trivializing grantmaking to achieve only readily quantifiable outcomes or trying to measure the unmeasurable. Albert Einstein got it right when he noted: "Not everything that counts can be counted, and not everything that can be counted counts."

We'll discuss the possibilities and limitations of counting later. Here we're really talking about an attitude: use your resources to achieve the greatest possible impact in achieving your objectives. At this level of generality, the point seems obvious, though implementing it may seem daunting. With due caution about thoughtlessly importing concepts from economics and business into the not-for-profit sector, the well-developed financial concepts of "return on investment" and "expected return" provide extremely valuable, if not essential, ways to understand philanthropic effectiveness.

The idea of a *social return on investment* (SROI) is simply that you want your (inevitably) limited resources to achieve the greatest possible impact. For most objectives—whether improving the graduation rates of disadvantaged youth, feeding the hungry, or preventing AIDS—the more you accomplish the better. The more you accomplish with the same resources, the greater the SROI.

Some organizations measure social return by looking at savings to governments resulting from philanthropically funded programs to employ former drug addicts or the developmentally disabled; others focus on the benefits to the individuals served (see Chapter 10). We use the term capaciously to describe the return on your philanthropic investment, whatever goals you may have.

The concept of *expected return* accounts for the risk involved in achieving your goals. It is a function of the magnitude of the impact times the probability of achieving it. The cost of a program and the expected return of its outcome together describe its cost-effectiveness. The impact of some philanthropic activities is pretty certain: if you are supporting a soup kitchen, you and the organizations you are funding will know at the end of the day how many people (who might otherwise have gone hungry) you are feeding and you can predict what the organization will achieve tomorrow. For many if not most not-for-profit activities, however, the impact is anything but certain. How many unwanted pregnancies will a teen-pregnancy-prevention program prevent? Will advocacy for campaign-finance reform result in legislation, will the legislation be implemented, and will it have more good than bad consequences?

Realistically, one can rarely calculate impact and probability with any degree of precision, which has led some people to criticize the ideas of SROI and expected return as misguided efforts to measure things that cannot be quantified. But forget about quantification for now, and consider SROI and expected return as the essence of an attitude that has at least the following benefits:

> It encourages philanthropists and the organizations they support to marshal their resources most effectively to accomplish shared objectives.
> It puts the administrative costs of the foundation and those of the organizations it supports in the proper context; specifically, those costs are justified to the extent, but only to the extent, that they contribute to an organization's impact. (More on this later.)
> It helps philanthropists recognize the risks of strategies and implementation in order to try to mitigate them.
> It justifies risky not-for-profit ventures whose potential benefits are high. Consider the likelihood of an organization succeeding in reducing global warming or of a medical research institute developing an AIDS vaccine. The probabilities are very low, but the potential payoffs are enormous.
> It encourages philanthropists to be realistic and candid about failure. "Failure" is almost a dirty word in our sector—for operating not-for-profits as well as foundations. Yet a large proportion of not-for-profit activities and foundation grants fail, not in the sense of the organizations falling apart—though that happens, too—but by having no impact. Without acknowledging failure, an organization loses one of its most important avenues of learning. At the Hewlett Foundation, we hold an annual contest for "the worst grant from which you

learned the most." Because of the foundation-wide learning that comes from it, the prize has become a sought-after honor rather than a mark of opprobrium.

➤ It helps philanthropists understand their own tolerance for risk. Some funders are prepared to take huge risks of failure. Others are quite risk averse. You can often find effective ways to achieve objectives that fit your tolerance for risk; for example, undertake several projects with different risk levels so that the overall "portfolio" is in line with your appetite for risk or choose different objectives that can be achieved without too much risk.

In fact, everyone goes through some sort of probability analysis when deciding to make a grant. It is usually informal, and often even unconscious. Bringing the analysis out in the open forces disciplined thinking when comparing and assessing proposals. It also highlights particular vulnerabilities in a program—aspects of the strategy where the probabilities seem particularly uncertain or noticeably low. In cases like these, it may well be worth the effort to gather more information or to design redundant strategies.

In nontechnical language, an SROI "attitude" involves getting the most bang for your philanthropic buck, or, once you factor in the uncertainties that generally exist in ambitious philanthropy, giving it your best shot.

Takeaway Points

➤ Strategic philanthropy consists of
   —clearly defined goals, commensurate with resources;
   —strategies for achieving the goals;
   —strategies that are based on sound evidence; and
   —feedback to keep the strategy on course.
➤ Strategic philanthropy deploys resources to have maximum impact— to make the biggest possible difference. This approach is captured by the idea of social return on investment, where "return" refers to improving the world rather than financial gain.
➤ All ambitious philanthropy is risky. A sound strategy makes success possible; its absence virtually ensures failure.

Chapter Notes

1. Robert Wood Johnson Foundation, *Fighting Back* (2007), http://www.rwjf
.org/reports/npreports/fightingback.htm#LESSONSLEARNED.

2. Ibid.

3. Much of this discussion draws on Raymond Domanico and others' evaluation, *Can Philanthropy Fix Our Schools? Appraising Walter Annenberg's $500 Million Gift to Public Education* (Washington, D.C.: Thomas B. Fordham Institute, 2000), http://www.fordhamfoundation.org/doc/annenberg.pdf, supplemented by reports and evaluations of the Bay Area School Reform Collaborative, available online at http://www.hewlett.org/Programs/Education/Achievement/BASRC.htm.

4. "The Challenge relies on *intermediary organizations* as agents of change. . . . As independent public-private partnerships, neither in the system nor wholly outside it, they cross organizational boundaries to intervene at critical points both up and down the educational system. They galvanize new resources from public and private sources. They educate, advocate, develop programs, and coach people in managing change. And they bring to school improvement the private creativity and civic mobilization that policy-driven reform alone cannot provide." Domanico et al., *Can Philanthropy Fix Our Schools?* 53–54 (quoting the Annenberg Challenge's midterm report).

5. Ibid., 1.

6. Ibid.

7. Ibid., 58.

8. See, e.g., Baruch Fischhoff, *For Those Condemned to Study the Past: Heuristics and Biases in Hindsight*, in *Judgment Under Uncertainty: Heuristics and Biases*, ed. Daniel Kahneman, Paul Slovic, and Amos Tversky (Cambridge, U.K., and New York: Cambridge University Press, 1982), 335, 341–342; and Phil Rosenzweig, *The Halo Effect . . . and the Eight Other Business Delusions That Deceive Managers* (New York: Free Press, 2007).

9. Domanico et al., *Can Philanthropy Fix Our Schools?* 57.

10. Foundation Center, *Statistical Abstract of the U.S. and Foundation Giving Trends 2000* (New York: Foundation Center, 2000).

11. *Leadership Dialogue: The Edna McConnell Clark Foundation and Harlem Children's Zone* (Washington, D.C.: Venture Philanthropy Partners, 2004), http://www.vppartners.org/learning/reports/report2004/report2004_hcz.pdf; and Bridgespan Group, *Harlem Children's Zone (HCZ): Transforming the Organization While Scaling Up in a Tightly Defined Local Service Area* (New York: Bridgespan Group, 2004), http://www.bridgespangroup.org/PDF/Clarkpdfs/HarlemChildrensZone.pdf.

12. Nancy Roob, e-mail message to Paul Brest, January 22, 2008. During the period discussed in the text, Michael Bailin was president of the EMCF.

13. Joel L. Fleishman, J. Scott Kohler, and Steven Schindler, *Casebook for The Foundation: A Great American Secret* (New York: Public Affairs, 2007).

14. John J. Miller, *Strategic Investment in Ideas: How Two Foundations Reshaped America* (Washington, D.C.: Philanthropy Roundtable, 2003), 40–49.

15. See Rick Cohen, *Strategic Grantmaking: Foundations and the School Privatization Movement* (Washington, D.C.: National Committee for Responsive Philanthropy, 2007), http://www.ncrp.org/downloads/ NCRP2007-StrategicGrantmaking-FINAL-LowRes.pdf.

16. Office of National Drug Control Policy, *Pushing Back Against Meth: A Progress Report on the Fight Against Methamphetamine in the United States* (Washington, D.C., 2006), http://www.whitehousedrugpolicy.gov/publications/ pdf/pushingback_against_meth.pdf.

17. Laura Hill, "Lassoing Montana Meth," *Philanthropy*, June 19, 2007, 26.

18. See generally Montana Meth Project, http://www.montanameth.org/About_Us/ results.php (accessed June 30, 2008).

19. Montana Attorney General's Office and Montana Meth Project, *Methamphetamine in Montana: A Preliminary Report on Trends and Impact* (2007), http://www.doj.mt.gov/news/releases2007/20070124preliminarymethreport .pdf. With Siebel's assistance, a number of other states are adopting similar programs.

20. See Kevin Bolduc et al., *Beyond the Rhetoric: Foundation Strategy* (Cambridge, Mass.: Center for Effective Philanthropy, 2007), http://www .effectivephilanthropy.org/images/pdfs/CEP_Beyond_the_Rhetoric.pdf.

21. Fleishman, Kohler, and Schindler, *Casebook for The Foundation*, 260–261.

22. Excerpts from the Grantee Perception Report are available at http://www .hewlett.org/More/Grantee%2BPerception%2BReport.

23. Fleishman, Kohler, and Schindler, *Casebook for The Foundation*, 67–69, 277, 238.

C h a p t e r   T w o

Choices in Philanthropic Goals, Strategies, and Styles

THE PHILANTHROPIST'S LOVE of humankind—or of art, nature, or God—must find expression in the pursuit of particular goals. You may enter philanthropy with a very specific set of goals and seek out organizations that are aligned with them, or you may have general interests in some areas and be responsive to a broader range of proposals. In either case, your goals are likely to change over time—in part through the very process of grantmaking, which will provide new perspectives on the problems that concern you.

The choice of philanthropic goals is essentially subjective. But different kinds of goals have very different implications for the nature of

---

Philanthropic Size and Scope

The Gates Foundation has invested over a billion dollars in developing an AIDS vaccine, which will have global, multigenerational impacts if successful. The Wallace Alexander Gerbode Foundation is an important funder of arts in the San Francisco Bay Area, enhancing the lives of thousands of people in the community. Both objectives are valuable, but they have profoundly different characters and scales.

your grantmaking. And as with the choice of a career, one can be more or less thoughtful about how to define one's goals. This chapter sets out some considerations about goals, as well as strategies, with the aim of helping you decide how to have impact in ways that best suit your own style.

The Scale of Philanthropic Goals

The most fundamental determinants of a donor's goals are his or her interests or concerns—whether supporting the Girl Scouts, renovating the high-school auditorium, promoting human rights, or reducing the threat of nuclear war. These are all legitimate and important pursuits, but they have different scales, requiring different sorts of commitments, and they tend to offer different kinds of satisfaction.

You can think of the problems a philanthropist might tackle in terms of three axes. The first axis captures the nature of the human needs the goal will satisfy.

1. Does the problem diminish quality of life, or does it threaten life itself?

Programs supported by foundations can range from those that nourish the human spirit and help cultivate creativity (neighborhood parks, the fine arts) to those that try to ensure the necessities of a good life (a nourishing diet, reliable shelter, clean air and water, freedom, justice) to those that try to make life possible, such as research into cures for HIV/AIDS and malaria or efforts to halt nuclear proliferation. You can think of a continuum along these lines:

Diminishes quality of life   Compromises necessities of life   Threatens life itself

We have little to add to centuries of philosophical debates about how to balance incommensurable values of these sorts. These are all legitimate and important pursuits and will appeal in different mixes to different philanthropists. But they have different implications for philanthropy and require quite different strategies.

A second axis deals with the duration of the problem.

2. How long will the harm persist?

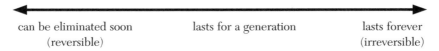

can be eliminated soon (reversible)	lasts for a generation	lasts forever (irreversible)

This axis is concerned primarily with the consequences of postpone-ment, compared with acting to prevent or mitigate a harm now. If you reduce conventional pollutants, such as soot and sulfur dioxide, the air will become clean and breathable within a matter of days. By contrast, even after the pollution stops, a lake may take decades to recover, with long-term damage to its ecosystems. And even with massive reductions of greenhouse gases, the earth may continue to get hotter for a half century or more, with long-term damage to agriculture, health, and habitats. The effects of today's poor educational systems may be passed on for a generation, but they will dissipate eventually if education is improved. By contrast, the loss of biodiversity is irreversible.[1]

The third axis involves the scope of the problem.

3. What is the scale of the problem?

small	large	vast

You can think of the scale of the problem in terms of the number of people affected or in terms of geography. The number of people affected may range from a few identifiable individuals (the orphans at the Casa de Niños) to a larger but graspable number (high-school dropouts in your community) to the unimaginably large (victims of a nuclear disaster).

The scope of the problem may be defined in other units as well—for example, by area. A park will improve your neighborhood. A land trust will protect local lands. A wilderness bill will create regional environmental protection. An effort to protect the Amazon rainforest could safeguard hundreds of millions of acres. An effort to reduce greenhouse gases is aimed at an immense amount of global real estate.

Problems such as war, human rights, poverty, and economic development in foreign countries are global for several reasons: they are abstract and often manifest themselves far away from home; they tend to involve vast numbers of anonymous people; and because they often require working in unfamiliar social and economic systems, they present complexities far beyond local problems.

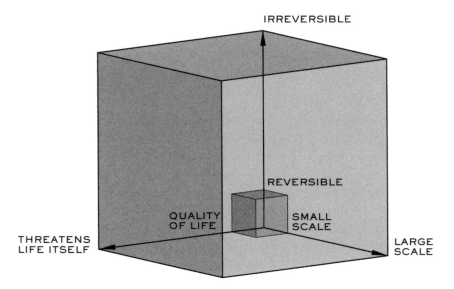

These three axes can be combined in a three-dimensional chart, shown here with one end of each of these axes anchored in the small cube, while the other ends extend infinitely outward, as suggested by the large cube.

We begin by considering the two extremes: work in the small cube, focusing on local, quality-of-life, reversible problems, and work at the outer edge of the big cube, covering global, life-threatening, irreversible problems. Many goals involve a mixture of elements. For example, working to prevent irreversible damage to a unique art treasure would be represented by a large value on the vertical axis, but is solidly inside the small cube on the other two axes. Still, when we consider the strategic differences, it is helpful to examine the extremes.

The Small Cube

At the core of the small cube lie programs that address the relatively near-term, non-life-threatening needs of a relatively small number of people. The small cube might include building a gallery in a museum or supporting a homeless shelter. Such philanthropy has several attractive characteristics:

> ➤ *The processes of change are direct and readily graspable.* Your money is the direct link between the need and its satisfaction.

➤ *The risks of utter failure are relatively low*. You know in advance that you will almost surely improve some people's daily lives.

➤ *Results tend to be visible, tangible, and discernible in the near term*. You can watch the museum gallery being built over the course of a few years and see beds in the homeless shelter filling up. Perhaps you will even observe a decline in the number of homeless people on the street.

➤ *Problems tend to be relatively easy to solve, and causal links between your philanthropy and the result tend to be clear*. You can readily trace the causal links between the actions supported by your gift and their effects.

➤ *The philanthropist's generosity is more likely to be recognized*. For many of these reasons, grants in the small cube often provide immediate, individual recognition.

The small cube has its limitations as well. The correlate of direct and immediate returns on your philanthropic investment is less leverage. Museum-goers in your city are better off, but statewide education in the arts may remain woefully inadequate. Although housing the homeless addresses the urgent needs of some residents, it does not necessarily prepare them for self-sufficiency. Moreover, immediate improvements can be swamped by other forces: an unusually cold winter could stress the available facilities for the homeless well beyond their capacity—a problem that more ambitious antipoverty strategies might mitigate.

The Big Cube

At the outer edges of the big cube are irreversible catastrophes that threaten life itself. The biggest advantage of philanthropy designed to address these problems is that you can improve hundreds of millions of lives or save hundreds of millions of acres for decades or centuries. The Green Revolution, supported by the Rockefeller and Ford foundations, was global in scale; it increased global agricultural productivity, saving untold numbers of people from starvation. (It must also be said that the Green Revolution had some serious downsides, and the story is not simple.[2]) The Rockefeller, Ford, Mellon, Hewlett, and Packard foundations' support for international family planning provides another example. Again, not without its controversies,[3] this effort had a role in

Seeing Big

Philanthropy toward the edges of the large cube may play a special role in goading businesses and governments into tackling certain problems. It is often difficult to get politicians and business executives to address the risks of serious, even catastrophic, harms such as global flu pandemics, nuclear war, and global warming. The late Speaker of the House of Representatives, Massachusetts congressman Tip O'Neill, famously remarked that "all politics is local." And it turns out that because global, long-term problems, even though potentially catastrophic, do not align with the rhythms or boundaries of our political systems or the incentives of managers, the thinking and action in these realms is disproportionately small. A politician or business executive may get no credit for preventing a catastrophe from occurring.

Philanthropists, then, even as small players, are among the most important and influential actors working on such issues as climate change, biodiversity, nuclear arms control, and global population. The fact that global warming is on so many governments' and businesses' agendas today is due in no small part to the Pew Charitable Trusts, the Energy Foundation, and a handful of other philanthropies that began addressing the issue in the early 1990s.

reducing the global fertility rate from five children per woman to just under three today. The so-called demographic dividend, partly attributable to this work, is credited for stimulating economic development in East Asia.[4]

Problems toward the edges of the big cube tend to require ambitious grantmaking, and require funders with a tolerance for ambiguity and complexity. Being larger in scale, they usually take more time to solve than other problems. Success often requires change to large systems.

For example, philanthropy can succeed in changing governmental and business policies toward climate change only if it is guided by a sophisticated understanding of the relevant decision-making processes, with an eye toward finding points of leverage where an intervention can make a significant difference. Philanthropists who take on large, complex problems need expertise in the dynamics of the systems they are seeking to change as well as knowledge of the problems themselves.

Work in the big cube also requires patience. The time frame for serious reform can be decades long, and attempts at quick fixes are unlikely to reap much beyond raised, then dashed, hopes. Conversely, sticking to a subject increases your ability to spend money well as you develop expertise in finding the best leverage points.

Work in the big cube almost always requires collaborating with others. This does not mean that individual philanthropists cannot take on large problems, but they must do so with a good sense of what others are doing to address the same problem and a willingness to combine resources toward common ends. They must also be willing to undertake risks and must realize that their particular efforts to solve global problems may not work. Even if the problem is solved, they may never know whether and how much they contributed.

Thus, if you mean to practice philanthropy in the big cube, you should recognize that

➤ *The processes of change are often indirect and complex.* Strategies for helping farmers in developing countries improve their productivity or sell their commodities abroad involve complicated technological, economic, and social interventions. Strategies for reducing AIDS or childhood obesity are similarly complex. And strategies for reducing nuclear proliferation or global warming often require indirect advocacy—efforts to induce citizens to induce policy makers or businesses to take action.

➤ *The risks of complete failure are high.* For every successful effort, like the Green Revolution, to bring about large-scale change, there are many strategies that have not succeeded (at least not yet)—for example, the reform of large urban school systems. We do not yet have an AIDS vaccine; poverty is still endemic in many communities at home as well as abroad; and the earth's temperature is rising: There is certainly risk in ambitious aims.

➤ *Results can be invisible, intangible, and a long time in coming.* The results of work in the big cube are often measurable only by small statistical changes, and even small changes may take many decades to emerge. Indeed, successes in the big cube that prevent catastrophes, such as a nuclear detonation, will go entirely unnoticed—like the curious incident of the dog in the nighttime.[5]

➤ *Causal links between philanthropy and the result can be obscure.* Efforts to achieve large-scale change typically involve many actors from both philanthropy and other sectors. Our own image of such ambitious projects, especially when they involve advocacy, is that of many people pushing a boulder up a hill. Even if they succeed, they will seldom know whether any one person's contributions made a difference.

➤ *The philanthropist's generosity is not likely to be recognized.* This follows from all the factors just mentioned—especially the intangibility of results happening in the distant future and the difficulty of attributing success.

But the advantages of working at the edges of the big cube are profound. When you are successful, your efforts will affect millions of people and can prevent irreversible damage. The patience, the risk, the indirectness, of such work can be compensated for by astounding leverage. If you do this right, your money will reach its fullest potential.

Although assessing philanthropic impact in terms of social return on investment does not always favor risky large-scale projects with long time horizons, we believe that philanthropy is underinvested in such projects—precisely because they *are* risky and distant in time and locale, and because many philanthropists desire the gratification of directly touching people's lives on a daily basis.

The Space Between the Cubes

Most philanthropy lies somewhere between the extremes of the small and big cubes. A program aimed at transforming K–12 education in California is somewhere in the middle on all three axes—the scope is substantial; the results of the work, if successful, will affect the current generation and their progeny; and the beneficiaries can be expected to have higher income, better health, and greater enjoyment of arts and culture.

The Ploughshares Fund

With a mission of preventing the use of weapons of mass destruction, the Ploughshares Fund has a budget of about $4 million per year. The fund, using its budget with strategic brilliance, made a principal contribution to the International Campaign to Ban Land Mines. Ploughshares grantees were instrumental in the renegotiations of the Nuclear Non-Proliferation Treaty. The fund supported high-level, off-the-record negotiations between senior U.S. analysts and North Korean officials that may have averted a war during the Clinton administration.

Ploughshares took on a hugely important realm of work that was not heavily supported by philanthropy. It built an expert board of directors, learned its field well, and has had an impact disproportionately large for its size. Given their ambitious choice of goals, it is evident that Ploughshares' donors have a tolerance for substantial abstraction and significant risk of failure.

Efforts to combat teen smoking and obesity are similar. To be successful, philanthropists will probably have to define a geography that is larger than a neighborhood and smaller than a continent. They will need to work in policy realms, from tax to public health. They will have to contend with powerful industries. They must understand the nuances of marketing to teenagers. And they will not know, until statistics show changing trends, whether their strategy is successful. But success could affect far more people, far more profoundly, than the same funds spent on building a new hospital wing.

Pursuing the Same General Goals in Different Places Along the Axes

The nature of the problems you are seeking to address plays a significant role in determining strategies, time horizons, and the other characteristics of philanthropy discussed above. But depending on how broadly you define your goals, you can often carve out approaches that suit your philanthropic resources and style.

Suppose that you are concerned with poverty in your community. On the home front, you might contribute to a food bank or support a job-training program or a "livable wage" campaign. Supporting direct services like these is paradigmatically in the small cube. It has immediate, tangible results and is relatively risk free: it is virtually certain that some people will be helped. The livable-wage advocacy strategy, in contrast, has risks. There are few organizations capable of carrying it out and no guarantees that it will succeed. Even if the policy is adopted, there remains the contested empirical question of whether a livable wage will actually improve the lives of the poorest people in your community. The job-training program lies somewhere in the middle. The payoff is less immediate and less certain than direct services, but it has the potential to move people out of poverty and is more likely to succeed—albeit benefiting a more limited population—than the livable-wage campaign.

Someone concerned with poverty or disease in developing countries has a similar array of strategies. Within the small cube—with immediate and visible results—you can provide disaster relief or subsidize the provision of AIDS drugs for residents of an African village. Further out on the axis—with complex strategies and uncertain payoff—you can support a campaign to prevent the transmission of the HIV virus.

On Fishing

An old saying goes: "Give a man a fish and you feed him for a day. Teach a man to fish and you feed him for a lifetime." Feeding someone for a day has immediate results and carries little risk of failure. Self-sufficiency has obvious long-term advantages but is not achievable by everyone—at least not in time to ward off starvation. (There are some other good variations on the adage, among which our favorite is "Give a man a fish, and you feed him for a day. Teach a man how to fish and he'll sit all day in a boat drinking beer.")

Preventing and Treating HIV/AIDS

Through a combination of sympathy for the identifiable victims of disease and U.S. antagonism toward international family planning, far more funds have gone into drugs for treating HIV/AIDS than into its prevention. However, studies suggest that combining prevention with treatment is cost-effective and will significantly reduce the number of deaths.[6]

Where you decide to intervene along this spectrum depends on where you think you can make the greatest impact given your financial and other resources. It also depends on how you weight the potential leverage of more abstract and riskier philanthropic investments compared with those that directly, visibly, and immediately touch human lives. Do you find it more compelling to cure individuals already afflicted with a disease, or to prevent others from getting it in the first place? To provide relief to the known victims of particular disasters, or to plan to avoid the recurrence of such disasters? Your own personal "style" may lead you to prefer one approach or the other, and that choice can lead to profoundly different effects.

Even philanthropists with relatively small resources can tackle large-scale problems by combining their resources with those of other funders—for example, by providing general support to a not-for-profit organization devoted to the problem. Although this usually requires forgoing the individual recognition that may come with being the sole funder of a project of more modest scale, collaboration in one form or another has been at the heart of many of philanthropy's great successes. Although your $20,000 grant may seem like a drop in the bucket compared with an organization's $3 million budget, it is only because of a number of funders like you that the organization can meet its budget.

There is no right philanthropic objective, but there are profoundly different choices. The choice of subject will substantially affect the character of the grants that must follow. Different individuals may differ not only in their philanthropic interests but also in their preferences for

Major Funder or Minor Contributor?

You may be among the lead funders of a large effort or be one of many relatively small contributors. Lead funders tend to be large foundations with staff members who have expertise in the subject. Lead funders tend to provide general support to key organizations in the field, supplemented by funds for particular projects that are often codesigned by the staff of the foundations and the organizations carrying them out.

Whereas a lead funder is likely to be in close communication with the organization's staff, a smaller contributor will have to rely more on the organization's reports and occasional meetings with its CEO or development officer. One great shortcut in deciding whether to invest in the organization: establish a relationship with a trusted lead funder who has done the extensive due diligence that a large investment requires.

where to position themselves on the axes described above. And some people may feel most comfortable having a mix of objectives. Our purpose in suggesting these axes is to provide some reference points as you consider where your own philanthropic interests lie.

Goals, Missions, Grant Guidelines, and Grants

So far, we have discussed concerns, goals, and strategic approaches in a very broad sense. At some point—in Chapter 5—these will become the bases for making grants. But first let's consider goals in terms of two other concepts: mission statements and grant guidelines.

An organization's *mission statement* expresses the organization's goals at a general level. The statement is often aspirational and sometimes even inspirational—for example,

The mission of the Julio and Maria Flores Foundation is to improve opportunities for disadvantaged youth.

Examples of Foundation Mission Statements

> "Improving the global environment"
> "Enhancing the human condition"
> "Supporting all aspects of the creative process for a worldwide community of artists"
> "Reducing global poverty"
> "Inspiring individuals to make responsible choices and take direct personal actions to achieve a peaceful and environmentally sustainable future"

For a foundation that has diverse goals, the mission can seek to tie those goals together.

Because *goals* serve as the basis for designing particular strategies, they are more specific than mission statements—for example,

The Flores Foundation seeks to improve the English reading skills of elementary-school students in the Greenville public schools.

Our own preference is for specificity, and for quantitative targets when possible. This provides a healthy accountability for you and your staff— an opportunity to explain to each other why you reached, exceeded, or fell short of a goal.

By 2010, we plan to increase the number of second-grade students who can read English at grade level from 75 percent to 90 percent.

What's the relation between goals and mission statements? Although having a mission statement is by no means essential for strategic philanthropy, the very process of drafting one can provide you and your family, advisers, or trustees an opportunity to discuss the core values that inform your work. The process of developing missions and goals is

Missions and Goals as More or Less Specific Destinations

If you've ever gotten driving directions, whether by asking a person, using an onboard navigation system, or referring to Google Maps or MapQuest, you know that the more precisely you specify your destination, the more specific the directions will be. Your philanthropic goals can be as specific as a street address—for example, keeping global CO_2 concentrations below 450 parts per million. Or they can be more general, like the location of a city (slowing global warming). A mission statement (improving the environment) is more like having a country as your destination. Although a mission statement may capture the spirit of your grantmaking, it cannot provide guidance for particular grants or, indeed, for organizations seeking your grant funds. Clarity of goals tends to focus your resources most effectively and provide a basis for accountability.

often recursive, with goals helping determine an organization's mission and the mission statement then providing a check—not a prohibition, but a moment of reflection—as you consider possible new goals.

The same goal can often be achieved through alternative approaches or strategies. *Grant guidelines* provide information to applicants to help them understand how well their work is aligned with your own approach. For example, the Flores Foundation might support after-school programs or teacher training. It might advocate that the district provide additional classes for English-language learners, or it might invest in innovative computer technologies for learning English. Or its general guideline for this area might state:

The Flores Foundation invites grant proposals by organizations with comprehensive after-school programs that center around English reading and writing skills.

By making the scope of your interests clear both internally and externally, grant guidelines focus your own staff's efforts, reduce the time wasted by potential applicants whose activities are far afield from your strategies, and reduce the time you spend reading and politely declining proposals. (To reduce is not to eliminate: hope springs eternal for every applicant that believes that it has a solution to your problem.)

In response to your grant guidelines, perhaps published on the Web, you will receive some proposals that are well aligned with your goals and strategies. As we discuss in Chapter 5, each proposal is the starting place for discussions that may result in a grant.

IT IS NOT unusual for new philanthropists to begin with a safe target and only later consider more complex and ambitious goals. Nor is it unusual for people who have come into great wealth to change their goals over time—sometimes as their interests evolve, sometimes through the very process of engaging in philanthropy and observing the outcomes. The philosopher H. L. A. Hart wisely observed that some "indeterminacy of aim" is inevitable in all human affairs.[7] But at any given time you need to know what goal you are pursuing. As the old adage goes, "If you don't know where you're going, any road will get you there."

Takeaway Points

➤ Philanthropy in the small cube addresses the relatively near-term, non-life-threatening problems of a relatively small number of people. It involves direct and readily graspable processes, a low risk of complete failure, visible and tangible results in the near term, and individual recognition.

➤ Philanthropy in the big cube addresses long-term, life-threatening global problems. It involves indirect and complex processes of change, a significant risk of complete failure, and invisible, intangible, and distant results, and it is less likely to lead to your particular contribution's being recognized.

➤ Different philanthropists may have different comfort zones for their goals and approaches.

➤ Whatever the nature and scope of your own approach, you will need to translate a general mission into specific goals, which will provide the basis for your strategies and grantmaking.

Chapter Notes

1.   For a rich discussion of the complexities of the concept of irreversibility, see Cass R. Sunstein, *Worst-Case Scenarios* (Cambridge, Mass.: Harvard University Press, 2007).

2.   See Chapter 3.

3.   See Matthew Connelly, *Fatal Misconception: The Struggle to Control World Population* (Cambridge, Mass.: Harvard University Press, 2008) and Martin Morse Wooster, *Great Philanthropic Mistakes* (Washington, D.C.: Hudson Institute, 2006).

4.   David E. Bloom and Jeffrey G. Williamson, "Demographic Transitions and Economic Miracles in Emerging Asia," *World Bank Economic Review* 12, no. 3 (1998): 419–455.

5.   In "Silver Blaze," a Sherlock Holmes story by Sir Arthur Conan Doyle, 1894, Inspector Gregory, the Scotland Yard detective investigating the case with Holmes, begins the dialogue:

> "Is there any point to which you would wish to draw my attention?"
>
> "To the curious incident of the dog in the night-time."
>
> "The dog did nothing in the night-time."
>
> "That was the curious incident," remarked Sherlock Holmes.

6.   John Stover et al., "The Global Impact of Scaling Up HIV/AIDS Prevention Programs in Low- and Middle-Income Countries," *Science* 311 (2006): 1474–1476; and Joshua A. Salomon et al., "Integrating HIV Prevention and Treatment: From Slogans to Impact," *PLoS Medicine* 2, no. 1 (2005), http://medicine.plosjournals.org.

7.   H. L. A. Hart, *The Concept of Law*, 2nd ed. (New York: Oxford University Press, 1994), 128.

Chapter 3 *Three*

Analyzing Problems and Developing Solutions

ONCE YOU HAVE a goal or objective* in mind, the next step is what we call problem analysis.[1] You can think of most philanthropy as either responding to a problem or seizing an opportunity. These are two sides of the same coin, but focusing on the problem tends to sharpen analysis. A problem can be understood in several different ways:[2]

➤ In its narrowest sense, a problem means that something has gone wrong; for example, a river is so polluted that fish are dying. Solving the problem would involve reducing or eliminating the sources of pollution and cleaning up the river.

➤ Sometimes nothing has gone wrong yet, but there is reason to believe that if an action is not taken, something may go wrong in the future; for example, if an earthquake or pandemic hits your city, thousands of people may die. Solving the problem would involve encouraging and assisting public agencies, businesses, and not-for-profit organizations to prepare to deal with potential disasters.

➤ Most broadly, a problem means that the world as it is varies from the world we would like. Solving the problem involves moving the world in a desired direction;[3] for example, you may believe that Americans should have a greater understanding of other nations and cultures. Solving this problem might involve educational programs on a grand scale.

---

* Throughout the book, we use *goal* and *objective* interchangeably.

Problem Analysis

Throughout this chapter, you may ask, *Who* needs to analyze problems and design strategies to solve them? Is this a task for philanthropists, or for the organizations they support? In later chapters, we consider how active a role you may wish to play vis-à-vis grantee organizations in determining the strategy for addressing particular problems. For now, though, even if you ultimately leave most of the responsibility to a grantee, you will need to undertake a thorough analysis to ensure that the organization's staff has adequately thought through the strategy and that it makes sense. If the tasks we describe seem daunting, we should note that you will seldom perform them all by yourself. There is almost no philanthropic ground that others—organizations and practitioners in the field, other funders, and academic experts—have not already trod. You would be wise to consult broadly to get a sense of the terrain and to avoid falling into known potholes.

Framing the Problem

After a very successful business career, Peggy Chau has started working part-time so that she can focus her attention on two small children and her new family foundation. Another motive for her decision was to avoid the grueling daily commute by car from her suburban home to the city center—a commute that has inspired her to do something to promote "smart growth" in her region.

Peggy makes an appointment to see a professor of urban planning at a nearby university. She mentions that she had visited some friends in a northwestern city that was a model of smart growth and prided itself on its light-rail system, and that she thinks that such a rail system would solve the problem here as well. The professor suggests that they first take a step back, and asks her, "What aspects of smart growth particularly interest you—or to put it differently, what problems would you like to work on solving?" Earlier that day, he had taught a class on the economic and social dimensions of urban growth, and he shows her a slide that lists some of the problems he discussed with the class:

➤ The boredom and social isolation of long commutes
➤ The "paving over" of the countryside, with the loss of scenic lands and the growth of strip malls

➤ The loss of lands devoted to agriculture and the loss of species' habitats
➤ The civic and cultural consequences of people being highly dispersed
➤ The effects on the inner city when residents move to the suburbs and exurbs

"All of these bother me to some extent," says Peggy, "but especially the commuting." As their conversation continues, she indicates that it's not boredom or social isolation that concerns her, but the congestion, which she has seen increase greatly on her own commute over the years. And why does this concern her? It's not the time it takes—people can amuse themselves by listening to the radio—but the increased pollution, the effect on global warming, and the rising cost of gas.

This leads to discussion of possible ways to reduce these costs of traffic congestion. Peggy realizes that light rail is not a solution here, because of the region's geography and the distances involved. But there may be other approaches, including zoning, that could at least mitigate the problems of future development. The professor suggests that Peggy contact a strong regional not-for-profit organization that is working closely with officials on these matters.

Reed Hastings's Education in Education

Most philanthropic interventions depend at least in part on facts about the real world. Recognizing the limits of her own knowledge, Peggy consulted with an urban-planning expert. If you plan to focus your philanthropy on a particular field, consider how the successful entrepreneur Reed Hastings prepared himself to become a partner in the NewSchools Venture Fund (http://www.newschools.org). When Hastings sought the advice of Stanford Education School professor Mike Kirst on how to use his philanthropic resources to create meaningful change in education, Kirst suggested that he go back to school to understand the roots of the current models of education. Hastings took the advice and enrolled in a masters program.[4]

Through her conversation with the urban-planning professor, Peggy deepens her understanding of the particular issue at hand, gains a deeper understanding of her own objectives, and learns something that will be useful in all her philanthropy: following the Zen practice of repeatedly asking why until you've gotten to the root of the question is a useful way to clarify the problem and expand the problem frame. Frames set boundaries on our thinking, defining what is "inside" and what is "outside" the scope of the problem situation. They not only tell us how to describe the problem but also indirectly inform us what goals and objectives the problem implicates and what solutions are possible. You can think of the problem frame as a window looking out on a broad vista. If you're on the far side of the room, the window is effectively smaller and you can see only part of the landscape; as you move closer to the window, your range of vision outside the window grows larger.

The first order of business is to make sure that you are trying to solve the right problem. People sometimes go about solving the wrong one because they do not frame the problem adequately. They may mistake symptoms for the problem itself, define the problem or solutions too narrowly, or—as in the case of Peggy's initial focus on a light-rail system—define the problem in terms of a ready solution without asking whether it is the best, or even an effective, way to correct the situation.

Here's another example. Joan and Fred Watkins, philanthropists deeply concerned with education in their community, are approached by Kevin Sloan, the president of the Ridge Community College Alumni Association. Kevin graduated from Ridge with honors and finished his degree at a liberal-arts college. He is concerned that the number of Ridge graduates going on to a four-year college is declining and asks the Watkinses to consider funding scholarships to enable Ridge graduates to attend college. The Watkinses decide to meet with the president of Ridge Community College to get a deeper understanding of the situation.

They learn that it's not just that Ridge graduates aren't going on to a four-year college; less than a quarter of its students even complete the community-college program. For most students, a four-year-college degree is far less important than the fundamental job-related skills learned in the two-year community-college program. But many students are pursuing basic job skills without having their eyes on a degree or certificate at the end of the coursework—a real error in terms of career opportunities. And many others are dropping out because of inadequate preparation, counseling, or financial support.

The Watkinses conclude that the problems are not peculiar to Ridge, but are endemic to community colleges throughout the state and are rooted in the structure of the community-college system. For example, state policies tie financial incentives to enrollment numbers rather than how many students actually receive a certificate or diploma. Because the community colleges are funded on the basis of the number of students registered for classes on a certain day, colleges understandably seek to fill seats. Students are allowed to register late for classes with no penalty; prerequisites are loosely enforced; and remedial courses can be postponed.

Without foreclosing the possibility of eventually supporting scholarships along the lines suggested by Kevin, the Watkinses decide to tackle what they now regard as the fundamental challenge facing community-college students whether or not they plan to go on to four-year colleges: obtaining two years of adequate and appropriately credentialed education. They realize that the problem calls for statewide systemic change, but they have never before used their philanthropic resources for something like this. The Watkinses decide to begin by contacting some foundations concerned with the issue with the hope of learning whether there is already work under way to change state policy, to which they might contribute.

The conversation with the community-college president didn't just expand the Watkinses' window; it gave them an alternative frame. Imagine that you're moving from the left side of the room to the right side and see quite different landscapes as you move from one vantage point to another. Consider these examples of differing frameworks:

➤ How do you think of the great expanses of the American West? As areas of natural beauty for the enjoyment of hikers or snowmobile enthusiasts? As parts of ecosystems that preserve biodiversity and provide essential services to communities? As sacred Indian grounds? Or as resources for ranchers or miners? By choosing different frames, philanthropists may choose to direct their resources to quite different purposes and to different kinds of organizations.

➤ How does a Mexican worker in the United States think of sending remittances back home—as support for his Mexico-based family, or also as support for his community? A number of foundations and not-for-profits in the United States and Mexico have been working with immigrants to expand their framework for providing aid through groups called "hometown associations." By pooling and sharing funds, not just with their own families but with entire towns, these associations create a support mechanism that connects many small donors on the U.S. side and helps them aggregate remittances and provide more substantial economic development aid to their communities in Mexico.

The metaphors we bring to a situation can have a powerful framing effect. Do you view negotiation as a game, a war, or a collaboration? In an interesting experiment, participants played a prisoner's dilemma–type game in which they had the choice of cooperating or defecting. Those who were told that the exercise was called the "Wall Street game" were more likely to defect than those who were told it was called the "community game."[5] Just thinking about the game one way or another changed the way they behaved toward the other participants.

As for philanthropic metaphors, consider the terms that foundations use to refer to their grantees: "customers," "partners," "agents." Although the term "customer" captures the importance of maintaining a good relationship, it ignores the fact that the real beneficiaries are the communities and individuals that the foundation and grantee are serving. The term "partner" captures some ideal aspects of the relationship, but it ignores the imbalance of power that often separates funders and grantees. The term "agent" captures the power relationship but understates the importance of the grantee's autonomy. Although we haven't heard the term used in philanthropy, one might also consider the grantee as a "seller" of services to the funder. You can't avoid using metaphors, but be conscious of their hidden meanings; don't become their prisoner.

By the same token, you can't avoid viewing problems through frames, but with effort you can become aware of how you are framing a situation and whether there are alternative ways of viewing it. You can also avoid some common pitfalls in framing problems, such as defining the problem in terms of a particular solution—as Peggy did with her suggestion that a light-rail system would solve regional congestion.

An old story tells of a farmer who drives to a neighbor's house to pick up some bags of chicken feed. The farmer drives up beside the barn and loads the feed into the back of his truck. As he goes to get back into the truck, he sees that his front left tire is flat—and then remembers that he has no jack in the truck. Feeling no small measure of exasperation, the farmer begins the long walk to the nearest gas station, without noticing that the barn's hay-lift pulley was perfectly positioned to lift the front of his truck.[6] The farmer erred in framing the problem too narrowly, which led to an inadequate solution. Specifically, he associated the problem ("How can I lift my truck?") with one particular solution ("Find a jack!").

To a person with a hammer, every problem looks like a nail. Philanthropists and the organizations they support are no exceptions to the universal tendency to use a set of stock approaches to one's work rather than being open to an array of possible solutions. For example, the dominant approach to reforming state financing of public schools for the past quarter century has focused on litigation—initially attempting to secure equal school expenditures among districts and more recently to assure an "adequate" education for every child. These lawsuits have dragged out over many years and have consumed many millions of dollars, yet they have not achieved much change in school finance policies, let alone in educational outcomes for disadvantaged children.

Frustrated by the lack of progress in California, a handful of foundations[7] began working with a bipartisan group of state leaders, including the Republican governor Arnold Schwarzenegger, the Democratic-led legislature, and the superintendent of public instruction, to understand the scope and nature of the problem and come up with some solutions. At the policy makers' request, the foundations funded a $2 million study of how California funds its K–12 schools. Though it is premature to know what results the study will produce, the fact that the research has broad political buy-in gives it a chance of success where litigation has failed.

Another common error is to frame multidimensional problems in a unitary way. For example, in response to the appalling statistic that 100 million children—mostly girls—in developing countries receive no education at all, many bilateral and multinational donor agencies initially framed the problem solely in terms of barriers to access to elementary education. But they neglected the scandalously poor education that often occurred within schools and the fact that merely removing barriers would stress systems that were already operating on or below the margin.

School fees were correctly understood as a significant barrier, and enrollment in Malawi jumped by 62 percent in the first year that the country provided free primary education. But the shock in demand exacerbated the overcrowding of classrooms, and shortages of teachers, textbooks, and materials. And this, in turn, led to a reduction in enrollment—not because of barriers to access but because ineffectual schooling didn't seem worth sacrificing the child's help with household work or tending the farm.

It is now understood that getting students into the classroom doesn't come close to ensuring that they are learning. Though lack of access is part of the problem, it is also a symptom of the problem. Obtaining an education depends on factors such as whether there are books in the classroom, whether the teachers are adequately trained, whether the teachers show up, whether students are physically healthy and sufficiently fed so that they can focus their minds on learning.

Diagnosing Causes

In many situations, solving a problem effectively requires accurately diagnosing its causes and relating them to possible solutions. Consider the following examples:

➤ If you are concerned about the depletion of salmon in the Pacific Northwest, you must understand why salmon are being depleted. Is it overfishing, pollution from farms running into spawning streams, dams on the spawning streams—or all three?

➤ If you are concerned about the high rate of teen pregnancies in your community, you need to understand why teenage girls get pregnant. Why are teenage girls and boys having sex at all? Are the pregnancies intended, and if so why? If not, why are the young people not taking adequate precautions? Are they aware of contraceptive methods? Do they have access to contraception?

➤ If you are concerned about the devastating effects of malaria, you must understand how the disease is propagated and the possible points of intervention—reducing the population of mosquitoes through poison, genetics, or the elimination of their habitats; protecting people from mosquitoes through bed nets; or developing better antimalarial medicines or a vaccine.

Unless you, or the organization you are supporting, know these things, you will not be able to develop effective strategies for solving the problem.

Imagine that you are a program officer for the Metro Community Foundation in a large northeastern city. Among your regular grantees is the Northside Neighborhood Center, which provides emergency assistance for some of the city's poorest residents—mostly Latino hourly workers in restaurants, big retail stores, construction sites, and the like.

In a meeting with staff from Northside to discuss renewing its grant for the next three years, they request a substantial increase for emergency financial assistance. For the past couple of winters, the center has seen a two-month surge in demand for food and other basic necessities. The center's staff attribute this to the lull in retail industries following the holiday season and to the nasty weather that hampers outdoor construction. The center's documentation of the seasonal surge is persuasive, but you have some doubts about the proffered explanation. You suggest that the center's staff conduct an informal survey of its clients.

Although they cannot rule out the labor-demand theory, it turns out that the families are beset by considerable illness during the winter—not surprising given that their apartments are poorly heated and ventilated and that medical advice and treatment are scant. Public clinics are available but not in the immediate neighborhood, and visits to them are few and far between.

At this point, the staff of both the Metro Community Foundation and the Northside Neighborhood Center begin brainstorming about a number of solutions, ranging from health insurance to persuading the city to open a clinic in the neighborhood. In a discussion with the city's health commissioner, a new hypothesis about the problem emerges: the surge of demand for emergency assistance coincides with flu season. Although the children get vaccinated through a school program, almost none of the breadwinners get flu shots. As a result, they miss work without paid sick leave and infect members of their families and their coworkers. Next year's flu is predicted to be especially virulent.

Developing Alternative Solutions

Before fixing on a particular strategy to solve the problem, you need to consider alternative solutions. Just as the best description of the problem is not necessarily the first to come to mind, so it is with potential solutions or strategies. Earlier we suggested continually asking *why*, to identify your goals. Now ask *how*, to generate solutions.

Putting their heads together and consulting with the health commissioner's office, staff from the Metro Community Foundation and the Northside Neighborhood Center consider possible ways to ensure that neighborhood families get annual flu shots. Vaccinations are available without charge at a public clinic that is reasonably accessible to the neighborhood. But many of the immigrant residents are leery of contacts with the government, especially where—as regulations require—they must provide their names and addresses. Last year, only about 7 percent of the adults in Northside were vaccinated, compared with a citywide average of over 30 percent.

Ultimately, the staff come up with a general strategy. The neighborhood center will send trained community health workers, known as *promotores*, door-to-door to sign people up to come to the center for flu shots. Unfortunately, the city's regulations do not permit municipal subsidization of any part of the process, but the foundation is willing to pay for this work, as well as for the vaccines, the nurses, the insurance, and the center's overhead. (For an example of developing alternative solutions in the context of global development, visit *www.smartphilanthropy.org.*)

Creativity in Developing Solutions to Problems

Developing alternative solutions requires creativity or innovation akin to that of a scientist or engineer—creativity that is goal-oriented, that aims to come up with pragmatic solutions to a problem.

Creativity requires an attitude or mind-set that is open to novelty, alert to distinctions, sensitive to different contexts, and aware of different perspectives—a mind-set that views problem situations from multiple perspectives.[8] This attitude is fostered by engaging in divergent thinking—imagining and generating a broad range of options—before evaluating and analyzing, criticizing, and narrowing down the range of alternatives.

Creativity usually entails crossing the boundaries of existing domains and combining elements of one with elements of another to create something new. Arthur Koestler wrote that Johannes Gutenberg invented the printing press after noticing the connection between applying force to impress script on paper and applying force to squeeze grapes in a wine press.[9] But innovations of this sort seldom result from the efforts of a single "creative" individual or from a sudden lightning-bolt insight. Rather, creative ideas are usually generated by people who have spent years of hard work within a field.

In its roughly one-hundred-year history, American philanthropy has played a role in developing many creative solutions that have had a real impact on society. In addition to those mentioned in Chapter 1, consider these examples from the twentieth century:[10]

➤ Using insulin to treat diabetes
➤ Releasing poor criminal defendants on their own recognizance
➤ Creating the profession of the nurse-practitioner
➤ Developing the 911 emergency telephone system

You have the potential to fund equally important breakthroughs in the twenty-first century. After all is said and done, of course, it may turn out that the best solution to a problem is a tried-and-true approach—but you can't know that until you have considered other possibilities.

Theory of Change
Underlying any strategy for solving a problem is what people call a *theory of change*—a theory of how the relevant part of the world works. A theory of change is fundamentally an analysis of the causal chain that links your philanthropic interventions to the goals you want to achieve. In the Northside example, the theory of change is based on several empirical hypotheses:

1. Influenza is responsible for breadwinners' missing days of work.
2. Vaccinations tend to prevent flu infections.
3. Breadwinners in this community are not getting flu shots because of their fear of government-run clinics.

The second hypothesis is well established by medical science. The first and third are hypotheses about social phenomena and are much more speculative. At this point they are based largely on intuition informed by knowledge of the community. They are, however, testable hypotheses, and if Metro and Northside are going to rely on them, the organizations can and should build at least some evaluation into the project.

A Theory of Change for This Book

Although we value scholarship for its own sake, this book is written with an instrumental purpose: to improve the effectiveness of your philanthropy with the ultimate goal of making the world a better place. Our theory of change is that this book will help readers who are already strategically oriented become even better and that it will whet others' appetites. Doubtless this is a speculative and somewhat optimistic belief. After all, for every thousand books written with the hope of making a difference in people's lives, let alone society at large, at most one or two succeed. But we think of our effort in terms of expected return just as we do "big cube" philanthropy: the probability of impact may not be high, but the potential magnitude of success is tremendous.

A theory of change is only as good as its empirical validity. An intuitively plausible theory of change is better than none at all—but the not-for-profit sector is littered with programs based on theories of change that seemed intuitively plausible but were not valid. Therefore, the more tested the theory of change, the sounder its use as the basis for a strategy.

From Theory to Action

Having figured out a plausible theory of change, it's time to outline a strategy for achieving your goal.

The Strategic Plan or Logic Model

The jargon for a strategic plan is *logic model*, meaning that it is the logical set of steps to achieve your goals. A logic model is a linked set of causes and effects based on the theory of change. Here's an example by someone who surely never used the term but who certainly understood the concept: Rube Goldberg.

Rube Goldberg gets his think tank working and evolves the simplified pencil sharpener.

Open window (A) and fly kite (B). String (C) lifts small door (D) allowing moths (E) to escape and eat red flannel shirt (F). As weight of shirt becomes less, shoe (G) steps on switch (H) which heats electric iron (I) and burns hole in pants (J). Smoke (K) enters hole in tree (L), smoking out opossum (M) which jumps into basket (N), pulling rope (O) and lifting cage (P), allowing woodpecker (Q) to chew wood from pencil (R), exposing lead. Emergency knife (S) is always handy in case opossum or woodpecker gets sick and can't work.

Of course, in its celebration of unnecessary complexity, Rube Goldberg's contraption is a parody of a logic model. But it nonetheless illustrates some important points.

➤ As you see, a logic model is nothing but a set of causal links—A causes B, which causes C, . . . which causes S—that ultimately lead to your goal.
➤ Albert Einstein described the ideal logic model when he said: "Everything should be made as simple as possible, but not one bit simpler." Of course, Rube Goldberg has made his contraption as complicated as possible. Yet it is not all that complicated compared with the strategies necessary to accomplish many social goals that philanthropists seek to bring about. For example, consider all the steps necessary to transport inexpensive contraceptives to a rural African village, sell them, and encourage villagers to use them.

➤ Rube Goldberg's logic model makes empirical assumptions about how the world actually operates—ranging from gravity, electricity, and other laws of physics to the behavior of woodpeckers and opossums. His intervention is only as good as his empirical assumptions. This is no less true of philanthropic interventions.

➤ Any break in Rube Goldberg's logic model will result in the entire project failing. This is true of some philanthropic projects as well. Note, however, that Goldberg has provided a degree of redundancy: an emergency knife in case the opossum or the woodpecker gets sick and can't work. Philanthropists can do this as well. But you can't know what redundancy to build in without having a thorough understanding of the causal chain.

➤ In Rube Goldberg's example, two interventions are necessary: opening the window and flying the kite. After that, nature takes its course, largely beyond Goldberg's control. That sounds simple enough, but now think about how hard it is to fly a kite while leaning out a window. So this part of the plan for implementing the strategy requires something beyond the basic logic model—it requires describing what confederates you will need outside the window and—well, how to fly a kite.

Risk Factors

You can think of a strategic plan in positive or negative terms—how to maximize the chances of achieving your goals, or how to minimize the risks of failure. Like opportunities and problems, these are just two sides of the same coin. We place risks in four categories:

➤ *Strategic risks*: the possibility that your strategy just doesn't pan out
➤ *External risks*: the possibility that external factors overwhelm your strategy
➤ *The risk of doing harm*: the possibility that your work leads to unintended bad consequences
➤ *Organizational risks*: the possibility that your grantee organization isn't able to carry out the activities to implement the strategy

We discuss the first three here and address organizational risks in Chapter 5 in connection with the due-diligence aspect of grant-making.

Strategic Risks

The fundamental strategic risk is that the underlying theory is flawed because it is based on natural or social science hypotheses that, however well founded, turn out to be wrong. In the Northside example, it may turn out that the flu has nothing to do with the families' seasonal crises. One way to mitigate strategic risk is to engage in careful problem analysis and planning. Another is to incorporate some redundancy: identify questionable elements of your logic model or theory of change and invest in more than one approach to achieving the result.

In Chapter 1, we described the Robert Wood Johnson Foundation's Fighting Back initiative as an example of a well-thought-out program that failed largely for strategic reasons. Because individual philanthropists and foundations do not devote significant resources to evaluating the outcomes of their grants, and because they tend to publicize successes more than failures, there are not many documented examples of strategic failures. One of the few exemplary case studies is the James Irvine Foundation's evaluation of its Communities Organizing Resources to Advance Learning (CORAL) project, a carefully planned and executed strategy that failed.[11] The goal of the eight-year, $60 million program was to improve educational achievement in low-performing schools in five California cities. The foundation believed that it could have the greatest impact by focusing on after-school programs created through a community-organizing and planning process that also incorporated parental involvement and collaboration with local not-for-profit organizations.

As the initiative proceeded, however, the programs that emerged from the community process were underenrolled, expensive, and of modest quality at best. They focused on enrichment activities (like the arts, music, and sports) rather than core academic subjects. But subsequent research suggested that after-school programs with an explicitly academic focus are far more likely to improve academic achievement. The foundation decided that a major overhaul was required and thus requested that the CORAL sites begin focusing attention on creating high-quality literacy-based programs. Although the results are not yet available, it is worth noting that only a foundation committed to continuous evaluation and research would have learned about the need for midcourse corrections.

External Risks

An external risk in Northside's vaccination program might be an unanticipated shortage of the flu vaccine or an economic recession that creates high enough unemployment to swamp any problem caused by the flu within the target population. When working in developing countries, widespread civil violence, pandemics, and other natural catastrophes can jeopardize any gains from programs aimed at improving economic conditions. For example, the unanticipated conflict in Kenya, following claims of a rigged election, put at risk some of the most promising development programs and achievements in sub-Saharan Africa.

The Risk of Doing Harm

Not only can philanthropists fail to achieve their intended results; sometimes they can do harm. Pursuit of a poor strategy may divert needed resources from the very population a philanthropist seeks to serve. Organizations or communities may become dependent on a particular funder who then pulls the rug out from under them with disastrous consequences. In the worst case, a well-intentioned effort may lead to economic, environmental, or physical damage.

Philanthropy played a role in the performance-based school-accountability movement that led to the enactment of the federal No Child Left Behind Act, which has had various unintended negative consequences. For example, the incentive to "teach to the test" has led to less time on topics and activities—such as the arts and physical education—that the tests do not cover. (Although CORAL's failure was attributed to emphasizing these activities to the exclusion of academic subjects, most educators believe that they are an important complement to academic studies.) Schools have also manipulated which students are included in or excluded from testing in order to enhance their apparent school performance. And high-school students on the cusp of failure have been pushed out so as not to compromise a school's score.[12]

Unintended consequences are a particular danger for donors and organizations working in the developing world. Success in international development often requires a deep understanding of local communities and their cultures. Ned Breslin, who works on development for the not-for-profit Water for People, cited a failed effort by an organization that had installed water pumps in Mozambique.[13] In one village, the hand pump broke fifteen months after it was installed, and though a few women in the village had been taught how to fix the pump, their training was inadequate and replacement parts were not readily available. The organization that undertook the project did not have the time or capacity to ensure its success; it acted on its own timetable without consideration for the realities of the community. The results were a bitter disappointment, especially for women whose community held them accountable for the failure.

The Carnegie Corporation, along with the United Nations and several other major foundations, supported the convening of a constitutional convention in Zimbabwe in 1999. The convention, however, was dominated by supporters of the nation's dictator, Robert Mugabe, and the constitution they produced was ultimately rejected by the people of the country. This defeat, a major embarrassment for the ruling party, backfired on the civic leaders who had been involved and may well have resulted in Mugabe's becoming a more authoritarian, more entrenched ruler. The Carnegie Corporation gave this candid assessment:

> In the case of Zimbabwe, while the grant produced the projected outputs—a public education and outreach campaign—the hoped-for outcome—a viable constitution acceptable to a majority of Zimbabwe's citizens—was not achieved.
>
> The lesson learned from the ill-fated grant to Zimbabwe is an old one that must be re-learned time and again: that leadership and program staff must weigh their aspirations against a realistic assessment of the limits of what they can accomplish in order to keep both in balance. "One has to find a way to be daring while also being realistic—to figure out how not to over-promise," [Carnegie's president, Vartan] Gregorian stresses.
>
> Looking back after seven years, constitutional reform was clearly a lost cause. . . . The Mugabe regime's intention was undoubtedly to co-opt the process without ever acceding to any of the public's demands. . . . The ruling party's humiliating loss led to even more intolerant and authoritarian policies. Analysts point to the failed referendum as a tipping point in Mugabe's slide into full-scale tyranny. Conditions in Zimbabwe have gone from bad to disastrous. According to the United Nations Development Program, Zimbabwe's GDP has contracted over 40 percent since 2000, and the inflation rate had reached a high of 1,913 percent as of May 2006. . . . Chronic food shortages continue and HIV/AIDS, brain drain, and stark poverty make a dismal situation bleaker still.[14]

We should note that proving that a philanthropic intervention caused harm is no easier than proving that it caused a positive result; the Carnegie Corporation probably played a minor role, at most, in Zimbabwe's disastrous decline. But the story emphasizes the importance of understanding the social and political dynamics of any system—whether a local community or a foreign country—in which one intervenes.

Of course, there may be disagreement about whether the consequences of particular interventions are beneficial or harmful—for example, whether school vouchers and many charter schools improve educational outcomes for disadvantaged students or whether they draw resources away from traditional public schools and exacerbate racial segregation.[15] Nowhere are these disagreements stronger than in international development. The so-called Green Revolution, led by the Rockefeller and Ford foundations, produced significant increases in agricultural production in developing countries from the 1940s to the 1960s and is credited with saving millions, if not billions, of lives.[16] Yet this work has been criticized for widening disparities between large-scale and small-scale farmers, for displacing small farmers from their land,[17] and for causing soil erosion and the loss of biodiversity.

Being willing to learn from failure is as important as having a good strategy at the outset. Acknowledging some of the environmental problems, the Rockefeller Foundation recently noted that "considerable effort has been made to mitigate these problems with much success in using integrated pest management and genetic resistance to reduce the need for pesticides."[18]

Implementing the Plan, Tracking Progress, and Assessing Success
The Northside Neighborhood Center's vaccination program (discussed above) requires a set of activities that are a lot more complex than flying a kite. The core of Northside's plan for implementing the strategy involves specifying these activities and identifying who will carry them out. In broad outline, its plan would include

➤ identifying the target audience for outreach;
➤ developing and implementing a communications strategy to alert the audience to the need for flu vaccinations and Northside's vaccination program;

> hiring and training *promotores* to visit households in the neighbor-
  hood, assigning households to be covered, and then conducting the
  visits;
> purchasing the vaccine and contracting with nurses;
> administering the vaccinations; and
> evaluating the success of the program.

A good implementation strategy will specify measurable goals for the
activities and milestones for achieving them. It will also describe how
one would know if the strategy was successful. After all, an organization
might undertake all the activities under its strategic plan but still not
achieve its objectives. For example, the *promotores* at Northside might
succeed in recruiting workers to get flu shots, yet the number of workdays missed because of illness may not decrease, or even if it did, it might
have no effect on the surge in the need for emergency assistance.

We should distinguish between evaluating ultimate success *in fact* and
assessing success *in principle*. With respect to the former, Northside does
not have either the expertise or the financial resources to evaluate the
ultimate impact of the vaccination program. If the Metro Community
Foundation is foresightful—more so than is typical of foundations—it
will work with Northside to find an organization that can do the evaluation, and then fund it.

We discuss how to evaluate actual outcomes and impact later in the
book. For now, though, let's consider how you would evaluate success in
principle, and why you would do this. Assume that you have unlimited
funds to invest in evaluation, that all the relevant data is readily available,
and that you have hired an independent expert to undertake an evaluation of the program. How would you respond when the expert asks, "Can
you tell me precisely what you consider to be the measures of success?"
What would be your ultimate measure of success for Northside? Perhaps
whether the program decreased the number of workdays missed?

There are two reasons for asking how you would evaluate success in
principle. One is to set appropriately high aspirations for the program.
Equally important, specifying the measures of success presses you to
clarify the goals that you are trying to achieve. For example, you may
decide that it's not just the number of workdays missed that matters, but
that reducing the incidence of flu is valuable in itself. Some of the best
strategies solve more than one problem at a time. But having several

positive outcomes does not in any way reduce the need to specify each one and measure progress against it. In effect, specifying what you would evaluate in principle provides an opportunity to double-check your goals to make sure that your theory of change and logic model are aligned with them.

Takeaway Points

➤ To solve a problem, you must first understand its causes. Solutions must be based on an empirically sound "theory of change," a theory of how the relevant parts of the physical or social world work.
➤ A solution is ultimately embodied in a strategic plan, sometimes called a "logic model," a causal chain leading to the desired outcome.
➤ A strategic plan should set clear goals defining what success would look like and should measure progress toward them.
➤ Every strategy has risks: the strategy may not work as you expected, grantees may not be up to the task, or the plan may have unintended bad consequences. Identifying the risks up front can help reduce them.

Chapter Notes

1. Some portions of this chapter are based on Paul Brest and Linda Hamilton Krieger, *Problem Solving, Decisionmaking, and Professional Judgment* (New York: Oxford University Press, forthcoming).

2. Charles H. Kepner and Benjamin B. Tregoe, *The New Rational Manager* (Princeton, N.J.: Princeton Research Press, 1981), viii; Gerald P. Lopez, "Lay Lawyering," *UCLA Law Review* 32 (1984): 1–2; and Allen Newell and Herbert A. Simon, *Human Problem Solving* (Englewood Cliffs, N.J.: Prentice Hall, 1972).

3. Lopez, "Lay Lawyering," 1–2.

4. Jeffrey L. Bradach and Nicole Tempest, "NewSchools Venture Fund" (Harvard Business School Case Study 9-301-038, October 13, 2000).

5. Varda Liberman, et al. "The Name of the Game: Predictive Power of Reputations Versus Situational Labels in Determining Prisoner's Dilemma Game Moves," *Personality and Social Psychology Bulletin* 30, no. 9 (2004): 1175.

6. J. W. Getzels, "Problem Finding and the Invention of Solutions," *Journal of Creative Behavior* 9 (1975): 12, 15–16.

7. The Bill & Melinda Gates, William and Flora Hewlett, James Irvine, and Stuart foundations.

8. See Ellen Langer, *Mindfulness* (Boston: Addison Wesley, 1992), 23.

9. Arthur Koestler, *The Act of Creation* (London: Hutchinson & Co, 1964).

10. Joel L. Fleishman, J. Scott Kohler, and Steven Schindler, *Casebook for The Foundation: A Great American Secret* (New York: Public Affairs, 2007).

11. Gary Walker, *Midcourse Corrections to a Major Initiative: A Report on The James Irvine Foundation's CORAL Experience* (San Francisco and Los Angeles: James Irvine Foundation, 2007), http://www.irvine.org/assets/pdf/pubs/evaluation/Midcourse_Corrections.pdf.

12. David N. Figlio and Lawrence S. Getzler, "Accountability, Ability and Disability: Gaming the System" (NBER Working Paper No. 9307, National Bureau of Economic Research, 2002). One study shows that following the introduction of the Florida Comprehensive Assessment Test in 1996, some Florida schools reclassified into special education students who normally performed poorly on the tests, because the special-education category was not used to grade the school.

13. Ned Breslin, "Water Projects: The Harm Caused by Well-Meaning Philanthropists," *onPhilanthropy*, August 1, 2007, http://www.onphilanthropy.com/site/News2?id=7181&page=NewsArticle.

14. "Looking Back at Zimbabwe," *Carnegie Results*, Winter 2007, http://www.carnegie.org/results/16/index.html.

15. Ron Zimmer and Richard Buddin, *Making Sense of Charter Schools: Evidence from California*, RAND Education Occasional Paper (RAND Corporation, 2006), http://www.rand.org/pubs/occasional_papers/2006/RAND_OP157.pdf.

16. Elizabeth Weise, "The Man Who Fed the World," *USA Today*, October 21, 2003, http://www.usatoday.com/news/world/2003-10-20-borlaug-usat_x.htm.

17. Vandana Shiva, "The Green Revolution in the Punjab," *Ecologist* 21, no. 2 (March–April 1991), http://livingheritage.org/green-revolution.htm.

18. The Rockefeller Foundation, "Frequently Asked Questions About the Green Revolution," December 2006, http://www.rockfound.org/initiatives/agra/agra_orig_gr_faq.shtml.

Solving Problems Through Program Strategies

T HE METRO COMMUNITY Foundation example in Chapter 3 involves designing and implementing a strategy for a single grant. An individual grant can be more or less strategic (with a small "s"), depending on how well you and the grantee analyze and address the problem at hand. But if you think about the examples in Chapter 1—both successful and not—you'll notice that achieving philanthropic goals often requires making a set of grants connected to an overarching Strategy (with a big "S"). This is true even of efforts to build the capacity of a single organization, for example the Edna McConnell Clark Foundation's work with the Harlem Children's Zone, which called for a mixture of project and general operating support grants as well as technical assistance from consultants and foundation staff. And it is certainly true of most efforts to protect the environment, improve education, and safeguard civil rights.

In each of these cases, achieving the goal requires a matrix of grants and other activities. Although the pieces never fit together with anything like the neatness of a jigsaw puzzle—and though they don't come precut in a box—a program strategy with a gaping hole is likely to be as unsuccessful as an incomplete puzzle is unrewarding. The essence of developing and implementing a program strategy consists of

1. specifying your goals;
2. defining a strategy for achieving the goals;
3. ensuring adequate resources to implement the strategy;

4. selecting grantees who will execute the strategy; and

5. assessing progress and making midcourse corrections.

To make this less abstract, we give an example of how a foundation put together a set of grants to achieve a particular goal, focusing on an initiative by the Hewlett Foundation called New Constituencies for the Environment.

Specifying Your Goals

California's population is expected to increase by 50 percent over the next fifty years. Without effective environmental policies, the impact on the state's increasingly stressed air, water, and land will be dire. Air pollution has already created serious health problems, including asthma, chronic and acute bronchitis, heart disease, and cancer, particularly for residents of the San Joaquin Valley and those living near the ports and trade corridors of Los Angeles and Long Beach. Among the major pollutants are ozone and soot emitted by trucks, diesel farm machinery, and ships in the Southern California ports. The health impact has fallen heavily on communities of color.

In 2004, both to address the immediate issues and to build institutional support for the environmental concerns of California's African-American, Asian-American, and Latino residents, the Hewlett Foundation launched the New Constituencies for the Environment (NCE) initiative. Foundation staff engaged in consultations with grassroots constituencies, elected officials, local and state environmental organizations, and health experts. As NCE evolved, it had two key objectives: (1) to reduce air pollution in the San Joaquin Valley and Southern California and (2) to increase the technical capacity, resources, and political effectiveness of organizations representing minorities and other disadvantaged groups.

Together with public-opinion polling, the foundation's consultations indicated that air pollution was the top environmental concern among communities of color. But they also revealed some challenges that the initiative would face:

➤ The agricultural and port-related industries saw higher air-quality standards as an economic threat. Their trade associations had considerable political power with local, regional, and state government agencies.

➤ The regional organizations most concerned with air pollution were small grassroots "environmental justice" groups. They had limited resources and little technical expertise. The state's expansive geography also presented a problem. Organizations working on similar issues in different regions were poorly linked and lacked the communications skills and policy know-how to have sustained impact in Sacramento. As a result, many elected representatives, including minority leaders, showed considerably less interest in air pollution than did their constituents.

➤ The membership and staff of California's more established environmental groups did not reflect the state's increasing demographic diversity.

The Hewlett Foundation's board was prepared to make a significant commitment to improve air quality in California. But it was evident that just providing additional money to individual organizations would not address these challenges: that would require strengthening these organizations' strategic, communications, and advocacy skills, improving collaboration, and adding technical expertise not currently within the purview of most of the environmental groups. The following case study focuses on one of the foundation's goals in this initiative, reducing ozone emissions in the San Joaquin Valley. Three of the cities in the San Joaquin Valley rank among the ten most polluted in the nation. None meet the so-called eight-hour standard for healthy ozone levels set by the U.S. Environmental Protection Agency.[1]

Defining a Strategy for Achieving Goals

In Chapter 3, we described the concept of a strategic plan or logic model for solving a problem. As background for understanding NCE's strategy for improving air quality in the San Joaquin Valley, it is helpful to understand the key regulatory agencies responsible for dealing with air pollution: local air-quality districts such as the San Joaquin Valley Air Pollution Control District, the California Air Resources Board (CARB), and the U.S. Environmental Protection Agency (EPA).[2] The air-quality districts develop regional air-quality management plans through a public process.

CARB combines these regional plans with statewide pollution-reduction measures to create a "state implementation plan" that it submits to the EPA, which gives considerable deference to the state agency.

Much of NCE's work was focused on the San Joaquin Valley Air Pollution Control District. This aspect of the initiative had the goal, or intended outcome, of reducing the number of days with unhealthy ozone levels. This would be achieved through particular strategies, each of which had its own subgoals, or intermediate outcomes. The strategies encompassed activities such as

> bringing pressure on the air-pollution control district from residents, media, and legislators and other public officials, by mobilizing residents in affected communities to turn out at hearings, educating legislators and officials, and persuading regional media to endorse more aggressive pollution clean-up;

> informing air-pollution control district board members and other stakeholders about the health and economic consequences of pollution, by commissioning and disseminating independent analyses and providing technical training to the environmental organizations; and

> providing information about practicable solutions to reducing pollution, by engaging pollution-control businesses and trade organizations.

Each of these strategies had indicators of progress so that the foundation and grantee organizations would know whether the initiative was on track—for example, actual resident turnout at hearings, the content of the technical reports, and sustained media attention to the issues.

Ensuring Adequate Resources to Implement the Strategy

If you run an airline company responsible for a flight from New York to London, you ensure that the plane has enough fuel to get there—and with a margin of safety. But many philanthropists start important initiatives without "sizing" the situation and assessing what resources will be necessary to see it through—with a margin of safety. Of course, the resources need not be yours alone. Other funders may be involved from the start or may be willing to take over at some point—midair refueling, to stretch the metaphor. But this is something that you would want to ascertain in advance rather than just hope for.

From the outset, NCE was a Hewlett Foundation initiative. Although other funders, including the California Endowment and the James Irvine Foundation, would support particular projects, the Hewlett Foundation felt responsible for ensuring that the expectations the initiative created in the region were met.

Given the challenging goals of building an environmental movement among "new constituencies" and cleaning up the air in the San Joaquin Valley and Southern California ports, the foundation knew it was in for the long term—at least a decade. Although none of the grants ran for longer than three years, the foundation anticipated that it would renew the grants to organizations that continued to contribute to these goals. Thus, although some organizations were eventually dropped from the portfolio, the majority of the grants have been renewed at least once. At the same time, the foundation has provided the resources for several grantees to hire fund-raising consultants to broaden their funding base so that they are not too dependent on any one source.

Selecting Grantees Who Will Execute the Strategy

The Hewlett Foundation made a series of grants to build the staff and strengthen the financial stability and technical capacity of regional organizations in the San Joaquin Valley, to increase coordination among regions, and to link regional initiatives with state-level efforts to address air pollution. The grants can be organized into the following categories:

➤ Regional advocacy
➤ State coordination
➤ Technical analysis
➤ Organizing and communication
➤ Organizational effectiveness

The grants were not, of course, made all at once. The need for some of them emerged only after the initiative evolved and the foundation and its grantees gathered feedback.

Regional Advocacy

Since 2003, the Central Valley Air Quality (CVAQ) Coalition has spear-headed efforts to improve air quality in the San Joaquin Valley. When NCE began, members of the coalition included

> the Center on Race, Poverty, and the Environment, whose staff of law-yers and organizers provided legal expertise, training, and organizing;
> the Latino Issues Forum, the only Latino organization in California with strong air-quality concerns and an organization that is skilled in community education and organizing Latinos;
> the Fresno Metropolitan Ministry, an interfaith organization that engages in community education and mobilization around the health of disadvantaged communities; and
> the Coalition for Clean Air, which had three decades of experience in advocating for air quality in Los Angeles.

The foundation funded these organizations and supported the addition of two nontraditional allies to the CVAQ Coalition:

> The Fresno-Madera Medical Society.[3] Statements about the health impacts of air pollution by the physicians and staff of this one-hundred-year-old institution added tremendous credibility to the argument that more aggressive action was needed.
> The Catholic Diocese of Stockton. Meetings held throughout the diocese heard parishioners' concerns and raised awareness about the health impacts of air pollution. In this religiously conservative region, the Catholic Church added a strong ethical dimension to the debate.

Coordination

According to its mission statement, the thirty-five-year-old Coalition for Clean Air (CCA) is "committed to restoring clean, healthy air to all of California and strengthening the environmental movement by promoting broad-based community involvement, advocating responsible public policy, and providing technical expertise." When the Hewlett Foundation launched NCE, CCA held promise as a statewide coordinator for the initiative, but it would need to expand substantially and to have a greater presence in the state capital to effectively assume this role. The foundation supported the retention of a not-for-profit management-consulting firm to develop a needs assessment and work plan for CCA's critical anchor role. With these in hand, the foundation made a three-year grant of $1 million per year to CCA. CCA quickly increased the diversity of its board and staff, broadened its Spanish-language communications capacity, and offered the assistance of its Sacramento office to other organizations working to reduce air pollution. These measures went a long way toward building trust with the local groups.

Technical Analyses

San Joaquin businesses had traditionally opposed air-pollution regulations on the ground that they would damage the economy to the disadvantage of the very communities of concern to CVAQ members. Skeptical about this argument, CCA suggested that the foundation retain Professor Jane Hall of California State University, Fullerton, to conduct an independent study of the economic impact of air pollution in the San Joaquin Valley—as she had done for Southern California years before. Grantees in the region thought that affiliation with a local institution would improve the study's credibility in this region, which was suspicious of outsiders. In collaboration with the Central Valley Health Policy Institute at California State University, Fresno, Professor Hall produced a report released in early 2006. It demonstrated that the health impacts of pollution cost the San Joaquin Valley economy a staggering $3 billion a year—and changed the terms of the economic debate.

The foundation also made a grant to the International Sustainable Systems Research Center (ISSRC) to propose technical solutions for reducing ozone pollution in the valley. The ISSRC's director, Dr. James Lents, one of the nation's leading air-pollution scientists, had previously headed Southern California's regional air-pollution agency and had helped shape the federal Clean Air Act. The ISSRC report, published in early 2007, recommended specific cost-effective measures to dramatically accelerate the timeline for clean air.

To enable CVAQ members to improve their own technical understanding, the grants supporting Professor Hall and Dr. Lents included provisions for educating the local groups about the issues discussed in their reports.

Organizing and Communication

The CVAQ Coalition had considerable experience in grassroots organizing, but less in engaging the media. The foundation therefore retained communications firms to assist the local organizations and to develop communications plans for the release of the technical reports. These efforts were successful in securing considerable coverage in the San Joaquin Valley media. The local organizations built on the publicity even after the press attention waned.

Organizational Effectiveness

The foundation supplemented some of the grants mentioned above with so-called organizational-effectiveness grants. Ranging from $5,000 to $40,000, they enabled grassroots organizations to retain consultants to assist in strategic planning, fund raising, information-technology systems, website design, and succession planning. As the CVAQ Coalition has developed a greater appreciation of the importance of communications, its members have increasingly requested and used organizational-effectiveness grants for strategic-communications training. Some of the member organizations are also participating in a peer-learning project, cofunded by the James Irvine Foundation, to help them strengthen their organizational capabilities.

Assessing Progress and Making Midcourse Corrections

The foundation expected to renew its grants if the organizations engaged in the agreed-upon activities and if the work showed some signs of movement toward the initiative's goals. Falling short of intermediate goals—as often happened in the first phase of NCE—was understood as a shared problem of the foundation and its grantees. It was not treated as a reason for not renewing a grant, but rather as an occasion for analysis and revision of strategies and tactics. Here are some examples of midcourse corrections made to date:

➤ *Scale and degree of collaboration.* The biggest divergence from the original NCE strategy involved advocacy on a statewide level. Plans for collaboration around a statewide campaign have been deferred for several reasons. Some local environmental-justice groups did not appreciate the importance of working at the state level and lacked the resources for engaging in it. These groups were hesitant to collaborate with CCA. Also, the institutional growing pains of CCA's expansion and the diversification of its staff and board absorbed more energy and time than expected.

➤ *Changing mix of grants.* A number of the initial NCE grants were not renewed, including grants to several environmental justice organizations, to a multifaith association, and to a medical advocacy group. In some cases, nonrenewal was the result of the grantee's failure to adhere to grant conditions (for instance, repeatedly not meeting reporting deadlines), concerns about lobbying activities, or the grantee's refusal to collaborate with other organizations. In other cases, the strategic assumptions underlying the selection of the grantee turned out to be incorrect: the organizations' activities seemed unlikely to produce policy changes.

➤ *Engaging technology businesses.* To assist grantees in pressing for implementation of specific recommendations in the ISSRC's report, the foundation contacted the manufacturer of a "selective catalytic reduction" technology and an industry group representing manufacturers of emissions-control technologies, which countered arguments that pollution-reduction technologies were too speculative.

This is as far as we'll go to illustrate the idea of putting together a program strategy. But if you are interested in what happened next, visit *www.smartphilanthropy.org.*

A Note About Measurable and Not So Measurable Goals

NCE's goal of reducing ozone pollution in the San Joaquin Valley was readily measurable; there are established standards of what constitutes healthy air. Philanthropic strategies concerned with K–12 education, after-school programs, and workforce development programs, to mention just a few, also lend themselves to measurable outcomes. Setting measurable goals not only allows for feedback and accountability, but the very discipline of trying to define measurable goals helps clarify what you're trying to accomplish.

In an insightful coauthored article, the late John Sawhill, former president of the Nature Conservancy, described the evolution of that organization's measurable outcomes from "bucks and acres" to an unwieldy ninety-eight-indicator system (which "promptly collapsed under its own weight") to a system that measures organizational performance in three areas: impact, activity, and capacity.[4] The measurement of impact is based on two indicators: biodiversity health and threat abatement. The former relies on scientific data (which has only improved over the years); the latter is more difficult to assess but reflects the risks that besiege the natural world. The authors emphasized the importance of goals that are both measurable and simple—easily collected and easily communicated. The measures need to focus on the highest-leverage strategies and allow managers to "compare performance across units as well as 'roll up' progress on a regional or national level. And most of all, measures of success had to address progress toward mission: how the organization's actions make a difference."[5]

But, especially at the start of an ambitious initiative, measurable goals are not always realistically possible, and it would be a shame to pass over any proposal just because it did not include them. For example, although one might define the goals of a civil rights movement—whether for African-Americans, women, gays and lesbians, the disabled, or others—in terms of "full equality," it would not necessarily be helpful to specify, let alone quantify, that capacious term at the very outset of the movement.

In addition to reducing air pollution, NCE had the statewide goal of increasing the technical and political capacity of "new constituencies" to address environmental problems throughout California. Assessing the achievement of this second goal is not as simple as measuring the reduction in ozone, but there are some indicators of progress:

➤ The not-for-profit sector's attention to problems of air pollution in California, and its ability to address those problems, has increased. During the course of the San Joaquin Valley initiative, the CCA has become more representative of California's diverse population and has become better accepted as an ally by many, though not all, local environmental organizations. It has developed the institutional and communications capacity to respond effectively to opportunities requiring swift collective action. The increasing expertise of the foundation's grantees has been recognized by others, as reflected by invitations to join committees that can influence policy, such as the governor's California Partnership for the San Joaquin Valley. The ISSRC has remarked on the increased sophistication of grantees' questions and comments.

➤ Though there had been individual champions, California's Latino organizations and policy makers as a whole had traditionally not given high priority to environmental issues. But in 2006, at the largest gathering of Latino advocacy organizations in decades, an entire day was devoted to the environment, under the banner of "broadening our agenda." Hewlett grantees were asked to serve on various panels, and Radio Bilingüe (itself a grantee) broadcast the proceedings live throughout the Central Valley and other regions. In late 2007, the Hewlett Foundation cohosted a "clean air summit" with the newly formed California Latino Legislative Caucus Foundation. Latino legislators, together with colleagues from the Black Caucus and key legislative committees, spent a day discussing the subject with environmental, business, science, and policy experts, as well as with grantee organizations.

It remains to be seen whether these early signs will result in a sustained interest in air pollution and other environmental issues, and a healthier environment for all Californians. The NCE initiative provides a clear example of the elements of an effective multigrant, multiyear philanthropic strategy. By focusing on the five key steps outlined at the beginning of this chapter, a foundation or philanthropic group can identify a problem, analyze it, uncover solutions, begin grantmaking to help fix the problem, and make midcourse corrections to improve the likelihood of a good outcome.

Takeaway Points

The strategy for a philanthropic program or initiative requires

➤ specifying goals—measurable where possible;
➤ defining a plan for achieving the goals;
➤ ensuring that you have adequate resources to implement the plan;
➤ selecting grantees who, in the aggregate, can execute the plan; and
➤ assessing progress and making corrections as appropriate.

Chapter Notes

1. This is the maximum amount of ozone to which an individual can be safely exposed during an eight-hour period. See U.S. Environmental Protection Agency, "8-Hour Ground-Level Ozone Designations," http://www.epa.gov/ozonedesignations (accessed July 1, 2008).

2. In addition, the Los Angeles and Long Beach port commissions play an important regulatory role for the Southern California ports.

3. In 2007, the Fresno-Madera Medical Society persuaded the California Medical Association (CMA) to take up the matter during its annual meeting. CMA's membership voted to do this and issued a press release with the headline "California physicians united in urgent call for clean air," calling for more aggressive efforts to reduce air pollution.

4. John C. Sawhill and David Williamson, "Mission Impossible? Measuring Success in Nonprofit Organizations," *Nonprofit Management & Leadership*, Spring 2001, 371–386.

5. Ibid., 375.

Chapter **5** *Five*

Grantmaking and Due Diligence

T HE PRECEDING CHAPTERS examined problem analysis and strategy. This chapter examines the nitty-gritty of making and monitoring a grant—from the application process through the final report. Much of the discussion parallels that of Chapter 3, focusing on the information a philanthropist needs in order to perform effective due diligence on a grant proposal and then track implementation.

The Proposal: An Overview

The proposal serves as the basis for discussions and negotiations between the funder and applicant and eventually for a contract between them. In its final version, the proposal is the grantee's commitment to what it will do and deliver.

Any proposal should include background information about the applicant's history, structure, leadership, and finances—all to help the funder understand the organization and determine whether it has the capacity to carry out the proposed activities. But the essence of a proposal is the applicant's answer to these questions:

1. Where are you going, and how will you know if you have arrived?
2. How do you plan to get there, and why do you think your plan will succeed?
3. How will you know if you are on course?

Note that the question "How will you know if you have arrived?" is at the beginning of the sequence. Although the actual arrival will happen only at the end—if all goes according to plan—it is essential that you and your grantee know in advance what success would look like.

Let's use the Metro Community Foundation's grant to the Northside Neighborhood Center as a starting place for elaborating these elements.

Articulating Concrete and Measurable Goals

Where are you going? The applicant must define the *goals* for the organization as a whole if the proposal is for general operating support, or for the specific project if the grant is for project support.

In our case, the Northside Neighborhood Center is asking for a project grant with the goal of reducing the economic crises faced by families when the breadwinners are beset by seasonal illness, particularly the flu.

How will you know if you have arrived? The applicant must explain how the organization will determine—at least in principle and ideally in fact—the extent to which it has achieved its goals.

Northside will use the incidence of flu among breadwinners in the neighborhood as an intermediate measure of the project's achievement. The ultimate measure of achievement, though, will be whether the demand for emergency family assistance during the flu season decreases.[1]

Clarity of goals and objectives lies at the very heart of strategic philanthropy. Here's a simple test of whether a goal is defined clearly: Can the applicant describe the goal with sufficient clarity so that you will be able to evaluate, in principle, whether the goal has been achieved? Better yet, can it be described so that an outsider would be able to assess success?

We discussed the *"evaluation in principle"* test in Chapter 3, but it's worth repeating here in the context of making particular grants. Actually assessing the impact of a grant may require undertaking an evaluation that is beyond your resources or—as in the case of mitigating global warming or nuclear proliferation—beyond your time frame (to put it euphemistically). So rather than worrying about what you can actually measure in the here and now, consider what you would measure if all the empirical evidence you could possibly want was available to you. This hypothetical test is mainly a way to ensure that you and your grantee know where you're going.

Goals and Mission Statements Redux

Earlier, we mentioned the differences between your goals and mission statements as a philanthropist. These differences also apply to your grantee organization: although an organization's mission statement may capture the spirit of the enterprise, unless it is as focused as NASA's original mission of "putting a man on the moon," it isn't specific enough to count as the goal for a grant.

Consider, for example, an organization with the mission to "improve the well-being and life opportunities of teenage girls." This is a pithy and inspiring statement, but it is far too vague for you to know, in retrospect, whether and to what extent the mission was actually achieved. Goals in line with this mission might be "reduce teen pregnancy rates" or "increase high-school graduation rates" within particular populations. The goals would be even better defined if the organization specified targets—for example, "increase the graduation rates among African-American girls at Hoover High from 40 percent to 70 percent"—but specifying a direction of change can suffice, at least if you have some baselines from which you can measure differences.

You might have less obviously measurable goals within the mission of improving teenage girls' life opportunities—for example, increasing their self-esteem or leadership abilities. Psychologists have actually developed quantitative assessments of self-esteem based on interviews and questionnaires.[2] If leadership is also a goal, the organization must develop indicators for this as well, even if they are more qualitative than quantitative.

Developing such indicators helps safeguard against confusing the organization's *activities*—for example, how many girls participated in a leadership training program—with *outcomes*—whether the program made any difference. As we'll see below, it is important for not-for-profits as well as their funders to determine which activities actually—and not just theoretically—lead to the desired outcomes.

Specifying precise goals will give you and your grantee a common benchmark of success and reduce the likelihood of arguments about whether the desired results were achieved. The trouble with an "I know it when I see it" approach to goals is that you and a grantee may see quite different things.

Specifying your shared goals in advance also makes it possible to build in evaluation from the start—a much easier task than retrofitting evaluation onto a project that's already in progress, let alone finished. For example, if one of the indicators of success of the program to improve girls' self-esteem is how participants are performing in school, obtaining advance permission from participants and their parents to see the students' grades is a lot more practical than scrambling to get them after the girls have completed the program (or dropped out). Planning in advance is even more important if the organization wishes to gain the school's cooperation in comparing participants in the program with classmates who did not participate.

Examples of Well-Defined Goals

Amy Smith's Fuel from the Fields project is an example of a proposal with clear and measurable goals. Designed to develop alternative charcoal in Haiti, the project won a $200,000 grant at the 2007 World Bank–sponsored Development Marketplace competition.[3]

In general terms, the project aims "to improve human health by creating micro-enterprises in Haiti that specialize in the production and sale of affordable, clean-burning cooking charcoal made from agricultural waste."

Dr. Smith describes the problem in terms that imply clear and measurable goals. "In Haiti, half of the population use wood and/or agricultural residues as their primary cooking fuel. Breathing the smoke from these fires leads to persistent acute respiratory lung infections, mostly in children." One indicator of progress is a reduction in the rate of these respiratory infections among children in areas treated by the program (compared with the rates of infections in untreated areas).

The sustainability of the project ultimately depends on making clean-burning cooking charcoal from agricultural waste (agro-charcoal) economically viable in competition with conventional wood charcoal. Thus, another measurable outcome will be the average market price of agro-charcoal in program-treated areas compared with that of wood charcoal in those areas. Success will be achieved when agro-charcoal is approximately competitive with wood charcoal.

An ancillary project goal is to stimulate the creation of at least one thousand local agro-charcoal production jobs in order to increase annual incomes for families participating in the program by $500. Success in this area will be achieved if (1) at least one thousand jobs are created that were not previously available and (2) the families who decide to work in agro-charcoal net $500 more in total income than families who continue to work in the participants' previous occupations.

Finally, the project aims to reach a production rate of 100 metric tons and to change the coal usage of ten thousand families after two years. Both of these goals are quantifiable and measurable.

Specifying Goals When Providing General Support for Multipurpose Organizations

How does the "evaluation in principle" test apply to an unrestricted grant to an organization that maintains a number of different programs in pursuit of its mission, each with its own strategy to achieve various goals? Consider, for example, a community center that provides various services for the elderly, an after-school program for children, a theater for adults, and so on.

Whether, as a funder, you are interested in all the community center's activities or some subset, there is no substitute for applying the "evaluation in principle" test separately to each activity of interest. If at first glance this seems reductionist—isn't the organization greater than the sum of its individual activities?—think of how the organization's own CEO and board think about its different programs. Without treating the senior and after-school programs separately, how would the organization be able to design and implement strategic plans, formulate budgets, and assess progress? Yes, the community center may be greater than the sum of its individual parts, but the parts are essential components of the larger whole.

The Need for Clear Strategies

The organization must articulate the key strategies it plans to use to achieve its stated goals.

Northside's key strategy will be to vaccinate the families' breadwinners. If it isn't self-evident, the organization must describe the reasons for believing that its strategies will succeed. Northside's strategy is based on the hypothesis that the incidence of flu causes lost wages and layoffs because of missed days of work. With sound medical evidence that vaccination provides immunity against the flu, vaccination should reduce the incidence of flu and hence reduce sick days and increase economic stability within families.

The organization must describe how it plans to implement its strategies.

> Northside plans to use *promotores* to encourage people to come to a
> free clinic where they will be vaccinated.

The proposal should lay out a strategy, or "logic model," as described in
Chapter 3. The logic model should be

➤ lucid and transparent;
➤ comprehensive, including every major step the applicant will take to
  achieve the goal; and
➤ based on sound empirical judgment—that is, on a sound "theory of
  change."

The key point is that the grantee organization must have a strong strategic plan for achieving its goals and must be capable of implementing
the plan.

**"I think you should be more
explicit here in step two."**

An organization's strategic plan is only as good as the theory of change on which it relies. In Chapter 3, we discussed the strategic risks inherent in grantmaking (the possibility that your agreed-upon strategy just doesn't pan out, because the theory of change is mistaken or the strategic plan is missing an essential component) and the external risks (the possibility that external circumstances change in an unforeseen way).

In addition to strategic and external risks, you and your grantees face the problem of organizational risk—the risk that the grantee organization lacks the financial or human resources necessary to implement the strategy. For example, there's a risk that the Northside Neighborhood Center won't be able to recruit, train, and deploy the *promotores*.

An important part of the due-diligence process involves identifying and reducing both strategic and organizational risks. (You usually can't do anything about external risks except take account of them and scrap the project if they unacceptably diminish its expected return.) To satisfy yourself that the grantee has a good chance of actually implementing the plan, you should make sure that the proposal describes both the resources necessary to pursue the strategy and how the organization plans to obtain and deploy them. But for all the importance of the written plan, nothing can substitute for site visits and other in-person meetings that allow you judge the organization's leadership and its capacity to undertake the strategy. These visits also benefit a grantee, who needs to understand your expectations, especially if the grant involves significant changes to its activities.

As we mentioned in Chapter 3, there are few publicly available case studies of strategic risks that led to failure. By the same token, it is difficult to find many examples of grants that failed because of organizational risks—though we know there are many, and we describe one from the Hewlett Foundation at the end of Chapter 6. A rare documented example is the W. K. Kellogg Foundation's experience with SeaChange, which reflects a combination of strategic and organizational problems.[4] SeaChange (not related to a new organization by that same name with lead funding from Goldman Sachs) was an innovative enterprise with a charismatic leader and an inspired set of ideas for connecting social entrepreneurs to funders (see Chapter 12). The Kellogg Foundation[5] knew that these ideas were untested but was willing to take a risk on the entrepreneurial not-for-profit.

As it turned out, SeaChange pursued too many ideas and never achieved focus, and the CEO lacked the management skills to implement his ambitious vision. The organization became mired in efforts to create an online technology without a well-thought-out business plan. The funders were perhaps too accepting of the risks they were taking and the possibility of strategic failure. They did not monitor the new organization closely enough and they assumed—wrongly, as it turned out—that its board was providing adequate oversight. Looking back, evaluators noted, "the experience of SeaChange does raise questions about the degree to which funders were examining the project themselves. Were they exploring the issues of governance, missions, or accountability in this start-up organization?"[6]

Assessing the robustness of an organization's strategies and its capacity to carry them out is an essential aspect of the due-diligence process, and so is coming to a judgment about the risks involved. One of philanthropy's distinguishing abilities is providing risk capital to the not-for-profit sector. A philanthropist interested in innovative or complex strategies must be willing to accept failure as part of the quest for success. But to acknowledge this role is not to invite unnecessary risk. As a philanthropist, you will try to mitigate risks through careful problem analysis and planning. When all is said and done, though, there remains a probability that the venture will fail to achieve its objectives. The *"expected return"* approach, outlined in Chapter 1, can be used to assess the risks of philanthropic investments. We cover this in further detail in Chapter 10.

Tracking Progress

The proposal must describe how the organization will track progress toward achieving the stated goals. An organization's strategic plan should provide major indicators of progress—for example, the number of workers signed up for flu shots by the Northside Neighborhood Center and the "show rate," that is, the proportion of those who sign up that typically show up. These indicators will provide information about whether the strategy is on course.

Northside will want to keep track of how many home visits the *promotores* conduct, how many residents they sign up for vaccinations, and how many residents are in fact vaccinated. These goals or milestones are sometimes described as *intermediate goals* to distinguish them from ultimate goals, or outcomes, of the program as a whole.

Just as a driver wants to know the car's speed, how much fuel is left in the tank, and whether the oil temperature is too high, the organization and its funders will want a dashboard of relevant indicators to assess a program. The possible breakdowns in implementation range from individual problems—a particular *promotora* who has a lower sign-up rate than others—to wholesale problems—significant slippage between the number of people who sign up and the number who actually come to the center for vaccinations. Without tracking information of this sort, Northside will have no clue about how the program is working and won't be able to make corrections to improve it.

We use the term *tracking* rather than *evaluation* to make the point that collecting information about an organization's progress is done not only when the program has ended but also on a regular basis, to provide the feedback necessary for strategic corrections while the program is being implemented. Tracking does not require social science studies by outside experts. Rather, it calls for the organization's own personnel to obtain systematic feedback.

Tracking progress is essential to managing any effective organization—whether a business, government agency, or not-for-profit organization. Tracking allows for midcourse corrections, for abandoning failing strategies and intensifying those that succeed. It lets managers understand their ability to meet their mission in real terms and in real time. Designing and implementing tracking systems can be costly, but a philanthropist who cares about the success of a program will not stint in funding them.

Dashboards

It is commonplace for businesses to use "dashboards" to track progress toward their goals, and not-for-profit organizations are increasingly using them as well. Typically, dashboards are Web-based tools that compile and display key metrics about the organization's performance, finances, and staff in an easy-to-understand manner. KaBOOM!, a national not-for-profit organization that supports community efforts to build playgrounds, uses a dashboard to track statistics, including the number of playgrounds built each year, the average number of volunteers per playground, the proportion of playgrounds built in neighborhoods with needy families, and the organization's various costs.[7] The dashboard has helped KaBOOM! ensure that it is serving low-income communities effectively. The key to building a successful dashboard is capturing data concerning the outcomes an organization cares about—data that can be used to make real-time programmatic, managerial, or financial decisions.

Some philanthropists have made substantial investments in grantees' dashboards after recognizing their importance to both the organizations and to the philanthropists themselves. For example, REDF (formerly the Roberts Enterprise Development Fund) supports a portfolio of not-for-profit businesses that employ people who would otherwise remain in long-term poverty. REDF has helped these businesses develop a management-information system to provide timely information to assess whether they are having the desired impact on the disadvantaged individuals being served. The system gathers and analyzes indicators of individuals' independence and stability, including information about jobs and income, housing, health and support networks, substance abuse, and the clients' own assessment of their achievement of personal goals.[8] The system also enables an organization to assess the performance of its own staff members,[9] and helps fulfill reporting requirements for its contracts with foundations and government agencies. With the support of other funders,[10] REDF covered most of the development costs, with the understanding that ongoing costs would become part of the organizations' cost of doing business and would be accounted for in their annual budgeting process.

If a grant proposal includes a comprehensive plan for implementing the organization's strategy, then much of the work to construct a dashboard relevant to the grant is already done. For example, a program designed to increase girls' self-esteem would likely include counseling activities. Indicators of progress might include

> the number of girls entering and remaining in the program during a semester;
> the number of counselors recruited;
> the number of counseling sessions scheduled and completed; and
> indicators of change in the participants' self-esteem.

The proposal would contain benchmarks for each of these activities, and the grantee's annual report to the funder would assess progress relative to these benchmarks. Of course, the report would also include qualitative information about the organization's activities and accomplishments, including an explanation for any significant deviation of actual performance from the benchmarks and plans for addressing any shortcomings of the program. When a grant provides general support to an organization, the core of the grantee's report would be indicators

In its youth-development programs, the Edna McConnell Clark Foundation characterizes its grantees' evaluation capacity in three developmental stages and provides the funding and technical assistance to help organizations move from one stage to the next:

1. Most of the organizations begin in the "apparent effectiveness" category, which means that they have anecdotal stories of success, a positive reputation in the community, a sound theory of change, and perhaps some data about who participates in their program. Often, however, these organizations do not collect systematic data about the populations they serve.

2. Over the three to six years of the initial grant, the organization is expected to reach at least "demonstrated effectiveness," in which data collection is rigorous. The youths' achievement can be compared to that of a control or outside group, and an external evaluator is hired or an internal capacity for evaluation is developed.

3. The highest level, "proven effectiveness," consists of statistically rigorous, scientific evaluation, such as randomized control studies.

For the Clark Foundation, an organization's evaluation system is important infrastructure and worthy of philanthropic investment.[11]

that the organization uses to measure its own success apart from any grant.

All of this suggests the value of a focus on goals, strategies, and evaluation by grantor and grantee alike. In the large majority of cases, such focus is a major factor in achieving real impact in your shared goals. However, there are instances when these constraints need to be relaxed—particularly in the earlier stages of building a new organization or field. We discuss this in more detail in Chapter 14.

Due Diligence and Good Philanthropic Behavior

A philanthropist's due-diligence process centers around the proposal. Beyond the formal legal aspects—for example, ensuring that the grant will comply with IRS regulations—the due-diligence process involves clarifying the organization's goals, strategies, and tactics and ensuring that its plans are sound and that it has the financial and human capacity to carry them out. Normally, this is done in conversations with the organization's staff and a review of its strategy, business plans, and budgets. As in the world of venture capital, a critical aspect of due diligence involves assessing the organization's leaders—through references and direct interaction—to develop the confidence necessary to entrust them with a grant.

As a philanthropist, you can pursue these matters in more or less depth. You may rely largely on intuition or trust in the organization's leadership, or you may engage in independent analysis and fact-finding using your own staff or consultants. Diligence is really a continuum, and how you allocate responsibility for the enterprise depends on your expertise and resources. You may hold some institutions closely to agreed-upon goals and standards and let others—those, say, with a good track record, a strong board of directors, and experienced leadership— essentially manage their own accountability. Seasoned grant makers find great relief, and show commensurable support, when they encounter organizations that clearly understand and regularly exercise this sort of oversight.

Of course, the due-diligence process is just the start. If it produces a grant, it will lead to a relationship that may last anywhere from a year to many decades. This relationship will involve reports, meetings, evaluations—the whole nine yards of grantmaking and the first few steps toward successful outcomes. Rather than say more about due diligence, though, we'll conclude this section with a few observations about the relationship between grantor and grantee.

Grantor-Grantee Relationship

No professional relationship is more important to a philanthropist than his or her relationship with a grantee. At its best, it is trusting, candid, and collaborative. But the relationship is founded on an imbalance of power.

From 1987 to 1999, Paul Brest, coauthor of this book, was the dean of Stanford Law School. During these twelve years, a day hardly went by when students, faculty, or alumni didn't tell him what he was doing wrong—and at least once in a while they were right. Then in 2000, he became president of the Hewlett Foundation and, within a matter of months, underwent a personal transformation and, by all external signals, achieved perfection.

The danger of his believing this was mitigated by a framed Yiddish proverb sent to him early on by a colleague at another foundation: "With money in your pocket, you are wise and you are handsome, and you sing well, too." But it is a constant danger. You don't hear criticism from potential grantees—and almost everyone you know, or who knows someone you know, is a potential grantee. And that can lead to an abuse of power. Shall we count the ways?

➤ *Not responding*—or not responding in a timely manner—to applicants and grantees.
➤ *Being abusive.* There is a fine line between being appropriately demanding and flaunting your power.
➤ *Allowing or encouraging an applicant to put lots of time and energy into a proposal without being sure that if the proposal meets your expectations you will fund it.* Of course, "due diligence" means just that, and its results are not inevitably positive. But a grant maker should signal concerns to applicants early on and should not lead them down a long garden path and off a cliff. (Before even

engaging with an organization, a grant maker should learn whether there are any obvious red flags.)

➣ *Subjecting an applicant or grantee to due-diligence or reporting processes that are disproportionately demanding relative to the size of your grant.* A funder whose grant dollars account for a small percentage of the organization's budget diminishes the value of its contribution by making disproportionate demands. Moreover, a relatively small funder can often rely on the diligence and evaluation of larger funders.

➣ *Abruptly exiting a field because of a change in interests* without taking account of legitimate reliance by organizations, other funders, and the beneficiaries of your work. A graceful exit allows for a soft landing rather than a crash.

Among its other services, the Center for Effective Philanthropy will survey a foundation's grantees and prepare a "Grantee Perception Report" that provides the foundation with considerable information about how it is coming across to grantees, while protecting grantees' anonymity. Though the grantor-grantee relationship is not a measure of the impact of a foundation's grantmaking, it is reasonable to think that poor relations between a foundation and its grantees are not generally conducive to effectiveness. At the end of the next chapter we tell a true story along these lines.

All of this said, we reject the metaphor of the grantee as a "customer." The real customers are the individuals or communities whose lives the grantee and grantor seek to make better. And it is this fact that not only justifies but also demands that due diligence be duly done.

Takeaway Points

➣ A proposal serves as the basis for discussions and negotiations between the applicant or grantee and the funder, and eventually serves as the basis for an agreement between them. The proposal should address
—the applicant's goals;
—the applicant's strategy for achieving those goals; and
—how the applicant will track progress toward its goals.
➣ In effect, the funder asks the same questions of an applicant that it asks of itself.

Chapter Notes

1. In this case, somewhat atypically, it may actually be easier to measure the ultimate outcome than the intermediate one.

2. Rick Hoyle et al., *Selfhood: Identity, Esteem, Regulation* (Boulder, Colo.: Westview Press, 1999), 82–85.

3. Catherine Laine, "Alternative Charcoal Project Wins Development Marketplace," Appropriate Infrastructure Development Group Blog, May 30, 2007, http://www.aidg.org/component/option,com_jd-wp/Itemid,34/p,496/ (accessed July 1, 2008). Other funding partners in the competition include the Bill & Melinda Gates Foundation, Conservation International, the Global Environment Facility, the John D. and Catherine T. MacArthur Foundation, the Joint United Nations Programme on HIV/AIDS, the Philippine Rural Reconstruction Movement, the Soros Foundation, the U.K. Department for International Development, and the U.S. Agency for International Development.

4. W. K. Kellogg Foundation, *Building an Organization to Last: Reflections and Lessons Learned from SeaChange* (2003), http://www.informingchange.com/downloads/seachange-0703.pdf.

5. Other funders also participated, including Echoing Green, the Ewing Marion Kauffman Foundation, and a number of private social investors.

6. W. K. Kellogg Foundation, *Building an Organization to Last*, 8. SeaChange eventually merged with another not-for-profit to create the Social Enterprise Alliance.

7. Debra E. Blum, "Checking the Dashboard," *Chronicle of Philanthropy*, October 12, 2006, http://philanthropy.com/free/articles/v19/i01/01mg0601.htm.

8. Michael E. Porter and Mark R. Kramer, "Philanthropy's New Agenda: Creating Value," *Harvard Business Review* November/December 1999, 121–130.

9. Fay Twersky, *An Information OASIS* (San Francisco: Roberts Enterprise Development Fund, 2002), http://www.redf.org/download/other/oasis.pdf.

10. The Charles and Helen Schwab Foundation, The William and Flora Hewlett Foundation, the Surdna Foundation, the Phalarope Foundation, and the Penney Family Fund.

11. Edna McConnell Clark Foundation, "Assessing the Impact of Programming: Three Levels of Effectiveness," http://www.emcf.org/pdf/how_levelsprogramquality.pdf (accessed June 30, 2008).

C h a p t e r Six

6

Beyond Grantmaking

P HILANTHROPY'S CORE ACTIVITY, grantmaking, is often
complemented by other activities that contribute to achieving
philanthropic goals. Consider the activities of Hewlett Foundation
program officers in designing and implementing the New Constituencies
for the Environment initiative described in Chapter 4:

> In addition to learning about the scientific and technological issues
related to air pollution, they learned about both the formal structure
of the agencies in which decisions affecting air quality were made
and the realpolitik of the decision-making process.

> They learned about organizations that were prepared to carry out
aspects of the strategies, organizations that could develop the necessary
capacity, and organizations that might have to be built from scratch or
(in the case of the Coalition for Clean Air) significantly expand their
scope of activities, to play a necessary role in the initiative.

> They learned about potential allies and opponents, both at the local
and state levels.

> Most of this learning took place in the field, in conversations with a
wide variety of citizens, activists, and other stakeholders. And once
the initiative was launched, program staff were constantly in the field
assisting organizations internally and by making connections with other
organizations, potential allies and opponents, technical consultants,
and decision makers, including local and state politicians. The staff
needed to understand, in real time, where the organizations needed

help in making these connections and also where they needed assistance in strengthening their own capacity. At the same time, they had to meticulously observe the legal restrictions on lobbying by private foundations.

➤ In many of these activities, the foundation was itself engaged in networking and in expanding and managing networks among its grantees and other stakeholders. The ability to gain the attention of people ranging from grassroots leaders to state policy makers was significantly aided by the foundation's reputation.

For another example of adding value beyond grantmaking, consider the recent efforts of a group of large, medium, and small foundations[1] to save the Great Bear Rainforest in British Columbia—the largest tract of coastal temperate rainforest left on earth. The foundations have supported a coalition of conservation and First Nations groups working with Canadian government bodies, industry, and residents to protect the Great Bear ecosystem and ensure economic opportunities for the coastal communities whose livelihoods depend on it. Much of this work has been hands-on, requiring the direct participation of the foundations in convening and cajoling groups with different interests. The foundations have also been an active—and successful—intermediary in the coalition's efforts to obtain funding from British Columbia and the Canadian government to protect these precious ecosystems in perpetuity.

Unlike grants, which are publicly reported, most activities of these sorts are not known outside of the foundation itself. Yet without them, much grantmaking would have little or no impact. This chapter focuses on the value of capturing and disseminating institutional knowledge, collaborating with other funders, and convening meetings of various stakeholders.

Developing and Disseminating Knowledge

The last decade has seen a great deal of interest in knowledge as a tool of philanthropy. As the Charles and Helen Schwab Foundation describes it, "knowledge management is the process through which organizations generate value from their intellectual and knowledge-based assets. Most often, generating value from such assets involves active sharing from within the organization, as well as with various stakeholders in the external community, in an effort to devise best practices and approaches."[2]

Managing Knowledge Internally

A foundation's ability to contribute knowledge to the field depends on its possession of that knowledge in the first place. A number of foundations have positions such as "knowledge officer" dedicated to capturing and organizing their internal knowledge and disseminating it externally. Tom Kern, director of knowledge services at the Annie E. Casey Foundation, observed that foundations have a great deal of *tacit knowledge*—knowledge that resides in the heads of founders, trustees, and staff members but that generally isn't written down.[3] When the individuals leave, their knowledge leaves with them. And even the large amount of knowledge that resides in written files is not generally codified to make it accessible and reusable.[4]

An article in the *McKinsey Quarterly* notes that "many philanthropists, fearing that a dollar spent internally is a dollar wasted, have neither the organization nor the systems to manage their knowledge properly."[5] Building and maintaining knowledge-management systems certainly can be costly and time consuming. Like every other aspect of one's philanthropic "infrastructure," it is only justified to the extent that it increases the likelihood of impact. But we suspect that foundations are significantly underinvested in this area.[6]

In 2001, the Annie E. Casey Foundation began a concerted effort to manage its knowledge better. The foundation was in the midst of staffing a major new initiative. Some of its program officers, who were experts on particular issues such as juvenile justice and child welfare, were about to lead cross-functional teams in several cities.[7] It became evident that only a fraction of the foundation's tacit knowledge in many areas had been captured in an accessible form. Staff members were spending substantial amounts of time looking for information, and experts were constantly answering the same basic questions. The foundation began to develop processes that would help the staff capture their knowledge efficiently. For example, it created simple templates for recording information from site visits—information that had been captured only in program officers' notes, if at all. The foundation eventually created an entire process for managing its knowledge resources, including what knowledge should be captured, who should be responsible for codifying it, how it should be maintained and disseminated, and to whom it should be made available.[8]

Disseminating Knowledge Externally

Some knowledge gathered by foundations is appropriately maintained only for internal use, but much of it can also be valuable to grantees, policy makers, and other funders. Although the social return on a grant is limited to some extent by the size of the grant, the value of knowledge can be multiplied many times over if there are good systems in place for disseminating it.[9]

For example, the Robert Wood Johnson Foundation (RWJF) regularly publishes reports on its grants, describing the reasons for making the grant, the problems addressed, its objectives and strategies, its results, and lessons for the field. As one RWJF staff member noted, "the people involved in the projects are surprisingly candid about their work and the evaluation of their projects."[10] RWJF also maintains other online publications, fact sheets, interactive maps (for example, on tobacco-settlement revenues), webcasts and podcasts, third-party evaluation reports on RWJF projects and programs, primers, and toolkits.[11]

In its work to "help vulnerable children and families succeed,"[12] the Annie E. Casey Foundation maintains an online knowledge center that includes data on key indicators of child, family, and community well-being, evaluations, case studies, and information about lessons learned and emerging practices. The foundation's overarching goal is to "provide advocates, policymakers, practitioners, the media, researchers, and community members with a range of Foundation resources developed either by Casey or one of our grantees. These resources capture the experience and learning of the Foundation in our efforts to improve outcomes for vulnerable children, youth, families, and communities."[13]

Knowledge dissemination is not the exclusive prerogative of large national foundations. For example, in the belief that "sharing lessons learned in practice is crucial to creating an environment that will encourage discussion and advance the field,"[14] the Marguerite Casey Foundation—started by Annie E. Casey's daughter—publishes reports related to its mission of improving the lives of low-income families. The Skoll Foundation maintains an online "community" primarily related to social entrepreneurship. The Barr Foundation publishes information relevant to its mission of enhancing the quality of life for Boston residents.[15]

Finally, knowledge is shared through the so-called affinity groups of grant makers with common interests. For example, Grantmakers in the

Arts, Grantmakers for Education, and the Funders' Network for Smart Growth and Livable Communities share information to improve their members' work.

Collaborating with Other Funders

Philanthropists operate in a social and economic space with many other participants—grantee organizations, governments, businesses, and other philanthropists. Even the paradigmatic philanthropic activity, grant-making, is a collaborative endeavor with the grantee and often other funders.

Merely being aware of the presence of other funders in your field creates opportunities to coordinate resources to achieve common ends. And in some circumstances, collaboration can significantly increase the participants' impact on social problems. Funders can work together to generate better ideas and build broader constituencies as well as increase the amount of money available to pursue common goals.

However, collaboration has inevitable up-front costs of time and effort spent in communicating and making decisions together with one's partners. The process can often be frustrating, and a beneficial outcome is hardly assured. As one funder remarked, "If I stopped to count the number of failed efforts at funding collaboratively, I'd be so depressed, I'd leave the business."[16] At the end of the day, the extra effort is justified only if it results in greater impact in achieving your philanthropic goals.

Since philanthropists are essentially investors, their most fundamental form of collaboration is the aggregation of dollars to make things happen on a scale beyond what any single funder could accomplish. An organization may approach a number of funders for general support or to support a particular project, or a funder may pitch an idea to peers. In any event, collaboration among foundations is at the heart of major philanthropic efforts, ranging from the Green Revolution to protecting the Great Bear Rainforest to restoring the salt ponds in San Francisco Bay. As another example, through the Youth Transition Funders Group, several foundations collaborate to improve the lives of vulnerable young people by ensuring that they are connected to institutions and support systems that will enable them to succeed throughout adulthood.

Philanthropists also collaborate in creating intermediary organizations that may engage in grantmaking and other activities. For example, the Energy Foundation, launched in 1990 by the Rockefeller and MacArthur foundations and the Pew Charitable Trusts, is now supported by nine different foundations and an increasing number of individual philanthropists. It develops strategies to improve energy efficiency in the United States and China and makes grants to dozens of not-for-profits in addition to providing technical assistance to governments. The Energy Foundation's staff serve as virtual program officers for its funders, providing a degree of expertise that would be difficult and expensive even for large foundations to replicate.

A recent effort, led by the MacArthur Foundation, provides an example of collaboration between foundations and government. In 1999, Chicago mayor Richard M. Daley undertook a $1.6 billion project to construct or renovate twenty-five thousand public-housing units. Characterizing this as "a historic opportunity to improve the quality of public housing; to diminish the isolation of public housing and its residents; [and] to support the development of well-designed mixed-income communities,"[17] the foundation created the Partnership for New Communities and established a donor-advised fund managed by the Chicago Community Trust,[18] to which a dozen other foundations, banks, and other businesses have contributed.[19]

In addition to contributing over $55 million to the project, the MacArthur Foundation has played a mediating role with respect to problems arising under the plan, such as the relocation of tenants. It has also provided resources to help streamline management systems and has supported research and evaluation of the project's successes and failures, with an eye to producing results quickly enough to be used to improve the project's implementation and management. The results to date have been very promising.[20]

For a detailed description of foundations' collaboration on Chicago public housing, visit *www.smartphilanthropy.org*.

Although foundations frequently collaborate in starting initiatives, there is considerably less collaboration—sometimes not even advance notice—in exiting from them. Funders may have good reasons for changing their interests. Absent dire circumstances, however, responsible philanthropists do not pull the rug out from under grantees or funding partners, but always provide reasonable notice and a ramp-down period.

For all of the potential benefits of collaboration, it is worth coming back to its costs, some inevitable and some not, and considering how they may be mitigated.

> *Group decision making.* Decision making by consensus is not an efficient process. The time consumed is a function of the number of collaborating funders, the number of staff members tasked to the joint enterprise, the participants' willingness to compromise on matters of procedure and substance, and the structure and leadership of the group. Therefore, the greater the number of collaborating partners, the greater the need to attend to the internal structure of the group and accord some deference to a steering committee or even a lead funder. Of course, agreeing on procedure itself takes time, but it has great potential payoff; in the absence of an agreement, procedural issues tend to be recycled ad nauseam.
> *Delegation of tasks.* Grantmaking involves a number of labor-intensive activities, including due diligence, monitoring, and evaluation. Avoiding duplication of these efforts can save both the funders and grantees time and money. To delegate any aspect of its grantmaking responsibilities, a fund must have confidence in its peers—confidence that ultimately can only be developed through ongoing professional relationships.
> *Fairness to grantees.* Collaborative grantmaking seeks to further the missions of both funders and their grantees. But potential grantees may feel at greater risk when their selection depends on the collective decision of a number of funders, which increases the chances of an all-or-nothing outcome. This danger cannot be entirely discounted, but our experience has been that funders are protective of their autonomy and that they tend to exercise independent judgment on basic issues such as the selection of grantees.
> *Organizational cultures.* The internal cultures of the participating institutions can have dramatic effects on collaboration. The effects are asymmetric, with pathologies detracting more from the common venture than good internal practices contribute to it.

In the end, only one's experience with individuals and institutions can determine who is a good collaborator and who is not. As attractive as the potential impact may be, experience sometimes teaches that the game with some players is just too frustrating to be worth the candle.

Convening Grantees and Other Stakeholders

Foundations have tremendous convening power. When foundation staff call a meeting, attendance is high not only because of their intelligence, thoughtfulness, charm, and wit, but also because people are attracted to money, to institutions with strong reputations, and often to places where people from different perspectives can sit down together and work out problems. When a philanthropist calls a meeting, people generally come, and they usually are on their best behavior to boot.

In the best of cases, funders, grantees, policy makers, and other stakeholders can add real value by sharing best practices, coordinating programs, developing new strategies, building trust, or reconciling warring parties. For example, the Marguerite Casey Foundation regularly convenes grantees to foster communication and collaboration.

➤ Two of the foundation's grantees, Latino Health Access in Santa Ana, California, and the National Association of Latino Elected Officials, launched a collaborative effort to increase voter-education and naturalization resources in the Latino communities of Santa Ana—a project that neither alone could have done as effectively.
➤ Two other grantees, the Hopi Foundation and Americans for Indian Opportunity, planned a future meeting of American Indian organizations, which resulted in a collaboration to address key issues in their respective communities.
➤ The foundation also used the regional grantee meetings as an opportunity to seek guidance on its evaluation framework and its movement-building work.[21]

The Charles Stewart Mott Foundation regularly brings together grantees pursuing common issues. For example, it invited a group of workforce-development organizations to discuss what's working, and what's not, to help workers stay in their jobs. The cognizant program officer noted that the grantees find the interaction so valuable that they remain in these "learning communities" even after a grant runs out.[22]

In 1997, the Peninsula Community Foundation,[23] the Sobrato Family Foundation, and the Charles and Helen Schwab Foundation created the Organizational Capacity Grants Initiative, under which they invited sixteen Bay Area not-for-profit organizations to create a learning community to improve grantees' organizational effectiveness. According to Alexa Culwell, then CEO of the Schwab Foundation, "We problem-solved together, we gave feedback, we listened to one another. We used our connections and networks, and we shared knowledge." Culwell reported improvements in most of the participants' capacity and effectiveness. "The concept of a learning community . . . enabled us to co-design the initiative from start to finish, involving all twenty-one partners in key decisions. A learning community levels the playing field because it brings everyone to the table to discuss issues of mutual importance, offering unique perspectives and insights."[24]

The Language of Philanthropy

Every field has distinct concepts and shorthand references. "Theory of change" and "logic model" are examples from philanthropy that serve useful functions. But it is easy to lapse into jargon that obscures rather than clarifies or that seems mysterious or just silly to outsiders. While the verb *to convene* and its related adjective or participle (as in *convening power*) are in common usage, *convening* as a noun is not used by ordinary people and does not—so far as we know—add anything not captured by common words such as *meeting, conference,* or *gathering.*

Toward a less pretentious vocabulary and for your utter enjoyment, we recommend Tony Proscio's three compendiums of philanthropic jargon—*In Other Words, Bad Words for Good,* and *When Words Fail*—commissioned by the Edna McConnell Clark Foundation.[25] Alas, his questionable words include *strategy.* We'll, nobody's perfect.

These are excellent examples of funders making productive use of their abilities to convene meetings of various stakeholders. But in fact, most meetings waste a good deal of time. Few are really carefully designed, or brilliantly run. And meaningful follow-up is the exception, not the rule.

For an outline of some basic principles of convening meetings, visit *www.smartphilanthropy.org.*

A Cautionary Tale About Strategy, Grantmaking, and Collaboration

In the spirit of learning from failure as well as success, we conclude the chapters so far with a true story that illustrates some of the complexities of engaging with grantees and collaborating with other organizations. It is a failure for which one of the authors, Paul, takes significant responsibility.[26]

From 1996 through 2006, The William and Flora Hewlett Foundation committed over $20 million to the Neighborhood Improvement Initiative, a program designed to improve the lives of residents in three Bay Area communities—West Oakland, East Palo Alto, and the Mayfair area of East San Jose. The Hewlett Foundation enlisted three community foundations as "managing partners," and it created new organizations as well as involving existing ones in the neighborhoods. Among the initiative's key goals were to "connect fragmented efforts to address poverty-related issues" and to "develop neighborhood leaders by creating a vehicle for increasing resident involvement in neighborhood planning and improvement strategies." The program was intended both to achieve tangible improvements for residents and to strengthen the long-term capacity of the community foundations and neighborhood organizations to sustain change.

Although the West Oakland project self-destructed early on, the neighborhood initiative left Mayfair and East Palo Alto better than it had found them and helped create organizations that continue to serve their residents in youth development, education, public safety, and other areas. Despite the huge investment of financial and human resources, however, the program fell far short of achieving the hoped-for tangible improvements in residents' lives. Although some stakeholders view characterizing the initiative as a failure as too harsh, it certainly was a great disappointment.

The work in East Palo Alto is illustrative. East Palo Alto is a poor city whose residents are mostly African-Americans, Latinos, Asians, and Pacific Islanders. As in the other communities served by the program, the foundation and its collaborators did not specify what poverty-related issues would be addressed or what results it hoped would be achieved, nor did they articulate a strategy for identifying and developing resident leaders. Rather, the initiative called for a diverse group of East Palo Alto residents to come together to develop a vision for the neighborhood and a general plan to achieve it, which the Hewlett Foundation would fund for six years at $750,000 per year.

Residents formed a new organization, One East Palo Alto (OEPA), which in turn formed task forces to discuss issues of individual and family support, neighborhood revitalization, and community building. Community leadership was in continual flux. Over the next three years, OEPA started thirty-nine projects involving dozens of local organizations. These projects were constantly modified and often abandoned. None of them achieved noticeable improvements in the community.

At the start of the initiative, the Hewlett Foundation had engaged the Peninsula Community Foundation (PCF) to provide technical assistance to the grantee organizations in East Palo Alto. During the first three years of the initiative, the Hewlett Foundation became increasingly skeptical of PCF's effectiveness in doing this, and Hewlett's staff intervened and communicated directly with the organizations. Relations between Hewlett and PCF soured to the point where they parted ways, and Hewlett staff members worked with the East Palo Alto organizations for the remainder of the grant period.

Confirming that it was up to the community to determine what particular projects to pursue, Hewlett nonetheless insisted that the community needed to focus on achieving only a few goals and to stick with them. OEPA regarded this not only as heavy-handed but as a breach of trust, and the relationship between funder and grantee became fraught with tensions. Hewlett provided consultants who helped specify the goals, design strategies to achieve them, and build in—as the original initiative had failed to do—indicators of progress.

The new goals focused on (1) improving the school performance of Latino pupils, 78 percent of whom scored below the 50 percentile on standardized school tests, and (2) teaching English to their parents, many of whom were not literate in any language, on the theory that this would enable them to help their children with homework and interact more effectively on their behalf with school teachers and administrators. These goals were pursued through an after-school program for the pupils and an evening program for their parents.

As it turned out, many of the pupils enrolled in the after-school program in East Palo Alto demonstrated an increased level of study skills, and a third of them showed improved literacy skills. Many of the adult students achieved a basic command of English, and a small but significant number achieved enough literacy to continue in English-as-a-second-language courses in a nearby community college. Both the youth and adult programs grew to accommodate an increasing number of students.

Almost surely, these outcomes could have been achieved with a fraction of the human and financial resources devoted to the effort and without the fracturing of relationships. But the major lessons of the story involve errors in the grant-making process from the beginning to almost the end.

➤ The story reinforces the critical importance of having a strong theory of change, clear goals, strategies, and indicators of progress—and of the need for all the participants in a joint venture to agree on these matters at the outset. (This does not foreclose significant course corrections along the way—but that term implies that there is a course to correct, and this was not always evident in the neighborhood initiative.)

➤ It is a story about inadequate attention to organizational and strategic risks and about the importance of focus and perseverance. All participants in the initiative, including the funder and the technical advisers, underestimated the challenges of building the capacity of community organizations to develop and stick with plans to deal with complex problems. The high failure rates of strategies in this realm should have served as a warning from the outset, but they were not adequately heeded.

➤ The story emphasizes the complexities of collaboration, especially when the collaborating partners have unequal power. The Hewlett Foundation was the exclusive source of funding for grantee organizations in East Palo Alto and a significant source for the Peninsula Community Foundation. What Hewlett thought of as the responsible and respectful exercise of power was perceived by others as throwing our weight around. Whether or not there's an objective truth here, it is certainly the case that even a suggestion or hint by a major funder can be overinterpreted by its grantees—and as the Hewlett

Foundation realized that the project was not going anywhere, it did considerably more than hint at or suggest the need for corrections. What Hewlett intended as helpful interventions were sometimes taken as capricious intrusions, and at the very least, the foundation did not handle the change of direction with adequate sensitivity to the community organizations or to PCF.

➤ This story highlights the importance of building a good evaluation system into the project from the start. The initiative was strong on "process" evaluation, which focused on how the organizations were relating to the community and developing internal capacity. But not until too late did the foundation focus on evaluating outcomes. It was too late not just because it is difficult to retrofit evaluation into an ongoing effort, but because it did not force the participants to ask the fundamental question at the outset: what would success look like?—a question that, if asked, would have revealed the absence of any agreement about the answer.

Consistent with the theme of sharing knowledge to improve practices in the field, the Hewlett Foundation published a detailed report on the Neighborhood Improvement Initiative, which is available on the foundation's website.[27]

Takeaway Points

➤ Philanthropists operate in a social and economic space with many other actors—grantees, other philanthropists, governments, and businesses. With due caution about the enervating effects of meetings and conferences that don't have clear goals and agendas, collaborative strategic relationships can contribute to net impact.

➤ Organizing and disseminating knowledge gained by foundations can contribute to social impact.

Chapter Notes

1. The David and Lucile Packard Foundation, The William and Flora Hewlett Foundation, the Rockefeller Brothers Fund, and the TOSA Foundation.

2. Charles and Helen Schwab Foundation, "Knowledge Management: Six Brief Essays on Lessons Learned." Under Alexa Culwell's guidance, the Schwab

Foundation was a leader in this area. In 2005, Ms. Culwell departed the foundation, and it significantly changed its grant-making strategy.

3. Grantmakers for Effective Organizations, *Leveraging What You Know: Knowledge Management Strategies for Funders* (2004), http://www.geofunders.org/document.aspx?oid=f978f512-e368-47e5-aeeb-6d85d99298f1.

4. Codification, according to the authors of an influential article, involves extracting knowledge from individuals, distilling the basic information useful to others, and creating a database that makes this knowledge accessible and reusable. This approach "opens up the possibility of achieving scale in knowledge reuse and thus of growing the business." Morten T. Hansen, Nitin Noria, and Thomas Tierney, "What's Your Strategy for Managing Knowledge?" *Harvard Business Review*, March/April 1999, 108.

5. Marla M. Capozzi, Stephanie M. Lowell, and Les Silverman, "Knowledge Management Comes to Philanthropy," *McKinsey Quarterly*, June 2003, 89.

6. Although at some point, knowledge management requires computer hardware and software, it begins with an organization's values and internal culture. Many foundations set aside "no travel" weeks to provide structured opportunities for staff members, who spend much time on the road, to exchange their tacit knowledge. Grantmakers for Effective Organizations, *Leveraging What You Know*.

7. Capozzi, Lowell, and Silverman, "Knowledge Management Comes to Philanthropy."

8. Ibid. See also Sidney Hargro, "May 2003 Knowledge Management in Action: The Columbus Foundation," http://site-b-com.i-dialogue1.com/Content.aspx?oid=9a7a0fff-59c2-48ca-ab08-5e295fb680ff (accessed June 30, 2008).

9. Lucy Bernholz and Kendall Guthrie, Commentary, "Knowledge Is an Asset, Too." *Foundation News & Commentary*, May/June 2000, http://www.foundationnews.org/CME/article.cfm?ID=412.

10. Robert Wood Johnson Foundation, "Grants Results."

11. See the Robert Wood Johnson Foundation Website, at http://www.rwjf.org/pr (accessed June 30, 2008).

12. Annie E. Casey Foundation, "Mission and History," http://www.aecf.org/AboutUs/MissionAndHistory.aspx (accessed June 30, 2008).

13. Annie E. Casey Foundation, "Knowledge Center," http://www.aecf.org/KnowledgeCenter.aspx (accessed June 30, 2008).

14. Marguerite Casey Foundation, "Resources," http://www.caseygrants.org/pages/resources/resources_index.asp (accessed June 30, 2008).

15. Barr Foundation, "About Barr Foundation," http://www.barrfoundation.org/about/index.html (accessed June 30, 2008).

16. Lucy Bernholz, *Creating Philanthropic Capital Markets: The Deliberate Evolution* (Hoboken, N.J.: Wiley, 2004), 100.

17. John D. and Catherine T. MacArthur Foundation, "Affordable Housing Grantmaking Guidelines," http://www.macfound.org/site/c.lkLXJ8MQKrH/b.943349/k.E82F/Domestic_Grantmaking_Affordable_Housing_Grantmaking_Guidelines.htm (accessed June 30, 2008).

18. MacArthur Foundation, "Public Housing." For more information about the Partnership for New Communities, go to their website, http://www.thepartnershipfornewcommunities.org.

19. Partnership for New Communities, "Investment," http://www.thepartnershipfornewcommunities.org/investment.html (accessed June 30, 2008).

20. J. Scott Kohler, "The Plan for Transformation of Public Housing in Chicago," in *Casebook for The Foundation: A Great American Secret*, by Joel L. Fleishman, J. Scott Kohler, and Steven Schindler (New York: Public Affairs, 2007), 264–265; Susan Lloyd remarks, 11/12/05; MacArthur Foundation, "Public Housing."

21. You can read more about the results of Marguerite Casey Foundation's 2006–2007 regional grantee meetings on the foundation's website, http://www.caseygrants.org.

22. Grantmakers for Effective Organizations, "GEO Action Guide: Leading Change; Transforming Grantmaker Practices for Improved Nonprofit Results" (draft October 8, 2007).

23. The Peninsula Community Foundation has since merged with Community Foundation Silicon Valley to become the Silicon Valley Community Foundation.

24. Alexa Cortes Culwell, "Building Stronger Grantee Relationships: How to Increase Impact" (keynote address, Donors Forum of Chicago Member Luncheon, Union League Club of Chicago, January 29, 2003), http://www.azgrants.com/articles/artdetail.cfm?ArticleID=49. Ms. Culwell is now CEO of the Stupski Foundation.

25. These publications are available on the Edna McConnell Clark Foundation website, at http://www.emcf.org/pub/otherresources.htm.

26. See Prudence Brown and Leila Fiester, *Hard Lessons about Philanthropy & Community Change from the Neighborhood Improvement Initiative* (Menlo Park, Calif.: William and Flora Hewlett Foundation, 2007), http://www.hewlett.org/NR/rdonlyres/6D05A0B4-D15E-47FA-B62E-917741BB9E72/0/HewlettNIIReport.pdf.

27. William and Flora Hewlett Foundation, *Special Projects: Neighborhood Improvement Initiative*, http://www.hewlett.org/NR/rdonlyres/D5CEA1CA-7EE0-4140-9AE6-3472A3D13918/0/NII04.pdf.

Chapter Seven

Forms of Grant Funding

THIS CHAPTER FOCUSES on the different forms of support that grants may take and how responsibilities for strategic planning and implementation are allocated between you and your grantees. These matters are largely determined by two factors:

1. The breadth with which you define your philanthropic goals and strategies
2. The presence of organizations whose activities are aligned with your goals and strategies

More heat than light has been emitted over the question of the appropriate forms of funding, with some asserting that supporting an organization's overall activities rather than particular projects is the only responsible form of philanthropy, and others arguing that such general support is inherently unstrategic. Our unequivocal view: it depends. What it depends on is the degree of your alignment with a grantee organization. Before we defend this simple conclusion, let's define the major categories of philanthropic funding.

Forms of Funding

General operating support—the philanthropist as public investor. General operating support—also called "core" or "unrestricted" support—is analogous to an investment in a for-profit company, the obvious difference being that philanthropists seek social rather than financial returns on their investments.

Unrestricted annual gifts to colleges, symphony orchestras, museums, and various charitable and environmental organizations are paradigmatic examples of general operating support. Such support allows the organizations to allocate resources to their own highest priorities, as well as to support back-office operations, pay utility bills, and the like.

Like financial investors, philanthropists who provide general operating support must have confidence in the grantee's overall expertise, strategy, management, and judgment. In the best case, that confidence is based on a thorough assessment of the grantee's leadership, management structure, strategies, and so on. But the philanthropists need not have deep substantive or strategic expertise in the grantee's fields of work. They leave to the organization the decisions about how to approach its work.

Exit, Voice, and Loyalty, the title of Albert O. Hirschman's insightful book, succinctly describes the basic ways that people can address their concerns with organizations in which they have a stake. Like typical small investors in for-profit companies, most donors who provide general operating support have no voice in the decision-making process and can only choose between loyalty and exit. Their interactions with the organizations are typically passive—writing checks, reading newsletters and annual reports, and listening to talks at fund-raising dinners. Depending on their satisfaction with these experiences, donors may increase, decrease, maintain, or end their financial support of the organization.

Support for an organization's self-defined unit, division, or program has many of the characteristics of general operating support. If you are an alumnus of the Yale School of Management, you may prefer to make an unrestricted grant to that school rather than to the entire university. By the same token, a philanthropist who is particularly interested in urban environmental issues may make a grant to the Natural Resources Defense Council's urban program rather than the organization as a whole. Since these units run numerous programs themselves and have their own overhead and administrative costs, supporting them with an unrestricted grant is much like providing general operating support.[1]

Negotiated general operating support—the philanthropist as large shareholder or venture capitalist. A philanthropist who intends to make a large grant, especially one that accounts for a significant proportion of an organization's budget, need not choose between loyalty and exit, but may decide to exercise his voice through negotiated general operating support. The organization still has unrestricted use of the funds, but before making the grant, the funder engages in a due-diligence process. This culminates in an agreement about the outcomes that the organization plans to achieve, the strategies it will employ to achieve them, and how it will assess and report progress.

The business analogy would be a large shareholder or a venture capitalist—someone with a significant stake in the venture who also may have substantive and management expertise in the enterprise.

The Hewlett Foundation's grantmaking abounds with negotiated general operating support grants to education, environmental, and family-planning organizations and performing arts groups. These grants manifest the foundation's confidence in the organizations' choices about how best to spend the grant funds while ensuring that their work is congruent with the foundation's goals. If the organization has multiple programs, the foundation may ask for detailed reports only about selected areas deemed particularly important to the foundation's goals.

Project support—the philanthropist as purchaser of services or as architect or general contractor. If you want to support medical education and research in general, you might make an unrestricted grant to Stanford Medical School. But if you want to help develop a cure for a particular form of cancer, you would likely support the work of particular researchers at Stanford or their laboratory. To continue the private-market analogy, we might say that rather than investing in a company, you are purchasing services.

In contrast to funders who provide general operating support because they are interested in the organization's overall or long-term impact, a project funder is typically interested in the success of a particular project—whether research to create a new antibiotic, the composition and performance of a new symphony, or assistance for the victims of Hurricane Katrina.

An institution will often seek funders for projects that it has initiated. In many cases, it has the expertise and capacity to design and carry out the projects without any guidance from the donor. You simply provide support for the initiative, with some percentage of your grant available for overhead costs. Alternatively, you may have projects in mind and, through word of mouth, professional networks, or a formal request-for-proposals process, identify experts to carry them out.

Sometimes a philanthropist may have a project in mind that requires bringing together the capacities of several different actors. In these cases, you can think of the philanthropist as a combination of architect and general contractor, hiring disparate subcontractors—carpenters, electricians, plumbers—and coordinating their work to get the job done. For example, one of the goals of the Hewlett Foundation's Environment Program was to reduce pollution from heavy-duty construction equipment. There was no single not-for-profit organization that had this as a major goal or that had the capacity to take on the work by itself. Thus, the program director (Hal) made grants to various organizations with expertise in technology, health, and federal regulatory matters, with the aim of persuading relevant industries and the Environmental Protection Agency to reduce harmful emissions. These efforts were successful. The Hewlett Foundation also played an architect or general contractor role in its New Constituencies for the Environment initiative (discussed in Chapter 4), with the plan, however, of giving the grantee organizations increasing autonomy. The Lynde and Harry Bradley Foundation's support for school vouchers, described in Chapter 1, provides a similar example.

As it happens, the organizations mentioned in these examples were not-for-profits, but there's no magic in that. A foundation acting as architect or general contractor may find that the best purveyor of a service that has great social impact is a business—for example, a public-relations firm that can effectively convey a message about teen obesity. As long as they are specifically for a philanthropic purpose, the IRS permits foundations to carry out what it terms "direct charitable activities" through any agent, including business organizations. A key aspect of the Siebel Foundation's campaign to reduce methamphetamine abuse in Montana (mentioned in Chapter 1) centers around conventional media outlets.

The Alignment of Philanthropic Goals with Organizations in the Field

When your goals are well aligned with those of an organization in your area of interest, general operating support is almost always the preferred form of funding. A philanthropist who finds a strong, well-aligned organization is fortunate indeed—as is the organization that receives the philanthropist's support.

But the breadth of your philanthropic interests affects the likelihood of alignment, and hence of the appropriate form of funding. Consider two hypothetical foundations, both concerned with domestic environmental issues. The Floodlight Foundation's mission is to sustain and improve the environment throughout the American West; its interests include land and water conservation, endangered species, national parks, fisheries, and air and water pollution. The Pacific Spotlight Foundation has only one area of interest: protecting salmon in the Pacific Northwest.

To understand how the foundations relate to the field, consider this sample of organizations:

➤ The Wild Salmon Center focuses on protecting salmon fisheries in the Pacific Northwest.
➤ Resource Media is a communications firm that works on many environmental issues.
➤ The Environmental Defense Fund (EDF) is a national organization whose western regional office is concerned with air quality, clean water, energy, open space, and dams throughout the West.
➤ The Northwest Chamber of Commerce and the Northwest Sportfishing Industry Association are concerned with salmon fishing as part of a much broader set of issues.

Now imagine each of the two foundations seeking organizations in its area of interest. The Floodlight Foundation casts its wide beam on the first three organizations, providing Wild Salmon Center and Resource Media with general operating support, and providing unrestricted program support for EDF's work in the West. In general, Floodlight's broad interest in the environment conduces to general operating support grants to a wide variety of environmental organizations. Indeed, unless a foundation with broad interests has a large staff, it is best suited to make general operating support grants and put trust in the grantees' strategies, because it lacks the expertise to independently design and assess strategies in its many areas of its interest. The Northwest Chamber of Commerce and Northwest Sportfishing Industry Association are not likely to come to Floodlight's attention.

By contrast, given its narrow focus on Pacific salmon, the Pacific Spotlight Foundation will provide general operating support only to Wild Salmon Center, and will support the particular projects of the other organizations, including the Chamber of Commerce and Sportman's Association, that help protect salmon.

Spotlight's single-mindedness allows its staff members to develop expertise in its area of focus. They understand the ecological systems involving salmon, the economics of salmon fishing, and the regulatory and legislative policies that bear on salmon. And they know the major stakeholders—commercial and sports fishermen, indigenous tribes—as well as the particular officials who can affect the relevant policies and how to influence them. Indeed, Spotlight staff members may have at least as much expertise in these areas as the not-for-profit organizations they fund. Hence, grantmaking to these organizations tends to involve considerable collaboration.

And Spotlight may sometimes act like an architect or general contractor to design an overall strategy and make grants to organizations to carry out particular components. For example, it may engage researchers at a university to study how dams affect the spawning of a particular species of salmon, and it may contract with a communications firm to disseminate the findings or make a grant to a firm or a not-for-profit organization to advocate against the relicensing of a dam.[2]

We should note that the Pacific Spotlight Foundation's focus on salmon does not mean that it will never make general operating support grants to multipurpose organizations. It may understand that the viability of salmon depends on the broader ecology in which they spawn and live and that salmon are better protected when there are strong environmental organizations in the field. But these organizations have a different place in its strategy, and their funding will be subject to different considerations.

Different Forms of Support Within the Same Foundation
Given the essential role that the alignment of the grantor's goals and the grantee's activities plays in determining forms of support, it is not surprising to find variations in forms of support not only between foundations but also among different programs in a foundation and even within a single program.

Because acting as architect or general contractor is so time consuming, even a foundation with very focused goals welcomes the opportunity to make general-support grants. In many cases, it will fund "anchor" institutions in a field at the same time as it supports particular projects—for example, supporting both the American Cancer Society and a particular research lab. The success of the Hewlett Foundation's particular project grants in family planning and reproductive health ultimately depend on organizations that constitute the infrastructure of the field, such as the Population Council, Population Reference Bureau, and Planned Parenthood. These organizations receive general operating support as well as grants for targeted projects such as HIV/AIDS prevention.[3]

A Presumption Favoring Reliable General Operating Support

We have been examining forms of philanthropic funding by asking the core strategic question, what best achieves your goals? Without losing this focus, we examine how the form of funding affects grantee organizations—a matter of genuine concern to strategic philanthropists, who care about the vitality of the fields in which they work. It is this concern that leads to a presumption in favor of general operating support.

Unrestricted support is the lifeblood of a not-for-profit organization. A well-run organization will have developed its own strategic plans. Its ability to innovate and its very integrity depend on the organization's having control over a substantial portion of its budget. But funders with particular projects in mind often ask an organization to engage in activities not central to its own mission. As the number of project-oriented funders increases, the organization's own plans can become fragmented and distorted. An organization that depends heavily on project support must engage in fund raising that cobbles together grants of interest to particular funders, while trying to maintain some semblance of a coherent plan. Many organizations find it difficult to "just say no" to any source of substantial funds.

Unrestricted funds enhance an organization's own resilience in the face of unexpected events and enable it to respond flexibly to changing needs. For example, Enterprise Corporation of the Delta, a community-development financial institution, was able to respond quickly to the devastation of Hurricane Katrina in 2005 only because it had flexible support from the F. B. Heron Foundation and others.[4] Enterprise Corporation of the Delta provided bridge loans to individuals and businesses, using its flexible capital, while victims waited for the slower bureaucracies of FEMA (Federal Emergency Management Agency) and insurance companies to reimburse them.

Similarly, the International Council on Clean Transportation (ICCT), which helps nations establish laws and strategies to reduce pollution from cars and trucks, was able to respond quickly when Governor Arnold Schwarzenegger became interested in a "low carbon fuel standard" that would progressively de-carbonize transportation fuels. ICCT used its unrestricted funds to help analyze the proposed policy. Within weeks of the project's launch, the European Union sought help to consider a similar policy. ICCT was able to send staff members to Europe, undertake a quick analysis of the situation, and add substantially to the E.U. staff capacity. ICCT could not have responded to either request had it relied solely on project support.

It is not just general operating support but reliable funding—grants of several years' duration with the prospect of renewal—that contributes to an organization's sustainability. Reliable support over a period of years permits grantees to engage in long-term planning, which is a boon for virtually any organization.[5] By contrast, project grants can require grantees to continually create new programs or recast old ones in order to win funding. A study by the Center for Effective Philanthropy notes that restricted dollars "create an environment in which not-for-profits lack the infrastructure they need to perform effectively; there is widespread burnout among not-for-profit leaders."[6] Putting it positively, Grant Oliphant of the Heinz Endowments says that multiyear funding "provides predictability for both funder and grantee that is critical for the grantee to do planning around staffing and programming. . . . It's a little like a business that knows it has a fairly reliable revenue stream versus living three months out from oblivion."[7]

The New-Land Foundation, which makes about $2 million per year in grants, has been a mainstay of support for regional environmental groups in the Rocky Mountains. This unstaffed foundation recognizes that some of the most important environmental work in this area requires local organizing, assessing and commenting on national-forest plans (forest by forest), proposing land for federal or state protection, and keeping officials accountable. The foundation's trustees therefore spend time finding strong local groups in the Rockies, and when such groups are found, the foundation supports them for many years, even decades. Of course the foundation must ensure that each group continues to have strong management and good plans, but since the bulk of the foundation's grants are renewals, this is fairly light work. To keep paperwork to a minimum, the New-Land Foundation does not require special proposals or reports, relying instead on the materials the organizations prepare for other funders. This foundation has a clear goal and good quality control—and manages with minimal costs.[8]

You may wish to ensure that an organization does not become too dependent on your funding and may therefore impose a cap on the proportion of funds you contribute to its total operating budget. And you may also wish to foster competition for your funds to ensure that a grantee remains among the best of its kind and to allow or even encourage new organizations to enter the field. But there is tremendous value in an organization's being able to count on continued funding as long as it continues to perform well.

Long-term support allows organizations to hire staff of higher quality—as the best staff will be able to demand a degree of job stability. It allows them to dig more deeply into their chosen subjects and to take on more ambitious projects that have longer time frames. Almost all important social change takes substantial time to accomplish; and sustained support of high-quality organizations equips them to deal with this reality. Thus, many not-for-profits are at least as concerned with having long-term commitments as they are with having general operating support.[9]

A recent study by the Center for Effective Philanthropy asserted that general-support grants also contribute to openness and trust between grant makers and grantees.[10] One reason for this is suggested by interviews with California foundation executives, who indicated that "general operating support grantmaking meant that the foundation engaged in more of a partnership model than a supporter of specific programs. The foundation had to identify the key individuals and organizations that they wished to nurture, and then ensure that they continued to do work that was important to the foundations' key priorities."[11]

Thus, when interests are well aligned, general operating support serves funders, grantees, and the individuals and communities that are their ultimate beneficiaries. Indeed, the benefits are so great that even a funder with specific goals should stand willing to provide long-term

General Operating Support as Virtual Collaboration

In Chapter 6, we discussed collaboration among foundations. Much joint funding often takes place without any explicit collaboration, simply by virtue of foundations' independent core support for an organization. For example, the Hewlett Foundation, along with many individual donors and other foundations, is a cofunder of performing-arts organizations in the Bay Area. It is not the funders but the organizations themselves who create this virtual collaboration. When it is feasible, general operating support is a highly efficient form of virtual collaboration that reduces the costs and potential pathologies described in Chapter 6.

general operating support to an organization whose activities encompass but are not limited to the funder's particular goals—even at the cost of some "slippage" between the funder's strategic focus and the organization's operations. General support coupled with an agreement that the organization report on the particular activities of interest to the funder often provides a workable middle ground.

Yet many foundations are reluctant to make general operating support grants. Here are some of the reasons that have been articulated, along with our comments on them.

My contribution is too small to make any difference to the organization. A grant of general operating support often accounts for only a small fraction of an organization's budget, so the funder may wonder just what difference its particular grant makes. But this misunderstands the role that a grant has in social change. No single grant, whether for a specific project or general operating support, is likely to have a discernible effect in solving an important problem. You and your grantee will seldom, if ever, be able to take credit for success; all you can hope for is to be part of the winning team.

General operating support grants cannot be evaluated and are therefore intrinsically unstrategic. The evaluation of a narrowly defined project is determined by the nature of the project itself. If your goal is to increase the number of wild salmon in the Pacific Northwest, you count the salmon. A philanthropist who makes a general support grant to an organization in effect accepts the grantee organization's mission as his own and evaluates the success of the grant essentially as the organization's CEO and board evaluate their own performance.

In other words, when you make a general-support grant you are investing in the organization's overall success. The F. B. Heron Foundation, which focuses on asset building in low-income communities, notes that its core support grants are evaluated on the basis of the grantee's planning documents,[12] and the foundation thus measures progress in terms of the organization's own ambitions and plans. As noted in Chapter 5, the Edna McConnell Clark Foundation builds strong evaluation into its general operating support grants to youth-development organizations to measure the programs' impact on their intended beneficiaries.[13]

If you are a major funder of a multipurpose organization, negotiated general operating support can provide an ample framework for evaluation. Even if your grant is unrestricted, you can agree that evaluation of the grant will focus on a particular subset of the organization's activities.

The point, ultimately, is that foundations that give general operating support grants can and often do take evaluation seriously. Rather than characterizing these grants as impossible to evaluate, they see them as an opportunity to build deeper, more trusting relationships with the grantees and to encourage improvements of the grantee's own evaluation system. As a result, general operating support grants can be strategic and yield measurable results.

General operating support creates an entrenched position for some organizations to the disadvantage of others. Because the most valuable sort of general operating support is multiyear and renewable, philanthropists may be concerned that offering general operating support is tantamount to a perpetual commitment. Some foundations deal with this problem by limiting general operating support to a fixed number of years. But if you are contributing to the impact of a successful organization, this is counterproductive.

The better way to resolve the dilemma is to be very clear, both internally and with grantees, that general operating support will be renewed if and only if it is justified by performance along the lines agreed upon and that proposals for renewals must be competitive with possible grants to other organizations in the field.

In sum, we think, not entirely kindly, that some of the resistance to renewable general operating support grants comes from the fact that it is more fun for individual philanthropists, foundation board members, and program officers to move from one project to another. Novelty is intriguing, but steadiness is more likely to win the day.

Takeaway Points

➤ Philanthropic grants fall into two broad categories:
   —*General operating support* (also called "core" or "unrestricted" support) grants leave it to the organization to determine how to spend the funds in pursuit of its mission.
   —With *project-support* grants, the funder supports some but not all of the organization's activities.
➤ In either case, the funder and grantee organization may agree on goals and indicators of progress toward them.
➤ The philanthropist's choice among forms of funding depends on how well aligned the funder's goals and strategies are with the grantee's mission and activities—the better the alignment, the stronger the case for general operating support.
➤ When alignment is strong, long-term renewable general operating support benefits both the funder and its grantees by allocating authority and responsibility to organizations that are often closer to the ground.

Chapter Notes

1. However, a foundation's support for a unit or program of an organization that does any lobbying may have different consequences, under Treasury regulations, than general operating support.

2. The example focuses on federally licensed dams. Treasury regulations prevent a foundation from advocating for the passage of a particular piece of legislation, but such regulations do not limit advocacy before administrative agencies.

3. Internally, the Hewlett Foundation refers to this as "general operating support-plus," the "plus" being the project support to help an anchor grantee strengthen its involvement in particular areas.

4. F. B. Heron Foundation, *Core Support* (New York: F. B. Heron Foundation, 2006), 8, http://www.fbheron.org/documents/ar.2005.viewbook_core_support.pdf.

5. Judy Huang, Phil Buchanan, and Ellie Buteau, *In Search of Impact: Practices and Perceptions in Foundations' Provision of Program and Operating Grants to Nonprofits* (Cambridge, Mass.: Center for Effective Philanthropy, 2006), 15, http://www.effectivephilanthropy.org/images/pdfs/CEP_In_Search_of_Impact.pdf.

6. Grantmakers for Effective Organizations, *General Operating Support: A GEO Action Guide* (Washington, D.C.: GEO, 2007), 13, http://www.geofunders.org/generaloperatingsupport.aspx.

7. Grantmakers for Effective Organizations, "GEO Action Guide: Leading Change; Transforming Grantmaker Practices for Improved Nonprofit Results" (draft October 8, 2007).

8. Hal Harvey is the president of the board of directors of the New-Land Foundation.

9. Huang, Buchanan, and Buteau, *In Search of Impact*, 19.

10. Grantmakers for Effective Organizations, *General Operating Support*, 13.

11. Carol Silverman, Kevin Rafter, and Kathleen Fletcher, *General Operating Support: Research on Grantmaker Policies and Practices* (San Francisco: USF Institute for Nonprofit Organization Management, 2006), 16, http://www.usfca.edu/inom/research/Fnd_General_Operating_Support.pdf.

12. F. B. Heron Foundation, *Core Support*.

13. Neil F. Carlson, *Making Evaluation Work*, Youth Development Fund Learning Series No. 2 (New York: Edna McConnell Clark Foundation), http://www.emcf.org/pdf/oldprog_ls2_makingevalwork.pdf.

C h a p t e r **8** *E i g h t*

Mission Investments: Investing for Social Impact

T
HE PREVIOUS CHAPTER focused on grants, the paradigmatic form of philanthropic funding. Here we consider the use of the two basic business funding instruments—loans and equity investments—to achieve social impact. We begin by considering their potential positive benefits, and then question whether you can make the world a better place by *refraining* from supporting businesses whose activities you believe to be harmful.

The financial instruments available to a philanthropist may be arrayed in these categories:

1. *Grants*, which are intended to achieve social impact without financial returns.
2. *Mission investments*, which are intended to achieve both social impact and financial returns.
   a. Below-market-rate investments are intended to sacrifice financial returns or accept higher risks to achieve social impact and are typically made as "program-related investments."
   b. Risk-adjusted market-rate investments are intended to achieve social impact and market-rate returns.
3. *Conventional investments*, which are intended to achieve financial returns but no particular social impact.

We have already discussed grants. Conventional investments need no discussion in this book, because you already know how and why to make them. This chapter examines the second category, mission investments, beginning with below-market-rate investments and concluding with the intriguing category of social-impact investments that are designed, or expected, to make market-rate returns.

Investments with Below-Market Rates of Return

For many social-purpose organizations, including those that generate revenues by providing services, grants are the only plausible source of regular philanthropic funding. However, not-for-profit organizations are sometimes in need of loans. And to the extent that an organization's business model allows for some form of ownership, it may be open to equity investments as well. In the large majority of cases, such loans or equity investments incur greater risks or lower returns than you would demand of transactions that did not have a social mission.

The difference between the risk-adjusted market financial of such an investment and the financial return on what we'll call an "ordinary" investment is the conceptual equivalent of a grant. Under the Internal Revenue Code, the entire amount of a socially motivated below-market-rate investment can be treated as a grant[1] and counted toward a foundation's mandatory 5 percent payout if the investment qualifies as a *program-related investment* (PRI).

To qualify as a PRI, the investment must (1) have the primary purpose of achieving an exempt[2] goal of the foundation, (2) not have a significant financial purpose, and (3) prohibit use of such funds for political purposes.[3] Any income from a PRI will be included with the rest of the foundation's investment income, but any amounts received or accrued as repayments of PRIs, such as repayment of loans or proceeds from sale or redemption of equity, must be paid out in the year of receipt or accrual in addition to the 5 percent required payout. Legal considerations aside, making a PRI reflects the judgment that the foregone income available for your future grantmaking is (at least) compensated for by the social return from the PRI.

Perhaps because they call for a mixture of social and financial returns and often require more legal analysis than a conventional grant, PRIs are relatively infrequent in the philanthropic world. They constitute a tiny percentage of philanthropic grants, with four foundations—the Ford Foundation, the David and Lucile Packard Foundation, the John D. and Catherine T. MacArthur Foundation, and one other foundation—

accounting for the large majority of all PRIs.[4] Typically, PRIs fall into one of three categories:[5]

> ➤ *Direct loans.* The most common form of PRIs, loans, have been made for such purposes as mortgage financing and predevelopment costs of housing and business ventures designed to help the poor.
> ➤ *Equity investments.* PRIs can be used to purchase common and preferred stock in business ventures and bank holding companies— again, mainly designed to benefit the poor.
> ➤ *Loan guarantees.* Foundations have served as guarantors of financial institutions' loans or lines of credit to not-for-profits, to mitigate the real or perceived risks of lending to such organizations.

Accepting Low Returns

Most PRIs are made in the form of loans (63.1 percent of PRIs, amounting to 43.7 percent of foundation PRI dollars); another substantial amount of PRI funds go to real estate equity investments (36.2 percent of dollars, though only 5.2 percent of individual investments).[6] For instance, The John D. and Catherine T. MacArthur Foundation has awarded more than $200 million in PRIs primarily to support community-development financial institutions such as Shorebank, which makes real estate loans to help provide affordable housing as well as loans to small businesses that create jobs in underserved communities. Among the MacArthur Foundation's recent PRIs are a $3 million investment in BRIDGE Housing Corporation in San Francisco for the acquisition of affordable rental housing, and a $2 million investment in the Calvert Social Investment Foundation to capitalize new loans in international microfinance organizations.

The Packard Foundation's funding for conservation easements to protect large tracts of land from development provides another example of low-return PRIs. Protecting private land generally requires an agreement for restrictions on the land's use, funds to compensate the landowner for forgone uses, and oversight by a land trust. This process requires extensive negotiation, deals with government agencies, and private and public fund raising, all of which may take considerable time. The Packard Foundation regularly lends money at concessionary interest rates to land-conservation groups like the Trust for Public Land to provide bridge funding to compensate a landowner before the complex

Acumen Fund's Approach to PRIs

Here's how one development-oriented investment fund thinks about its below-market-rate investments. Acumen Fund is a not-for-profit venture fund that supports businesses bringing health, water, housing, and energy to people living on less than $2 a day through grants, loans, and equity investments. Acumen Fund evaluates investments according to their social impact, financial viability, and breakthrough insights:

	SOCIAL IMPACT	FINANCIAL VIABILITY	BREAKTHROUGH INSIGHTS
Poor	It is less cost-effective than other available social options.	It has provided an incomplete return of capital to Acumen Fund.	There are no additional insights from the investment.
Good	It provides more social impact per dollar invested than other options.	There has been a full return of capital to Acumen Fund.	It has influenced Acumen Fund's other investment activities.
Better	It has proven itself scalable (at least 10x).	The enterprise's core operating cash flows are positive without subsidies.	It has provided unique insights that are broadly shared with the field.
Best	It has served more than one million individuals and materially improved the issue target.	The enterprise has been able to tap into commercial capital markets (catalyzing new dollars).	It has stimulated external replication or behavioral shifts.

Extracted and adapted from "Acumen Fund Metrics," http://blog.acumenfund.org/wp-content/uploads/2007/01/Metrics%20methodology1.pdf.

deals have been worked out and the funds have been raised to put a permanent solution in place. Packard gets its money back when the land-trust organizations repay the debt following a successful fund-raising campaign or the sale of the conservation easement to a government agency or a conservation buyer. To make this work, however, the

Packard Foundation must offer the loans at a lower interest rate and sacrifice financial return. In doing so, the foundation forgoes the difference between the low interest rate and what its market-rate investment portfolio would produce, which results in a smaller budget for conventional grants. But the PRIs have enabled the foundation to protect sizable swaths of land at the relatively low cost of the forgone income—and with very low rates of default.

This is just one example of the Packard Foundation's use of PRIs. Drawing on examples from the foundation's conservation work, its president, Carol Larson, gives seven reasons why PRIs are useful:[7]

1. ***Access to financing.*** There is no easy access to capital for conservation projects, especially for smaller land trusts. Any commercial financing that might be available would be much more expensive than a PRI, often prohibitively so.
2. ***Commercial loan terms.*** Commercial lenders typically require collateral in the form of a deed of trust against the conservation property purchased, and conservation organizations are uncomfortable placing the property at risk of foreclosure. They are comfortable granting the same security to the Packard Foundation because its social mission makes it more likely that the foundation will work to ensure the success of the project and less likely to foreclose. For example, the foundation will work with borrowers to extend loan terms or modify payment schedules due to reasonable project delays or changed circumstances.
3. ***Grants can displace public funding.*** Many conservation acquisitions need bridge financing only for the period between acquisition and public funding. In these circumstances, a grant would not be the best use of a foundation's assets, because it would displace public funding.
4. ***PRIs extend programmatic reach beyond the grants budget.*** PRIs provide an additional tool and source of funds for the foundation to accomplish its program objectives. For example, a PRI to Ecotrust capitalized a loan fund for small Alaskan fishing communities to buy quota shares—rights to a portion of the allowable catch—through community quota entities. This was in addition to the Packard Foundation's fisheries grants budget.
5. ***PRIs can catalyze other funding, both commercial and private.*** Commercial lenders viewed loans to the newly formed community quota entities described above as too risky and expensive. The loan

fund capitalized by the Packard Foundation PRI allows the community quota entities to preserve their community fishery and build equity in their quota shares over time, at levels sufficient to support commercial refinancing of the Packard Foundation–financed loans. This program should also bring more commercial credit to the industry over time, creating greater growth potential for these fishing communities.

6. **PRI funds come back.** As PRI loans are repaid, they can be lent again in support of other important conservation projects. Because PRIs are repaid and the funds are then paid out again, the Packard Foundation views them as relieving its grant budget rather than decreasing it.

7. **PRIs build organizational capacity.** Working with small conservation organizations that are first-time borrowers typically involves organizational capacity building. The Packard Foundation understands conservation organizations better than most commercial lenders do, and can therefore provide more useful advice and design underwriting requirements that reflect the needs of conservation deals. The foundation works closely with the borrower's staff throughout the due-diligence, document-negotiation, loan-funding, and loan-monitoring phases of the project, identifying transactional issues and ways to resolve them.

The Packard Foundation's PRIs are not limited to conservation. For example, it purchased bond anticipation notes that allowed the California Institute of Regenerative Medicine to begin funding stem-cell research in California while the institute was under threat from various lawsuits. And the foundation's PRIs played a key role in making emergency contraception available in the United States. The so-called morning-after pill is designed to prevent pregnancy after unprotected intercourse. In 1977, Dr. Sharon Camp founded the Women's Capital Corporation to bring emergency contraception to market in the United States under the brand name "Plan B" with the objective of permitting over-the-counter (OTC) sales. Because of the political issues surrounding emergency contraception, the company could not obtain commercial funding. The Wallace Global Fund made an initial interest-free loan of $450,000, which was followed by a series of interest-free loans from the Packard Foundation amounting to

$8.5 million. The loans provided funding for obtaining FDA approval of Plan B as a prescription drug—a necessary step toward OTC status—and for a marketing campaign. In 2004, the company was sold to Barr Laboratories Inc., which repaid the loans. Two years later, notwithstanding conservative opposition, the FDA approved OTC distribution of the pill.

Taking High Risks for the Short Term

As some of these examples show, early-stage investments have the potential for creating social benefit but are perceived as too risky by private investors. For example, in the case of microfinance, investors didn't believe that you could make money from giving loans to the poor. But the Ford Foundation, along with other donors, gave Grameen Bank the funding necessary to demonstrate the viability of microfinance.[8] Once the bank showed a profit, the investment community welcomed Grameen Bank and the new microfinance industry with significant amounts of capital.

High-risk philanthropic investments can subsidize the cost of developing a technology with important social benefits that otherwise would not come to market. For example, the Hewlett Foundation joined a number of "angel investors" in supporting Hypercar Inc. (now Fiberforge), which aims to develop high-performance, low-cost, advanced composite materials for use in automobiles. Because carbon fiber is many times stronger per unit weight than steel or aluminum, the company believes it is possible to build cars that are far lighter than today's fleet, with great energy savings, and without sacrificing safety or functionality.[9]

Recently, Google.org has undertaken a campaign to make renewable energy less expensive than coal. Labeled RE<C, this initiative includes investments and grants to develop promising technologies that will eventually compete with coal in unsubsidized markets. For example, Google.org has invested in eSolar Inc., which is developing modular solar power plants that are inexpensive to install, maintain, and expand. Another company, Makani Power Inc., is developing high-altitude wind energy. One of Google's founders, Larry Page, expressed the hope that if RE<C meets its goal "and large-scale renewable deployments are cheaper than coal, the world will be able to meet a substantial portion of electricity needs from renewable sources and significantly reduce carbon emissions."[10]

Most high-risk philanthropic R&D investments seek to prove concepts that will eventually find their way into conventional markets and attract nonphilanthropic investors.

Investments with Market Rates of Return

Mission investments with market rates of return represent a win-win strategy, where you can get a social return on a financial investment without sacrificing any financial return whatsoever. We examine below whether and when this might be possible (we're agnostic) and also examine the suggestion that you can sometimes achieve the amazing result of beating the market at the same time as you achieve social impact (we're skeptical).

Typically, investing in enterprises with market rates of return adds nothing to the social benefits implicit in making any type of investment. Your marginal investment in Toyota because it manufactures hybrid cars (we'll leave aside its gas-guzzlers) will not affect the number of hybrid cars it produces or their cost. At least for publicly traded companies, a foundation's investment has only symbolic value, because if the foundation doesn't invest in a particular company, someone else will. Although symbols can be deployed for social change, in this case the symbolic investment is more likely to lead to self-congratulatory complacency than to changing the world.

As we see it, the only way to generate market rates of return, or better, and create social impact—to have an effect beyond that of any ordinary investor—is to have unique knowledge about the value of an investment. This seems plausible with respect to some private equity investments. But for investments in publicly traded securities, we see no reason to doubt the efficient market hypothesis, which holds that individuals lack such unique knowledge (unless they are making illegal use of "inside" information).[11] We discuss the issues in more detail below.

Market-Rate Investments and Private Equity
The efficient market hypothesis may not be as applicable to private equity as it is to the public markets, especially for investments in local or regional enterprises. For example, New Cycle Capital, LLC, an early-stage venture capital firm, invests in what it calls "domestic emerging markets"—businesses that either focus on low-income and ethnic populations or lack access to traditional sources of risk capital.

New Cycle was a key investor in Sneaker Villa, a specialty retailer of urban-inspired apparel and footwear products that operates in inner-city neighborhoods. In addition to hiring local employees, Sneaker Villa has social programs, such as Turn In Your Guns, which exchanges merchandise for guns, and it provides discounts for students for each "A" on their report card. New Cycle provided the financial capital and management expertise to help Sneaker Villa expand.

There are other such socially oriented funds that seek market-rate venture capital returns. Pacific Community Management focuses on expanding small businesses in California that benefit low- and moderate-income communities.[12] DBL Investors invests in companies that provide "social and environmental improvement in the San Francisco Bay Area's low and moderate income neighborhoods."[13] The Baltimore Fund focuses on creating jobs for low- and moderate-income workers in Baltimore.[14] Philanthropies, including the Open Society Institute, the Annie E. Casey Foundation, and the W. K. Kellogg Foundation, are among the major investors in such funds. The possibility that these mission investments will achieve market-rate returns seems to lie in the fund managers' specialized knowledge. Such familiarity with these community-based non-technology-related businesses is analogous to the specialized knowledge of venture capitalists with expertise in biotech, electronic media, and the like.

To the extent that you can create real social impact through market-rate investments, all the more power to you and the enterprises you support. In order to assess whether you are actually making market-rate investments, however, you need to evaluate the performance of your entire portfolio of such investments rather than cherry-pick those that succeed. In calculating return, you should consider—as in the case of PRIs or grants, for that matter—the information and transaction costs of making the investments. This is not to detract from the value of these investments; even if, with all costs included, your returns are below market, you presumably are having social impact. But for your own sake and that of the field, it's important to be accurate in reporting on your returns.

Market-Rate Investments in Public Markets

In the investment world, alpha describes the additional return from an investment above and beyond the expected market rate of return. Some portfolio managers think that they can both beat the market and generate social return. Is it possible? We're somewhat skeptical. Many managers who seek only financial returns have historically devoted themselves to capturing alpha in the public markets. For the most part, they have not beaten passive portfolios based on market indexes—at least not for long.[15]

That said, some wise people believe that taking account of social considerations can lead to better-than-market returns in the long run. For example, former vice president Al Gore and David Blood, a former head of Goldman Sachs Asset Management, have formed a new investment firm, Generation Investment Management LLP, in the belief that conventional markets don't take adequate account of a company's long-term sustainability. By using a positive screen based on environmental, social, and governance (ESG) factors—from climate change and human capital to corporate governance and stakeholder engagement—Generation Investment Management believes that it can reduce the risks of its investments and above-market returns.

Innovest Strategic Value Advisors provides another example. Founded in 1995 with the mission of integrating sustainability into financial analyses by identifying nontraditional sources of risk and value potential for investors, Innovest has done research that links companies' ability to manage the associated risks and opportunities of climate change with their financial performance.[16] It has also developed the Access to Medicine Index, which will help investors analyze the link between pharmaceutical companies' provision of essential drugs in developing countries and their profitability.[17]

A common belief underlying these alpha-seeking mission investments is that "sustainable" or "socially responsible" practices will make businesses more profitable in the long run. By itself, investing in alpha-seeking portfolios has little social impact, but if the market realizes the importance of ESG factors, then asset managers will pay more attention to long-term valuations and extrafinancial considerations, which will cause companies to give more consideration to the value of practices like environmental risk management, employee retention, and community relations. However, there is some question whether it is social responsibility that leads to profitability or vice-versa.[18] And for every investor who's been successful at capturing alpha, there are many others—whether or not socially motivated—who have not.

Negative Screens on Your Investments: Socially Responsible Investing

We turn now to the obverse of affirmative financial investments for social good. Can you advance your philanthropic goals, or at least avoid compromising them, by avoiding certain investments? Should a philanthropist with strong environmental concerns hold stock in Newmont Mining Corporation, which releases millions of pounds of arsenic from its mining operations every year at a horrendous environmental cost? Should a philanthropist concerned with child welfare in developing countries hold stock in an apparel company whose products are produced by child labor?

Many foundations, including our own, have been criticized for their indifference to these concerns in their financial investments.[19] An article in the *Los Angeles Times* accused the Bill & Melinda Gates Foundation of inconsistency in supporting the vaccination of Nigerian children against polio and measles while owning stock in a company whose oil refinery's fumes impair the health of the very same children.[20]

In 2007, the Hewlett and Gates foundations independently reviewed their investment practices. Taking into account the complexities and costs of meaningful negative screening and doubts about its effectiveness in changing corporate behavior,[21] they decided to limit screening to businesses, such as tobacco companies, whose profit model is centrally tied to egregiously harmful activities. (The Gates Foundation no longer has any holdings in the companies identified for disinvestment by Harvard, Yale, and Stanford because of their activities in Sudan.[22])

But some other foundations—including the Educational Foundation of America, the Merck Family Fund, the Presbyterian Foundation Group, through New Covenant Mutual Funds and the Tides Foundation—do screen their investments.[23] In 2000, the dollar volume of socially screened investments—which variously exclude alcohol, defense, gambling, guns, pollution, pornography, and tobacco—amounted to $2 trillion, or more than 20 percent of institutional funds.[24]

So does socially responsible investing (SRI) help philanthropists in their attempts to advance the well-being of humanity? Here are some factors relevant to formulating your own policy.

The Nature of the Screens
Different indexes exclude companies on different bases. For example, one of the first screened funds, the Pax World Fund, which was founded in

1971 by Luther Tyson and Jack Corbett of the United Methodist Church, got its start by screening out companies supplying military equipment for the Vietnam War. KLD Research & Analytics Inc.'s popular Domini 400 Social Index, an index of large-cap companies taken mainly from the Standard & Poor's 500 index, excludes companies involved beyond specific thresholds in alcohol, tobacco, firearms, gambling, nuclear power, or military weapons; it gives affirmative weight to companies with positive social and environmental records in community relations, diversity, employee relations, human rights, product quality and safety, the environment, and corporate governance. The Sierra Club Stock Fund employs over twenty social and environmental screens. The Ave Maria mutual funds, which seek investments that do not violate core teachings of the Catholic Church, screen out companies involved in abortion and pornography or that provide benefits to employees' nonmarital partners.

Some screens seem to have very large holes. For example, the Dow Jones Sustainability World Index, which screens for the top 10 percent of firms within each industry in terms of their sustainability and environmental practices,[25] includes Newmont Mining Corporation, Barrick Gold Corporation, and Weyerhaeuser Company—companies that have been frequent targets of criticism by environmental activists. More generally, Paul Hawken, a well-known corporate and environmental activist, writes:

> Because SRI mutual funds have no common standards, definitions, or codes of practices, many investors express concern and disappointment about their investments. The disappointment does not stem from portfolio losses, but from the lists of companies in the portfolios themselves (Enron, General Electric, Lockheed Martin, McDonald's, etc.). . . . The cumulative investment portfolio of the combined SRI mutual funds is virtually no different than the combined portfolio of conventional funds. . . . The screening methodologies and exceptions by most SRI mutual funds allow practically any publicly-held corporation to be considered as an SRI portfolio company. . . . Fund names and literature can be deceptive, not reflecting the actual investment strategy of the managers.[26]

The Financial Consequences of Screening Investments

There is no definitive evidence about whether screening your investments provides lower-than-market-rate, market-rate, or above-market-rate returns. Some studies indicate that screening provides close-to-market or above-market rates of return. From 1990 to 1998, three of the largest screened index funds—the Domini 400 Social Index,[27] the Citizens Index,[28] and the CREF Social Choice Account[29]—outperformed the S&P 500.[30] Depending on their exclusions, screened funds arguably avoid the potential liabilities of tobacco lawsuits, superfund site cleanups, and product liability for assault-rifle mayhem. Furthermore, "socially responsible" companies may have competitive advantages in managing their brands, assessing environmental risks, or hiring talent. Business-school graduates say that they would be willing to forgo considerable compensation to avoid working at companies not concerned with their communities and the environment.[31]

However, the performance of different funds varies widely, as has the performance of a given fund in different time periods. Among the ten largest socially responsible mutual funds reported in the Social Investment Forum—a national membership association dedicated to advancing the concept, practice, and growth of socially and environmentally responsible investing—the average annual returns ranged from 24.68 percent (Bridgeway Ultra-Small Company Tax Advantage) to –7.30 percent (Dreyfus Premier Third Century).[32]

Meir Statman, at Santa Clara University's Leavey School of Business, writes that "the returns of the [Domini 400 Social Index] were higher than those of the S&P 500 during the overall May 1990–April 2004 [period] but not in every sub-period. In general, SRI indexes did better than the S&P 500 Index during the boom of the late 1990s but lagged it during the bust of the early 2000s."[33] Similarly, David Vogel, at the Haas School of Business of the University of California, Berkeley, notes that "during the latter part of the 1990s, many social funds showed relatively strong returns due to their heavy exposure in financials, 'clean' technology, health care, media, and communications. But their performance was then negatively affected when the value of many of these firms declined."[34]

In any event, it is not clear whether the better performance of some screened funds is a direct result of their "ethical" management philosophy or just a manifestation of Wall Street's random walk. If corporate social responsibility provides a competitive advantage, it seems likely to be reflected in current stock prices. Unless a screened fund takes factors into account that the market has not already considered, it is not evident why the funds should outperform, say, the S&P 500.[35]

The Costs of Screening Investments

The management and other associated costs of SRI funds are not greater than those of traditional mutual funds.[36] However, an SRI strategy does restrict the breadth of investments for foundations that employ managers to invest in publicly traded securities. At least at present, there are few firms that are both excellent financial managers and well versed in the nuances of socially responsible investing.

The Social Impact of Screening Investments

The rationale for negative screens is to remove financial support from companies whose practices, products, or services are inconsistent with your mission. Avoiding "dirty hands" may be intrinsically or symbolically important for you or your trustees or for external constituencies. And when integrated with strong corporate campaigns of the sort discussed in Chapter 13, disinvestments may change the behavior of companies or an entire industry.

But individual institutions' divestment practices are unlikely to affect the stock price of a company, let alone the cash flows relevant to its operations.[37] Typically, other money, not restricted by any sort of screening, will rush in to fill the gap. Absent concerted action by a large number of investors, refusing to own stock in a business is an attenuated lever for influencing change.

Takeaway Points

➤ Mission investments are financial investments that seek social impact as well as a financial return.

➤ Mission investments are typically made in private markets, either as direct loans, equity investments, or loan guarantees.

➤ Some mission investments qualify as "program-related investments" and count toward a foundation's required 5 percent payout under the Internal Revenue Code.

➤ Although screening out investments in companies whose practices you abhor may serve institutional values, the practice is largely ineffective in achieving social impact.

Chapter Notes

1. "Expenditure responsibility" and various other administrative requirements would obtain.

2. Basically, one or more religious, charitable, scientific, literary, or educational goals. 26 U.S.C. § 170(c)(2)(B).

3. 26 C.F.R. § 53.4944-3. If the PRI requirements are not met, the investment must be measured against the requirements for investments that do not jeopardize the foundation's purposes, which include exercising "ordinary business care and prudence, under the facts and circumstances prevailing at the time of making the investment, in providing for the long- and short-term financial needs of the foundation to carry out its exempt purposes. In the exercise of the requisite standard of care and prudence the foundation managers may take into account the expected return (including both income and appreciation of capital), the risks of rising and falling price levels, and the need for diversification within the investment portfolio (for example, with respect to type of security, type of industry, maturity of company, degree of risk, and potential for return). The determination whether the investment of a particular amount jeopardizes the carrying out of the exempt purposes of a foundation shall be made on an investment by investment basis." 26 C.F.R. § 53.4944-1(a)(2). PRIs are also governed by state laws regarding prudent investments by trustees.

4. Sarah Cooch and Mark Kramer, "The Power of Strategic Mission Investing," *Stanford Social Innovation Review* 5, no. 4 (2007): 44.

5. Ford Foundation, *Investing for Social Gain: Reflections on Two Decades of Program-Related Investments* (New York: Ford Foundation, 1991), 10, http://www.fordfound.org/archives/item/0198.

6. Sarah Cooch and Mark Kramer, *Compounding Impact: Mission Investing by US Foundations* (FSG Social Impact Advisors, 2007), 17, http://www.fsg-impact.org/images/upload/Compounding%20Impact(3).pdf. The fourth foundation requested not to be named in the study.

7. Correspondence from Carol Larson, February 24, 2008. On file with the authors.

8. Ford Foundation, *Investing for Social Gain*, 34.

9. Some of the nonphilanthropic angel investors may expect competitive market rates of return. Even so, if the company lacks the funds to pursue effective R&D, and if the foundation reasonably believes that its investment is likely to produce external social benefits, this is an appropriate PRI in both social and legal terms.

10. Google, "Google's Goal: Renewable Energy Cheaper than Coal," http://www.google.com/intl/en/press/pressrel/20071127_green.html.

11. The efficient market hypothesis asserts that financial markets are "informationally efficient," or that prices on traded assets—for example, stocks, bonds, or property—already reflect all known information and therefore are unbiased in the sense that they reflect the collective beliefs of all investors about future prospects. See Eugene Fama, "The Behavior of Stock-Market Prices," *Journal of Business* 38, no. 1 (1965): 34–105.

12. See Pacific Community Ventures, LLC, http://pcvfund.com (accessed June 30, 2008).

13. DBL Investors, "About DBL Investors," http://dblinvestors.com (accessed June 30, 2008).

14. See Open Society Institute, "OSI Announces Baltimore Venture Fund," news release, July 16, 2002, http://www.soros.org/initiatives/baltimore/news/venturefund_20020716.

15. Rex A. Singuefield, "Active vs. Passive Management" (opening statement, Schwab Institutional Conference, San Francisco, October 12, 1995), http://www.dfaus.com/library/articles/active_vs_passive.

16. Innovest Strategic Value Advisors, *Carbon Beta*™ *and Equity Performance: An Empirical Analysis* (2007), http://www.climateactionproject.com/docs/carbonbetaequityperformance-delivered.pdf.

17. The idea behind the Access to Medicine Index is to determine whether a failure to properly address health crises around the world may hurt a company's reputation and its license to operate in certain markets—and ultimately, its bottom line. Innovest Strategic Value Advisors, *Access to Medicine Index Scoping Report & Stakeholder Review* February (2007), http://www.innovestgroup.com/images/pdf/atm%20index%20scoping%20report%2022-02-07.pdf.

18. David Vogel, *The Market for Virtue: The Potential Limits of Corporate Social Responsibility* (Washington, D.C.: Brookings Institution Press, 2005), 29–33.

19. Harvy Lipman, "Meshing Proxy with Mission," *Chronicle of Philanthropy*, May 4, 2006, http://philanthropy.com/free/articles/v18/i14/14000701.htm.

20. Charles Piller, Edmund Sanders, and Robyn Dixon, "Dark Cloud Over Good Works of Gates Foundation," *Los Angeles Times*, January 7, 2007.

21. For a critical and balanced academic review of the performance and impact of socially responsible investing, see Michael L. Barnett and Robert M. Salomon, "Throwing a Curve at Socially Responsible Investing Research: A New Pitch at an Old Debate," *Organization & Environment* 16, no. 3 (2003): 381–389.

22. Bill & Melinda Gates Foundation, "Our Investment Policy," http://www.gatesfoundation.org/AboutUs/OurWork/Financials/RelatedInfo/OurInvestmentPhilosophy.htm (accessed June 30, 2008). The rationale for looking to the decisions of these universities is that they already have the infrastructure for scrutinizing investments.

23. State Street Global Advisors, "A Case for Socially Responsible Investing," *Council of Michigan Foundations 2004 Conference Recap* (2006), 3.

24. Bernell K. Stone et al., "Socially Responsible Investment Screening: Strong Evidence of No Significant Cost for Actively Managed Portfolios" (paper, Moskowitz Prize Competition, 2001), 2, http://www.socialinvest.org/resources/research.

25. *Investopedia*, s.v. "Dow Jones Sustainability World Index," http://www.investopedia.com/terms/d/djones-sustainability-world.asp (accessed June 30, 2008).

26. Paul Hawken, *Socially Responsible Investing: How the SRI Industry Has Failed to Respond to People Who Want to Invest with Conscience and What Can Be Done to Change It* (Sausalito, Calif.: Natural Capital Institute, 2004), 5, http://www.responsibleinvesting.org/database/dokuman/SRI%20Report%2010-04_word.pdf.

27. Between 1990 and 2006, KLD's Domini 400 Social Index was a float-adjusted, market capitalization-weighted common stock index, whose holding consisted of companies that have "positive environmental, social, and governance (ESG) performance." The ESG performance evaluation considered issues such as alternative energy, climate change, community relations, human rights, accounting, and transparency. KLD, "KLD's Domini 400 Social Index," http://www.kld.com/indexes/data/fact_sheet/DS400_Fact_Sheet.pdf. In November 2006, the Domini 400 Social Index was renamed the Domini Social Equity Fund in a transition to an active management strategy. See http://www.domini.com/domini-funds/Domini-Social-Equity-Fund/index.htm (accessed June 30, 2008).

28. The Citizens Index, created and maintained by Citizens Advisers, was a market-weighted portfolio of common stocks of "approximately three hundred companies chosen for industry representation, financial soundness, and corporate responsibility." Steve Schueth, "Social Investing," Social Funds Learning Center, http://www.socialfunds.com/education/article.cgi?sfArticleId=1 (accessed June 30, 2008).

29. The CREF Social Choice Account is a variable annuity account that seeks a favorable long-term rate of return that reflects the investment performance of the financial markets while giving special consideration to certain social criteria. The account typically invests about 60 percent of its assets in stocks and other equity securities and about 40 percent in bonds and other fixed-income securities. In the case of equities and corporate bonds, the account invests only in companies that meet its social criteria. Companies with revenues from alcohol, tobacco, gambling, weapons production, or nuclear power are excluded. Remaining companies are evaluated on a number of issues, including environmental stewardship, human rights, community relations, employee relations, workforce diversity, product safety and quality, and corporate governance. CREF Social Choice Account, http://www.tiaa-cref.org/pdf/fact_sheets/cref_social_choice.pdf (accessed June 30, 2008). As a variable annuity account that "seeks a favorable long-term rate of return that reflects the investment performance of the financial market," the CREF Social Choice Account invests "about 60 percent of its assets in stocks and other equity securities and about 40 percent in bonds and other fixed-income securities." In its selection process of equities and corporate bonds, the portfolio management team account rules out companies with revenues from alcohol, tobacco, gambling, weapons production, or nuclear power, and assesses potential holdings on issues such as environmental stewardship, human rights, community relations, employee relations, workforce diversity, product safety and quality, and corporate governance. Teachers Insurance and Annuity Association – College Retirement Equities

Fund (TIAA-CREF), "CREF Social Choice Account," http://www.tiaa-cref. org/pdf/fact_sheets/cref_social_choice.pdf.

30. The returns of the three funds from inception to 1998 are as follows: Domini 400 Social Index, 333.03% vs. S&P 283.77% (since May 1, 1990); Citizens Index, 176.26% vs. S&P 139.23% (since December 31, 1994); and CREF Social Choice Account (equity, or stock, portion), 290.18% vs. 274.05% (since April 1, 1990). Steve Schueth, "Social Investing," Social Funds Learning Center, http://www .socialfunds.com/education/article.cgi?sfArticleId=1 (accessed June 30, 2008).

31. David B. Montgomery and Catherine A. Ramus, "Corporate Social Responsibility Reputation Effects on MBA Job Choice" (Stanford Business School Research Paper No. 1805, 2003), https://gsbapps.stanford.edu/ researchpapers/library/RP1805.pdf.

32. Vogel, *The Market for Virtue*, 37.

33. Meir Statman, "Socially Responsible Indexes: Composition, Performance, and Tracking Errors" (paper, Leavey School of Business, Santa Clara University, 2005), http://www.haas.berkeley.edu/responsiblebusiness/documents/ SociallyResponsibleIndexes_Statman.pdf.

34. Vogel, *The Market For Virtue*, 36.

35. See CharitySRI, "Financial Returns," http://www.charitysri.org/ for_charities/financial_returns.html#studies (accessed June 30, 2008).

36. See John B. Guerard, Jr., "Is There a Cost to Being Socially Responsible in Investing?" *Journal of Investing*, Summer 1997, 31–35; J. David Diltz, "Does Social Screening Affect Portfolio Performance?" *Journal of Investing*, Spring 1995: 64–69; and J. David Diltz, "The Private Cost of Socially Responsible Investing," *Applied Financial Economics* 5 (1995): 69–77.

37. Andrew Samwick, professor of economics at Dartmouth College, provides a clear overview of the issue in his post "Some Economics of Divestment," posted to his blog Vox Baby on October 26, 2005, http://voxbaby.blogspot.com/2005/10/ some-economics-of-divestment.html.

C h a p t e r *N i n e*

Assessing Progress and Evaluating Impact

I N CHAPTER 4, we saw that a philanthropic initiative often requires making a coordinated cluster, or suite, of grants. And in Chapter 5, we discussed assessing the progress and impact of individual grants. In this chapter, we combine these processes to ask how a philanthropist can assess the progress and impact of an initiative as a whole. This involves a mixture of qualitative and quantitative measures. It is useful to separate the assessment into three categories:

➤ Monitoring performance
➤ Tracking progress
➤ Assessing impact

Monitoring performance and tracking progress are means for getting the feedback necessary to make midcourse corrections to a strategy. Ideally, assessing impact can also contribute to corrections, though its time horizons are often very long.

Monitoring Performance

A grant agreement is essentially a contract: the grantee organization usually commits to undertake certain activities or to produce specified deliverables. Assuming that the strategy underlying the grant is based on a sound theory of change, meeting these commitments is essential to achieving impact. By monitoring the grantee's performance, a funder ensures that the grantee is doing what it agreed to do.

A funder obtains information about a grantee's activities mainly through written reports, supplemented by conversations and site visits. A report may consist of both quantitative information and a narrative description of matters not captured or explained by the quantitative data alone. For example, a grant for an after-school mentorship program might set targets for the number of students enrolled, mentors recruited, and mentorship sessions per student. In addition to reporting the particular numbers achieved, the report might include the executive director's broader thoughts about the program, including challenges and opportunities the program faces, and the report would explain any differences between the targeted and actual numbers.

You would not usually make a grant if you didn't believe there was a good chance that the grantee organization had the capacity to carry it out. But an organizational problem may arise during the course of the grant. Perhaps the demands of the work were not fully appreciated at the outset, or the organization suffered an unanticipated setback, like the departure of its executive director. An organization's inability to meet agreed-upon targets may signal problems of this sort. A funder who has a trusting and candid relationship with a grantee and stays apprised of the organization's progress is not likely to have to wait for a formal report.

The program officer's close monitoring of the cluster of grants in the Hewlett Foundation's New Constituents for the Environment initiative (Chapter 4) provided feedback that led to many course corrections. In the course of a program to reduce teen obesity, the Atlanta-based Arthur M. Blank Family Foundation convened its grantees every five weeks to address common challenges. A staff member noted that, as a result, "you can never have problems that are more than five weeks old. . . . This way we can make adjustments to create better performance as soon as we realize there is an issue."[1]

Tracking Progress—and Revising Strategic Plans

A strategic plan provides a necessary starting place for a philanthropic initiative. But when a plan encounters the real world, it almost inevitably requires revision. Tracking the implementation of a strategic plan provides the feedback necessary for midcourse corrections. Consider this example from an initiative by the Ball Foundation to improve under-performing Chicago high schools. Srik Gopalakrishnan, the lead evaluator of the initiative, explained:

> We started out with a "cascade model" of professional development—a group of 40 lead teachers from a few schools go through professional development and then take their new skills back to their schools to train other teachers. Unfortunately, we found that this cascade model wasn't working. The lead teachers were learning and growing, but they weren't spreading the information once they got back to their schools. We learned from our surveys and focus groups that our model needed rethinking—the lead teachers said it was very hard, with all they were doing on a daily basis, to distribute the learning. There were issues that we hadn't thought about at the beginning such as substitute teachers and union contracts. We redesigned the program, and in our new schools we have implemented coaching at the school level to recreate the experience that the lead teachers went through.[2]

Similarly, the Health Foundation of Central Massachusetts learned that teachers' neglect to obtain signed parental permission slips was hindering an in-school oral-health program.[3] And in a program to address family homelessness in the Puget Sound area, the Bill & Melinda Gates Foundation learned that the absence of play space in housing units contributed to kids' getting into trouble, which in turn contributed to the eviction of families.[4]

In virtually every respect, the process for tracking the progress of an initiative or a cluster of grants mirrors the process for an individual grant. Just as a grant proposal calls for the articulation of goals, strategies, and indicators of progress, so does the strategic plan for an initiative—except, of course, that the plan precedes making individual grants. In Chapter 4, we summarized the plan for New Constituencies for the Environment (NCE), which included indicators of progress. And we described how feedback during the first couple of years of NCE shaped subsequent grantmaking.

Dashboards provide a useful tool for tracking progress. The dashboard may capture information about a particular group of grants or about the foundation's work as a whole. As part of an evaluation of the

Bill & Melinda Gates Foundation's high-school reform efforts in fifty school districts across the country, FSG Social Impact Advisors created dashboards to enable the foundation to identify the districts in which improvements occurred.[5] The indicators, which track groups of students by race and ethnicity, include promotion and dropout rates and reading and math proficiency, all shown graphically over a five-year period. On a foundation-wide basis, a dashboard may capture such things as[6]

> ➤ indicators of progress for particular strategies and clusters of grants;
> ➤ changes in national indicators (for example, health, employment, housing) in areas of grantmaking;
> ➤ the number of individuals served by a foundation that supports direct services;
> ➤ grant proposals received, accepted, and declined;
> ➤ administrative expenses;
> ➤ investment performance;
> ➤ staff compensation and satisfaction; and
> ➤ satisfaction of external stakeholders.

For cluster evaluations as a method for assessing progress, visit *www .smartphilanthropy.org*.

Evaluating Impact

We begin with the technical but critical distinction between achieving the intended outcome of a strategic plan and achieving impact. Recall the cartoon of the wolves baying at the moon in Chapter 1, and consider this old story. A man rode the Fifth Avenue bus to work every day. And every day, when the bus stopped at Forty-Second Street, he opened the window and threw the sports section of the newspaper into a litter basket. After many years, the bus driver asked why he did this, and the man replied: "I do it to keep the elephants off Fifth Avenue." "But there aren't any elephants on Fifth Avenue," said the bus driver, to which the man responded: "See, it works!"

The passenger relentlessly pursued a strategy to achieve a particular outcome, and the desired outcome regularly occurred. Admittedly, your authors do not fully grasp the underlying theory of change behind his actions; nonetheless, we're pretty skeptical that his strategy had impact. Impact assumes causation—that the outcome would not have occurred without his intervention.

So, how do you test for impact? The easy but unfortunate answer is that if you don't see signs of progress in the indicators accompanying a strategic plan, you are unlikely to be achieving your intended outcome, let alone having impact. On the hopeful side, signs of progress and even achieving those outcomes may be suggestive of impact. But, the elephants aside, it is usually impossible to establish impact without undertaking some sort of evaluation, which is likely to be time consuming and expensive.

One way to avoid the costs of evaluation is to base your interventions on strategies that others have shown to work in similar situations. What sometimes makes this difficult, though, is determining what counts as "similar." For example, a substance-abuse prevention program that is very successful for wealthy suburban children may have little impact in a poor urban area, or vice versa. This may seem obvious, but often seemingly insignificant differences in the populations you are trying to affect, or in implementation, means that a strategy that worked in one context won't work in another.

Approaches to Evaluation

Common among all approaches to evaluating impact are the goals of establishing (1) that a particular intervention is *correlated* with the outcome and (2) that the intervention *causes* the outcome—for example, establishing that the rate of malaria infections in a village goes down (1) *when* residents use bed nets and (2) *because* they use bed nets.

Establishing what the outcome actually was and its correlation with the intervention is often hard enough—for example, it may be difficult to gather the data necessary to establish a baseline of malaria infections and then to track the number of infections over time. Establishing causation is usually more difficult, because even if there is a change, it may be due to factors besides the introduction of bed nets—perhaps the weather was drier than usual, thus producing fewer mosquitoes, or perhaps other antimalaria interventions were introduced at the same time.

Randomized controlled experiments are the gold standard of evaluation. Although observational and econometric studies can also shed great light on the outcomes of social interventions, they seldom can establish causation.

Randomized Controlled Studies

In randomized controlled studies, participants from the population of interest are randomly assigned to either the treatment group—those who receive the intervention—or a control group.[7] After collecting data on the two groups' outcomes, you see if there are sufficiently large—statistically significant—differences between the two. Statistical significance is a function of the magnitude of the differences and the size of the groups. Too small a sample may make it difficult to draw any conclusions one way or the other. But if you find statistically significant differences, you can conclude that the intervention had an impact because the random assignment controlled for other factors.

The U.S. Food and Drug Administration requires that most new pharmaceutical products be subject to randomized controlled studies before being introduced into the market. Participants in clinical trials receive either the new drug (the treatment) or a control (a placebo, or conventional treatment if there is one), and researchers analyze whether the health of those receiving the new drug improves more—or less—than the health of those in the control group. Randomized controlled studies are not mandated for social interventions, and they are seldom done. But when feasible, they can provide essential insights into the actual effects of social programs.[8]

Observational, or Quasi-Experimental Studies

There are two main sorts of observational studies. One looks at the same group *before and after* the intervention. The other takes a *cross-sectional* approach and compares the treatment group with a similar group, identified in the existing world rather than randomly assigned.

Both suffer from the weakness that they cannot control for factors other than the intervention that may have changed at the same time. The so-called broken windows theory provides a famous example of the problem: New York's zero-tolerance policy for vandalism and other petty crimes in the 1990s was claimed to have resulted in a significant reduction of all crimes, including felonies. But it turned out that crime rates declined simultaneously, and to approximately the same extent, in other U.S. cities that had not adopted this approach. The decline might have resulted from the waning of the crack epidemic, or the increase in the number of drug offenders in prisons (and therefore not on the streets), or the general demographic decline in the number of young males.[9]

This was a case where a cross-sectional comparison contradicted the findings of a before-and-after study. But cross-sectional studies have problems of their own. For example, a large cross-sectional study in the 1990s found that hormone replacement therapy (HRT) for postmenopausal women significantly reduced the risk of heart disease.[10] But a later randomized controlled trial found that HRT actually increased the risk of heart attacks.[11] The later study randomly assigned 16,608 postmenopausal women to groups of roughly equal size and gave one group the hormone combination and the other a placebo. It turned out that the original studies had not controlled for the fact that women on HRT "were also more likely to see a doctor (which is how they were put on hormone therapy in the first place), and probably more likely to exercise and to eat a healthful diet, than women who were not taking the drug."[12] Thus, the relationship wasn't that taking hormones made women healthy, it was that healthy women took hormones.

There are variations on quasi-experimental studies, including an approach that compares the difference between data on the treatment group before and after the program with the difference between data on a similar group that wasn't exposed to the program.[13] And one can sometimes use statistical analysis to establish correlations that, together with one's knowledge of how the world works, at least hint strongly at causation. The popular book *Freakonomics* is based largely on analysis of this sort.[14] Rather than go deeper into theory and methodology, we'll give a few examples that shed light on how these approaches might be relevant to philanthropy.

The Benefits and Limits of Evaluation
In this section, we look at some cases where evaluation has demonstrated conclusively that a particular intervention works or that it doesn't work. We then discuss the pervasive problem of inconclusiveness and ask about the implications of all of this for your work as a philanthropist.

The Good
The Abdul Latif Jameel Poverty Action Lab (J-PAL), a research center at the Massachusetts Institute of Technology, specializes in conducting

randomized controlled studies in developing countries. J-PAL randomly assigned girls in Kenya either to a group that was promised merit-based scholarships and a cash grant for school supplies if they scored well on academic exams, or to a control group. It turned out that just being eligible for scholarships led the girls to think of themselves as "good students" and led to higher academic grades. In fact, both student and teacher attendance improved in eligible schools, and even boys showed improved test scores.[15]

In 2004–2005, SRI International employed a cross-sectional approach in evaluating the outcomes of the Bay Area KIPP (Knowledge is Power Program) charter schools, whose "pillars" include high expectations, parental choice, long school days, autonomous school leaders, and a relentless focus on results. (Although a randomized controlled study is now under way, KIPP and its sponsors also wanted this early, formative assessment of its impact to detect any obvious need for midcourse corrections.) Using two standard state tests, the SAT 10 and CST, experimenters tracked KIPP students' achievement over two years and compared their achievement with that of students in comparable California schools. The report explains the limits of the methodology:

> In an ideal world we would make two comparisons as a basis for determining if KIPP students are performing better than if they were not attending KIPP schools. The first would be to compare achievement growth of KIPP students to their growth trajectory prior to KIPP. However, this requires individual student data for several years prior to enrollment in KIPP that is not publicly available. . . . The second would be to compare KIPP students' achievement with that of a comparison group of students, defined based on KIPP school waitlists (which do not yet exist), or matching students in the district based on demographic characteristics. Again, this comparison requires access to student-level data for both KIPP and non-KIPP students.[16]

With these limitations, the report noted:

> The spring 2005 CST data indicate that the overall percentage of students performing at a proficient level or above is consistently higher for KIPP schools than for comparable schools in the district—in some cases dramatically so. Similarly, when comparing students in KIPP schools to all

students in the state, more fifth graders in two of the five KIPP schools scored at or above proficient in ELA (English language arts) than students statewide; in three of five KIPP schools, the percentage of fifth-grade students who scored at or above proficient in math was higher than for the state. Likewise, in three of the four KIPP schools with sixth-grade scores, a higher percentage of sixth-grade students reached proficiency in math and ELA compared to the state as whole. In the one KIPP school with seventh-grade scores, the percent proficient in both ELA and math exceeded the state.

Although not conclusive, the size of the differences was great enough to strongly support the hypothesis that the KIPP approach made a real difference in children's academic outcomes—sufficient to justify continuing and even expanding the program while conducting more precise studies.

The Bad

The next best thing to learning that a social intervention succeeds is determining conclusively that it does not succeed—so that funders will seek better options rather than pouring money down the drain. A famous example of a demonstrably ineffective intervention is the Drug Abuse Resistance Education (DARE) program, which sought to prevent youth substance abuse through classroom instruction. Randomized controlled studies of the DARE program consistently showed that students in treatment and control groups had the same rates of both short- and long-term drug use.[17]

In another case, the evaluation firm Mathematica Policy Research Inc. was commissioned to conduct a randomized controlled evaluation of federal abstinence education initiatives designed to prevent teen pregnancy. Mathematica worked with four different states to randomly assign schools either to receive or not to receive abstinence education, and then analyzed students' self-reported sexual activity rates. The results, released in 2007, show that students whose schools received abstinence programs were just as likely to be sexually active as students whose schools did not.[18] James Wagoner, the president of Advocates for Youth, said of the results: "After 10 years and $1.5 billion in public funds these failed abstinence-only-until-marriage programs will go down as an ideological boondoggle of historic proportions."[19]

The Inconclusive

In 1997, the New York City Voucher Experiment randomly assigned two thousand low-income families with K–4 students to either a treatment group or a control group. Families in the treatment group received school vouchers for private-school tuition, worth $1,400 per child per year, for four years,[20] while families in the control group did not receive vouchers. After three years, researchers administered math and reading tests to students in each group and analyzed the results. It turned out that vouchers did not significantly affect children's test scores in the aggregate, though they had a small positive impact on the test scores of African-American children. Most other studies of voucher programs have shown similar results.[21]

The voucher experiment did not show that vouchers are ineffective. Rather, methodological problems, especially the small sample size, made it hard to draw a conclusion one way or the other.[22] Given the difficulty of designing and implementing studies of social interventions, you should be prepared for inconclusive results much of the time. This can happen, for example, because samples that were originally of reasonable size diminish as a result of attrition—for example, families in the control group move away and the experimenters lose track of them. Or the control group coincidentally receives some interventions from another source—whether similar to or different from the "treatment" group.[23]

UNFORTUNATELY, MANY NEGATIVE and inconclusive results never see daylight—the former, for reasons of motivation; the latter, for lack of interest. Even knowing about inconclusive results is useful, since a subsequent study may be able to learn from the first and remedy some of the defects that militated against a clearer outcome.

What does all of this mean for the philanthropist? Sometimes you can assess the effects of your grants without complex measures, especially where the theory of change is pretty straightforward. A donation to a soup kitchen feeds someone otherwise likely to go hungry. If you make a gift to a symphony orchestra to allow youngsters to attend without charge, a simple before-and-after comparison may give you all the information you need. For all of the importance of The Nature Conservancy's complex measures of biodiversity (see Chapter 4), a donor could learn something of value even from its earlier, more primitive, "bucks and acres" metric.

But formal evaluations are usually the only way to establish that an effort at social change is making a difference. Yet they often are beyond the reach of day-to-day philanthropy, for these reasons, among others:

> ➤ Philanthropic interventions frequently occur in situations that do not lend themselves to experiments or even to the data collection that would answer the questions.
> ➤ Randomized controlled studies, and even observational studies, are expensive.
> ➤ Even well-designed experiments may turn out to be inconclusive.
> ➤ It's usually impossible to separate your philanthropic contribution from the contributions of other forces, including other philanthropists. Most efforts at social change are like a tug of war, with the forces for change pulling on one side of the rope and all the forces causing the problem pulling on the other. It's often hard enough to know if your team has won, let alone whether it would have won even if you hadn't been tugging.

Evaluation of a Theory of Change or Strategy

The good news is that to the extent that an evaluation can demonstrate that a theory of change is valid and robust—that it is generalizable to other populations and locations and applicable outside of the specific context—then you have some assurance that an intervention based on it will achieve the desired effects. Sometimes an effect may be so easy to measure or so large that you can feel reasonably confident without a formal evaluation. At the very least—and this is not a trivial matter—if a particular strategy has been evaluated and found *not* to produce the desired effects, you needn't waste your grant funds on it.

The costs and complexities of evaluating impact may tempt you to throw up your hands and just rely on intuition. Before you yield to the temptation, consider the work of Dr. Joan McCord, a criminologist who evaluated programs for troubled youth.[24] Her best-known work was a longitudinal study comparing participants in programs that provided mentoring, health-care services, and summer camp to high-risk boys with a control group of similar youths. She found that boys in the program were more likely to become criminals, have employment and marital problems, and become alcoholics than those in the control group.

The evidence contradicted not only the expected outcome but also the participants' own belief that they had benefited from the program. (Dr. McCord hypothesized that the boys in the treatment group may have felt that they were given the attention because something was wrong with them, making it a self-fulfilling prophecy.) She found similar paradoxical effects from a "just say no" drug education program and from Scared Straight, a program designed to deter young people from following a criminal path.

In sum, if you are a philanthropist with a long-term commitment to a field, it is well worth putting your funds—and lots of them—into evaluation. In any event, if you are about to fund a program, find out what empirical validation lies behind its strategy.

Takeaway Points

➤ After a grant is made or a strategy launched, a philanthropist will
—monitor the grantee's performance to ensure that the grantee is doing what it agreed to do;
—track the grantee's and the philanthropist's own progress toward their shared goals, and make adjustments where appropriate; and
—attempt to evaluate the impact of the strategy.
➤ Impact evaluation is often complex and expensive, but it is essential in determining whether a philanthropic intervention is actually making a difference. An evaluation that seeks to demonstrate that a strategy has impact and is generalizable to other contexts can be of great value to a field and is worthy of philanthropic support.

Chapter Notes

1. Mark Kramer et al., *From Insight to Action: New Directions in Foundation Evaluation* (FSG Social Impact Advisors, 2007), 24, http://www.fsg-impact.org/app/content/ideas/item/488.

2. Ibid.

3. Ibid., 25.

4. Ibid., 26.

5. Ibid., 45.

6. Kristen Putnam, *Measuring Foundation Performance: Examples from the Field* (Oakland: California HealthCare Foundation, 2004), 11, http://www.chcf.org/documents/other/MeasuringFoundationPerformance.pdf.

7. Random assignment eliminates any systematic differences between the groups that could affect the outcome data in ways unrelated to your program.

8. The Coalition for Evidence-Based Policy maintains a terrific website on social programs that work, at http://www.evidencebasedprograms.org.

9. The literature on this theory is nicely summarized in *Wikipedia*, s.v. "Fixing Broken Windows," http://en.wikipedia.org/wiki/Fixing_Broken_Windows (accessed June 30, 2008).

10. Jane Brody, "New Therapy for Menopause Reduces Risks," *New York Times*, November 18, 1994.

11. Gina Kolata with Melody Petersen, "Hormone Replacement Study: A Shock to the Medical System," *New York Times*, July 10, 2002.

12. Susan M. Love, "Preventive Medicine, Properly Practiced," *New York Times*, July 16, 2002.

13. Joshua Graff Zivin, Harsha Thirumurthy, and Markus Goldstein, "AIDS Treatment and Household Spillover Benefits: Children's Nutrition and Schooling in Kenya," February 2007.

14. Steven D. Levitt and Stephen J. Dubner, *Freakonomics: A Rogue Economist Explores the Hidden Side of Everything* (New York: HarperCollins, 2005).

15. Michael Kremer, Edward Miguel, and Rebecca Thornton, "Incentives to Learn" (NBER Working Paper No. 10971, National Bureau of Economic Research, 2004), http://www.nber.org/papers/w10971. Another experiment by J-PAL demonstrates the failure of an intervention to achieve its intended goals, though it certainly did some good along the way. In a randomized controlled study to determine whether reducing the incidence of parasitic worms among children could lead to better attendance and, consequently, higher test scores, J-PAL administered low-cost deworming drugs to children at randomly chosen schools in a poor, densely settled farming region near Lake Victoria. The drugs worked well: after one year only 27 percent of children in treatment schools had moderate to heavy worm infections, compared with 52 percent of children in control schools. The effects on schooling, though, were minimal at best: though attendance rates in treatment schools were 7 to 9 percent higher than in control schools, the test scores of children in intervention and control schools were not significantly different.

16. SRI International, *Bay Area KIPP Schools, A Study of Early Implementation: First Year Report 2004–05* (Menlo Park, Calif.: SRI International, 2006), http://policyweb.sri.com/cep/publications/KIPPYear_1_Report.pdf.

17. Cheryl L. Perry et al., "A Randomized Controlled Trial of the Middle and Junior High School D.A.R.E. and D.A.R.E. Plus Programs," *Archives of Pediatrics and Adolescent Medicine* 157 (2003): 178–184.

18. Christopher Trenholm et al., *Impacts of Four Title V, Section 510 Abstinence Education Programs: Final Report*, report prepared by Mathematica

Policy Research Inc. for the U.S. Department of Health and Human Services, April 2007.

19. Advocates for Youth, "10-Year Government Evaluation of Abstinence-Only Programs Comes Up Empty," news release, April 13, 2007, http://www .advocatesforyouth.org/news/press/041307.htm.

20. Social Programs That Work, "New York City Voucher Experiment," http:// www.evidencebasedprograms.org/Default.aspx?tabid=143 (accessed June 30, 2008).

21. See Alan Krueger and Pei Zhu, "Another Look at the New York City School Voucher Experiment," *American Behavioral Scientist* 47, no. 5 (2003): 658–699; and Institute of Education Sciences, National Center for Education Evaluation and Regional Assistance, "Evaluation of the DC Opportunity Scholarship Program: Impacts After One Year," http://ies.ed.gov/ncee/pubs/20074009 (accessed June 30, 2008).

22. William G. Howell, book review, "Data Vacuum," *Education Next* 2, no. 2 (2002), http://www.hoover.org/publications/ednext/3366891.html.

23. See, for example, Paul T. Decker, Daniel P. Mayer, and Steven Glazerman, *The Effects of Teach for America on Students: Findings from a National Evaluation* (Princeton, N.J.: Mathematica Policy Research Inc., 2004), http:// www.mathematica-mpr.com/publications/pdfs/teach.pdf.

24. Douglas Martin, "Joan McCord, Who Evaluated Anticrime Efforts, Dies at 73," *New York Times*, March 1, 2004.

$$C\ h\ a\ p\ t\ e\ r\quad 10\quad T\ e\ n$$

Impact on Steroids: Measuring the Social Return on Your Philanthropic Investment

I N CHAPTER 1, we referred to Albert Einstein's quip that "not everything that counts can be counted, and not everything that can be counted counts." We recall it here because this chapter is all about counting—about efforts on the leading edge of quantitative impact assessment. Although some of these efforts may push the limits of what is considered countable, we begin with an example that is well within bounds.

Suppose that the Metro Community Foundation supports two soup kitchens in neighborhoods with similar demographic characteristics and clients. Serving the same food, they provide nutritious hot lunches to the neighborhoods' poorest residents. Northwest Kitchen has an annual budget of $325,000 and serves two hundred people every day of the year; South Kitchen has an annual budget of $250,000 and serves one hundred people.

It doesn't take much math to figure out that Northwest Kitchen's cost per person served is $1,625 per year, or about $4.45 per person per day, and that South Kitchen's cost per person served is $2,500/year, or about $6.85 per person per day. Both the foundation and its grantees will want to understand why South's cost per person is higher than Northwest's. Is South Kitchen just inefficient? Does Northwest Kitchen benefit from economies of scale because of its larger clientele? Or does South Kitchen provide services beyond food? If South Kitchen is merely less efficient, it may be able to learn from Northwest Kitchen. If the difference is due to economies of scale, perhaps the city's demographics make this inevitable, or perhaps South Kitchen can broaden its reach.

After considering the alternatives, the Metro Community Foundation might end up accepting South Kitchen's costs of feeding the hungry. But suppose that South Kitchen's $6.85 cost per person included other services—for example, job counseling. The foundation might reasonably ask whether the benefits of counseling were commensurate with its costs. And this requires estimating the dollar value of those benefits.

"Heartless?" you might ask. "Inevitable," we would answer. It's at least inevitable that you would do such a calculation intuitively, and that you would conclude that at *some* cost, the estimated benefits wouldn't be worth the investment. If so, then why not test your intuition with some actual estimates? The estimates may help you

> ➤ design new grant or program strategies;
> ➤ assess the outcome of a program to either improve its performance or decide whether to continue funding it; and
> ➤ decide which program among several to invest in, given the assessment of predicted or past performance.

Let us first return to the earlier example of the Metro Community Foundation's grant for the Northside Neighborhood Center's vaccination program, and then look at some examples from real foundations. The numbers in the hypothetical vaccination program are not intended to be realistic. Rather, we present this model to demonstrate the fundamental approach or methodology of an expected return analysis.

Northside's Vaccination Program

As part of their joint exploration of the value of the vaccination program described in Chapter 3, the Metro Community Foundation and the Northside Neighborhood Center held conversations with public-health and labor experts and learned from others who had engaged *promotores* to promote public health. This led them to make the following estimates:

> ➤ About 15 percent of unvaccinated adults will get the flu this year.
> ➤ On average, having the flu causes a worker to miss five days of work. At prevailing wages for workers in the target community, this amounts to an out-of-pocket loss of $480.

➤ In the absence of some sort of outreach program, almost none of the targeted workers will get vaccinated.

➤ Although the program aims to visit 3,000 people through its *promotores*, because it is new and untested, the program is likely to reach only 75 percent of the target population.

➤ An estimated 80 percent of those visited will likely sign up to get vaccinated.

➤ Of those who sign up, only about 60 percent will actually get vaccinated.

➤ The vaccine used is 90 percent effective at preventing the flu.

Given these facts, they computed the potential benefits of the program:

➤ *Promotores* will visit 75 percent of the 3,000 targeted workers, or 2,250 people.

➤ Of those visited, 80 percent, or 1,800 people, will sign up.

➤ Of those who sign up, 60 percent, or 1,080 people, will get vaccinated.

➤ An estimated 90 percent of those vaccinated, or 972 people, will be effectively protected against the flu.

➤ An estimated 15 percent of those protected, or 146 people, would have gotten flu without vaccination.

➤ These 146 workers would have lost a total of $70,080 in wages.

And what of the costs? Developing and implementing Northside's outreach plan will require recruiting, training, and hiring enough *promotores* to try to reach three thousand people. The cost of recruitment and wages will be $35,000, and the training program will cost an additional $15,000. The center's administrative costs are 15 percent of its direct costs, or $7,500 for the program. This brings the fixed cost of the program to $57,500. The cost of the flu shots, including the nurses' time and Northside's administrative costs, will be about $15 per person, and the vaccine is readily available on demand. Since we expect 1,080 people to be vaccinated, the total cost of vaccinations will be $16,200. Thus, the total cost of the program is $73,700.

You don't need to be a financial wizard to conclude that the cost of the vaccination program exceeds its benefits of $70,080, albeit by a small amount. Perhaps the difference is close enough that you think the cost is justified by the value of avoiding infecting others and the miseries or medical costs associated with having the flu—costs that are substantial even if difficult to measure. Given the largely fixed costs of the training program, one might improve the numbers by scaling up the program— but this seems unrealistic for an already ambitious pilot program. The mildly disappointing calculation may inspire the community foundation and neighborhood center to consider alternative strategies for encouraging flu vaccinations—for example, experimenting with a communications program that involves lower-cost outreach than the individual visits, or developing an insurance program for the workers.

Of course, all the numbers used in making this determination are the result of estimates, and the margins of error for some of them can be huge. But there's no reason to believe that the numbers underestimate rather than overestimate the impact. Indeed, people tend to be over-optimistic that complex projects like these will succeed. A step-by-step analysis of the sort we've just gone through requires you to be explicit about your assumptions, to test your intuitions against the best available evidence, and to do this in dialogue with others.

The Concept of Expected Return

The analysis done by the staff at Metro and Northside is captured by the benefit/cost ratio, which is the fundamental element in calculating expected return:[1]

$$\frac{Benefit}{Cost}$$

The benefit—more accurately, the *expected* benefit, since we are estimating the likely outcome of an untested program—is the value of the program's target, or hoped-for ultimate outcome, adjusted for factors that would diminish the likelihood of hitting the target. Typically those factors involve the intermediate outcome of each stage of the plan. For example, if the value of protecting one worker from getting the flu is $480, the benefit is the number of actual flu cases avoided multiplied by $480. As we saw in the last section, to estimate the number of flu cases avoided, you multiply the target population (in this case, 3,000 people) by the factors that select out the number of people who don't benefit from the program. The product is the number of people who would have gotten the flu but for the program.

To repeat the preceding analysis, you would multiply these factors in the numerator:

TARGET	VISITS	SIGN-UPS	VACCINATED	PROTECTED	WOULD HAVE CAUGHT FLU
3,000 ×	0.75 ×	0.80 ×	0.60 ×	0.90 ×	0.15

This yields an estimated 146 cases of flu avoided, for a total benefit of $70,080. Since the cost of the program is $73,700, the program has a benefit-cost ratio of slightly less than one—each $1 spent on the program only yields $0.95—meaning that the benefit is slightly less than the cost. (For the reasons mentioned above, this does not mean that the Metro Community Foundation shouldn't fund the project—though it should encourage a search for less expensive means to achieving the same end.)

As we will discuss later in the chapter, expected return is the benefit/cost ratio with the expected benefit discounted by the probability of achieving it:

$$Expected\ Return = \frac{Benefit \times Probability}{Cost}$$

REDF: The Pioneer of SROI Analysis

Before turning to the case studies below, we want to say a word about REDF, which led the way in the analysis of social return on investment (SROI). In Chapter 5, we mentioned the management-information system that REDF helped build for its portfolio of workforce training organizations. REDF's explorations of SROI in the 1990s had a profound influence on all subsequent efforts in the field.

Among the noteworthy and somewhat idiosyncratic aspects of REDF's approach to SROI was what it defined to be the "social" in social return—not the benefit to the individuals being trained of moving into productive jobs, but the cost savings to society through their increased tax contributions and reduced demand on publicly funded benefits and services.[2] By using these measures, REDF could demonstrate the value of its social investments to governments as well as private investors and philanthropists. REDF also concluded that these numbers constituted a more credible, consistent, and modest measure of that value than a measure of the benefits to individuals. Because REDF's organizations relied significantly on earned income from services provided by their employees as well as grants, an organization's costs consisted of its net operating losses plus the grants.[3] Although only a few of the organizations in REDF's portfolio broke even financially, all or most produced a net social return.

For various reasons—including that its grantee organizations were concerned with benefits to individuals and their families rather than with public cost savings—REDF has abandoned this approach to SROI. But REDF was the trailblazer in this area, and it continues to be an important and strategic investor in Bay Area workforce training programs.

Assessing and Comparing the Impact of Domestic Antipoverty Programs: The Robin Hood Foundation's "Metrics" Analysis

Established in 1988, the Robin Hood Foundation aims to reduce poverty in New York City through a combination of grants and management assistance in four program areas: early childhood and youth, education, job training and economic security, and basic survival, including health.[4]

In 2003, Robin Hood began a concerted effort to measure the individual benefits to poor clients created by its grantee organizations, with the aim of comparing the impact on grantees within a program area and, ideally, of comparing program areas with each other.[5] The problem, as described by the foundation, was, "How do we compare the poverty-fighting impact of apples (charter schools) with the poverty-fighting impact of oranges (job training for home health aides)?" The solution was to create a system for estimating the social impact of its grants to each organization.

Unlike REDF (but like our hypothetical Metro Community Foundation) Robin Hood measures its impact in terms of the personal benefits that accrue to their poor clients and their families. For example, in a job-training program for ex-offenders, the foundation estimates the impact of job placements on trainees' recidivism and their future earnings. When working with early-childhood programs, it estimates the impact of reading-readiness on high-school graduation rates and therefore the individuals' future earnings. For clinics that treat hepatitis, the foundation translates the number of adults diagnosed and treated into a dollar value of overall well-being.

Although Robin Hood has not published information about particular grantees, it demonstrates its approach through a fictional example, Bob's Jobs, a workforce training program for women. Bob's Jobs uses data based on a composite of Robin Hood's actual programs.

Here's how Robin Hood calculates the benefits of Bob's Jobs. Of one hundred and fifty enrollees, seventy-two complete the training program.

Forty-one of these newly minted construction workers retain their jobs at the end of three months (but not an entire year), and the other thirty-one still have jobs at the end of one year.

How much does the program benefit the trainees? Robin Hood compares the salary of each participant before she entered the program and after she graduates. The forty-one women with short-term employment enjoyed an average salary increase of about $2,900, or $120,000 in total. The average annual salary increase for the thirty-one women who hold jobs for at least a year was approximately $12,000. To compute the value of the program for these thirty-one women, Robin Hood makes the following assumptions:

➤ They will continue to be employed for thirty years.
➤ Their annual salaries will increase by 1.5 percent above inflation.
➤ Based on an average of 1.8 children each and research findings on the effects of parents' employment, each family will enjoy an intergenerational income boost of $56,000.
➤ The discount rate for calculating the present value of all benefits is 3.5 percent.

Based on these assumptions, Robin Hood estimated that the net present value of the benefits to the thirty-one long-term workers is $9.1 million. Adding the one-time benefit for the forty-one short-term workers, the total value of the program is $9.2 million.

But Robin Hood's grant accounts for only about half the funding for Bob's Jobs, which is supported by other donors, both private and public. The total benefits attributable to Robin Hood are, therefore, $4.6 million.

What about the costs? The grant to Bob's Jobs was $200,000. Robin Hood does not include the administrative costs of making the grant; they are not huge and they do not differ significantly from those of its other poverty-fighting programs. Dividing the numerator of $4.6 million by the denominator of $200,000, the benefit-cost ratio (or expected return per dollar) is 23. That is, for each dollar that Robin Hood spends on Bob's Jobs, trainees and their families gain $23.00—a very good return on investment.

The Robin Hood Foundation has performed similar calculations for its other poverty programs, including a program to help people manage budgets, bank accounts, and loans (benefit/cost ratio of 1.9) and a clinic that deals with asthma, hepatitis, and cancer (benefit-cost ratio of 12).[6]

While Robin Hood's work is informed by benefit/cost analysis, the Foundation recognizes that the calculations are not precise. Therefore, it continues to test its metrics against the informed intuitions of program officers and experts in the field at the same time as it induces them to justify their intuitions against the numbers generated by the analysis. (For a case study of Acumen Fund's use of SROI to assess investment opportunities in international development, visit *www .smartphilanthropy.org.*)

Using Expected Return to Assess Proposed Strategies: The Hewlett Foundation's Global Development Program

Just as benefit/cost, or expected return, analysis can help guide particular grants, it can also help develop philanthropic strategies—the frameworks for making grants. In a collaborative effort with Redstone Strategy Group, the Hewlett Foundation combined the conventional SROI components of cost and benefit with estimates of the likelihood of success to compare the expected return of possible strategies in its new program in global development.

The goal of the Global Development Program is to "improve the income and well-being of people living on less than $2 per day." In pursuit of this goal, program staff considered a variety of strategies in developing countries and selected three: (1) promoting transparency and accountability of governments in order to improve the provision of public services, (2) improving access to agricultural markets to improve economic conditions for the rural poor, and (3) improving the quality of education. Each of these strategies could be implemented in myriad ways within any one of the developing countries under consideration.

We illustrate the methodology using the example of promoting transparency and accountability to improve governance in Nigeria.[7] Despite $50 billion in annual oil revenues and $1 billion in annual aid, 92 percent of the population of Nigeria (over 120 million people) lives in abject poverty. Corruption is widely believed to contribute to this situation. Research suggests that decreasing corruption improves government effectiveness, increases gross national income per capita, and improves the well-being of the very poorest citizens by a fairly predictable amount.

Using expected return analysis to guide choices between investments requires a common metric. Oversimplifying, the foundation used the metric of doubling the incomes of people living under $2 a day. The expected return calculations summarized below produced a ballpark estimate of what the foundation could hope to accomplish in Nigeria with an initial commitment of $30 million over eight years. That amount covers a suite of grants for transparency and accountability activities such as expenditure tracking, budget monitoring, and "citizen report cards" on the quality of public services.

In calculating the expected return, the staff members considered the investment's potential benefits if it were completely successful, the estimated probability of success, the foundation's fractional contribution, and cost. Each of these measurements relied on the analyses of development experts and the foundation's on-the-ground experience supporting similar work in Mexico. The foundation used the following equation to calculate the expected return:

$$\frac{\textit{Benefits in a perfect world} \times \textit{Likelihood of success} \times \textit{Hewlett contribution}}{\textit{Cost}}$$

> *The benefits of complete success* were the social benefits that would be realized if the proposed theory of change succeeded perfectly. Relying on research and interviews with experts, the foundation's experience in Mexico, and trends in Nigeria, the foundation estimated that absent risk, transparency and accountability investments by the Hewlett Foundation and others could double the incomes of about eight million Nigerians currently living on less than $2 a day.

> *The likelihood of success* reflected the fact that virtually all philanthropic theories of change face strategic, organizational, and external risks, and the history of corruption in Nigeria exacerbated some of these risks. To calculate these risks, the foundation again consulted with experts and took into account its experience with transparency and accountability grantmaking in Mexico. Recognizing that the theory of change relied on many moving parts working together in just the right way, staff members gave the program's efforts to improve governance in Nigeria a 25 percent probability of success.

> *The Hewlett Foundation's contribution* was an estimate of the portion of success for which the foundation's effort could be credited,

both in terms of the *amount* of money invested and the *influence* of that money. Since the theory of change relied on donations by other foundations and many nonphilanthropic investments, the Hewlett Foundation's contribution would clearly be only one part of a larger effort. All told, the foundation's financial share of the theory of change would likely be less than 5 percent. Because its involvement was intended to be catalytic, however, the Hewlett Foundation estimated its contribution to be 10 percent for the purposes of the expected return calculation.

➤ *The cost* associated with the benefits under consideration included supporting nongovernmental organizations engaged in budget and revenue monitoring, in expenditure tracking, and in training government officials in the implementation of freedom-of-information laws. The costs also included the administrative costs involved in making, monitoring, and evaluating grants. As mentioned earlier, the foundation's theory of change required that it invest $30 million during an eight-year period.

Putting the benefits factors together, the Hewlett Foundation and Redstone Strategy Group concluded that the foundation's $30 million investment in transparency and accountability work in Nigeria could double the incomes of about 200,000 people now living on less than $2 a day.

BENEFITS OF COMPLETE SUCCESS		LIKELIHOOD OF SUCCESS		HEWLETT CONTRIBUTION		EXPECTED BENEFIT
doubling the income of 8,000,000 poor people	×	0.25	×	0.10	=	doubling the income of 200,000 poor people

Dividing the expected benefit by the cost yields the expected return:

$$\frac{8,000,000 \times 0.25 \times 0.1}{30} = 6,667$$

Thus, according to the expected return calculation, every $1 million that the Hewlett Foundation spent on improving transparency and accountability in Nigeria can be expected to double the income of about 6,700 poor people.

Similar analyses for an array of potential investments resulted in a range of outcomes, from very high expected returns for supporting impact evaluation of public services, to very low expected returns for reforming trade in emerging economies. Recognizing the imprecision of these estimates, the foundation ultimately decided to investigate a number of strategies with high expected returns—including transparency and accountability in Nigeria and elsewhere, impact evaluation of public services, improving agricultural markets, and education in certain developing countries. The Hewlett Foundation currently is using this type of analysis to determine where in Africa to pursue certain of these strategies.

Calculating Expected Return in Dollars per Dollar Invested

Because the actual measure used by the Global Development Program included well-being factors that were not measured in dollars, the Hewlett Foundation did not calculate the expected return on a per dollar basis for its decision making. This is possible with our simplified example, however. Here's how we might do this.

Data suggest that the average income of a person in Nigeria living on less than $2 a day is $644 per year, so doubling a person's income would yield an annual increase of that same amount. Let's assume (conservatively) that the person earns this income for ten years, yielding a total increase of $6,440 (not discounted). Thus, the calculation of expected return per dollar invested would be

$$\frac{8{,}000{,}000 \text{ } \textit{people} \times 25\% \textit{ likelihood of success} \times 10\% \textit{ contribution} \times \$6{,}440 \textit{ income}}{\$30{,}000{,}000}$$

This results in an expected return per dollar invested of about $43, which is substantial but perhaps not unreasonable considering the risks associated with the investment.

For a technical note on the expected return analysis, visit *www.smartphilanthropy.org*.

Concluding Thoughts About Expected Return

Expected Return and the Administrative Costs of Grantmaking
The foundations that have engaged in the expected return analyses summarized above have done so in the belief that it will both improve their own grantmaking and contribute beneficial knowledge to the

broader field of philanthropy. We think this is a good bet, though hardly a foregone conclusion. That said, planning strategies, conducting due diligence, and monitoring and evaluating grants—and certainly engaging in expected return analysis—cost more than making grants without these procedures.[8] Every dollar of administrative costs reduces the funds available for making grants. Does this mean that you should try to minimize administrative costs? Our answer is decidedly no. You shouldn't minimize them, but rather you should seek to *optimize* them in terms of achieving impact.

Thus, the value of doing an expected return analysis in effect depends on its expected return in terms of achieving impact. Even if the margins of error of an analysis are huge—as they are with the Hewlett Foundation's strategic planning for its work in global development—the expected return is one's best guess: there's no a priori reason to believe that the estimate either over- or understates the actual outcome. Equally important, as Brian Trelstad, Acumen Fund's chief investment officer notes, the value of the analysis "is not in the number . . . that is spit out at the end, but in forcing the team to think through the marginal analysis of whether or not we really are generating significantly more social impact for our philanthropic dollar than prevailing approaches."[9]

The Risk of Utter Failure

Some philanthropic investments may have a positive, indeed very high, expected return but nonetheless be susceptible to complete failure. Indeed, failure may be more likely than success, but the expected return may nonetheless justify the investment. This is true of many advocacy initiatives.

For example, consider an environmental advocacy initiative that has a 40 percent chance of releasing $50 million in state funds for new parks and that has a 60 percent chance of utter failure. If it costs $250,000 to run the initiative, then

$$\textit{Expected Return} = \frac{(\$50 \text{ million} \times 40\%)}{\$250,000} = 80$$

This is a lot of potential bang for your 250,000 bucks—but with a 60 percent chance of failing. Expected return analysis is fundamentally indifferent to risk. The expected return is also 80 for a $250,000 advocacy initiative that is 88.9 percent likely to gain $22.5 million in park funds. Whether you should make the long-shot bet depends on your tolerance for risk.[10]

Impact and Attribution

Many thoughtful commentators on evaluation caution that efforts to attribute credit for a particular outcome are usually fruitless.[11] The causes of social change are usually too complex and the actors too many to claim that any single grant, or even a series of grants, tipped the balance. Doubtless, there are exceptions—especially when interventions are local and highly targeted, as in the case of some job-training programs. But, at the other extreme, if you are supporting a civil rights movement or working to reduce poverty in a developing country, just forget about attribution.

Even with the strongest, most evidence-based theory of change, your marginal contribution often is, well, marginal—at least when others are working toward the same end. Does this undercut the very thesis of this book that strategic philanthropy is all about impact? Assuredly not. The concept of expected return suggests the more nuanced view that strategic philanthropy is about *expected impact*. It is about ensuring that your philanthropic interventions will give you a reasonable shot at making a difference—even though you may never actually know the effect of your particular dollars. Enough dollars on the margin can add up to something decidedly nonmarginal.

The Hazards and Values of Expected Return Analyses

Bruce Sievers, formerly the executive director of the Walter and Elise Haas Fund and now a visiting scholar at Stanford University, has been a vocal critic of expected return analysis. His essential criticism is that an emphasis on "measurable outcomes . . . may distort an organization's program or actually cause more important, intangible aims to be overlooked."[12] The concern would be exemplified by a foundation that supported the performing arts and evaluated grantees only in terms of their audience size or box-office receipts to the exclusion of the quality of their performances. Sievers goes on to note:

> The environmental movement, the rise of the conservative agenda in American political life, and the movement toward equality for the gay and lesbian communities, all aided by significant philanthropic support, have transformed American life in ways that lie beyond any calculations

of "return on investment." Of course, we believe that there *have* been calculable returns on investments in these issues, but the point is that these movements have recast the American moral landscape, resulting in enormous change in the way society functions and understands itself, with consequent changes in policy. Commitment of philanthropic resources to these issues was not merely a matter of analyzing increments of inputs and output; it was a moral engagement with wooly, unpredictable issues that called for deeply transformational action.[13]

We agree entirely with this point. Some programs lend themselves better to metrics than others, and some not at all. It would be a tragic error for a philanthropist to distort his or her mission in order to seek only measurable outcomes. And even when an expected return analysis seems valuable, the margins of error can be huge.

With all these caveats, we think that such analyses have helped clarify rather than distort the work of the Robin Hood and Hewlett foundations, and others, and can be helpful to you as well. For one thing, an expected return analysis presses you to clarify your goals, to make your assumptions explicit, to be realistic about the power of philanthropy to effect social change, and to be aware of the risks involved along the way. An expected return analysis can inform and test your intuitions about the effectiveness of a particular strategy or grant. And it provides a focus for conversations with colleagues about all these matters.

On the whole, we imagine that expected return analysis is more appropriate for relatively mature or developed fields rather than those at early stages. But efforts at expected return analysis are themselves in their infancy, and we hope that funders will continue to develop and apply models to many areas of grantmaking and will inform others of their findings.

Takeaway Points

➤ The benefit/cost ratio of a philanthropic investment is the ratio of the social benefits to the amount of the grant and related costs.

➤ When the benefits are uncertain, the expected return formula takes into account the possibility that the benefits won't be achieved.

➤ People intuitively predict expected return in their personal and professional lives. Even when it is not possible to estimate expected return with any precision, the exercise sharpens your intuitions.

Chapter Notes

1. Unlike the benefit/cost ratio, the expected return formula puts the net benefit (benefit less cost) in the numerator:

$$Expected\ Return\ =\ \frac{Benefit\ -\ Cost}{Cost}$$

The "benefit" portion of the formula is reduced to the extent that the probability of achieving the benefit is less than 100 percent.

2. For a discussion on the disadvantages of using public-sector savings as a measure of success, along with other criticisms about SROI by REDF, see Cynthia Gair, *A Report from the Good Ship SROI* (San Francisco: REDF, 2005), http://www.redf.org/publications-sroi.htm.

3. REDF, "REDF's SROI Analysis: The Process," Chapter 3 in *SROI Methodology* (San Francisco: Roberts Foundation, 2001), 30, http://www.redf.org/download/sroi/sroi_method_3.pdf.

4. Much of the text that follows is based on Michael M. Weinstein with the assistance of Cynthia Esposito Lamy, *Measuring Success: How The Robin Hood Foundation Estimates the Impact of Grants,* (New York: Robin Hood Foundation, 2008).

5. Robin Hood Foundation, *Quarterly Update*, 4th quarter 2004, 4–7, http://www.robinhood.org/images/results/updates/Q4_2004.pdf.

6. Calculating the benefits of the clinic is particularly interesting and complex because of the conversion of health benefits into dollars. The Robin Hood Foundation used units of quality-adjusted life years (QALYs), assigning $100,000 to each QALY, which is in line with the valuation used by some federal agencies. A QALY is a unit commonly used in medical economics. One QALY is equal to a year of perfect health, whereas a QALY less than one is equal to a year lived in pain, discomfort, or disability. See *Implementing QALYs*, What is . . .? series 2, no. 1 (Hayward Medical Communications, 2004), http://www.evidence-based-medicine.co.uk/ebmfiles/ImplementQALYs.pdf; and Maria Segui-Gomez, "Overview of Preference Based Health Status Measures" (keynote, third international conference on Measuring the Burden of Injury, Baltimore, Md., May 15–16, 2000), http://ntl.bts.gov/lib/11000/11400/11433/keynote_4.htm.

7. The example is taken from Redstone Strategy Group, *Making Every Dollar Count: How Expected Return Can Transform Philanthropy.*

8. International programs, grantmaking to individuals, and direct charitable activities, as well as larger staff size, raised expense levels at independent foundations, especially at smaller foundations. Elizabeth T. Boris et al., *Foundation Expenses and Compensation: How Operating Characteristics Influence Spending* (Urban Institute, Foundation Center, and Philanthropic Research, 2006), http://www.urban.org/UploadedPDF/311281_Foundation_Report_final.pdf.

9. E-mail correspondence with Paul Brest, January 5, 2008.

10. Our example ignores the opportunity cost of that state money; it might be stripped from other worthy programs, or it could cause taxes to be raised, thereby dampening economic growth. These issues should be considered in setting desired outcomes, lest one program's success come at the cost of another. However, we see no reason that a foundation should be other than risk neutral in its grantmaking.

11. Mark Kramer et al., *From Insight to Action: New Directions in Foundation Evaluation* (FSG Social Impact Advisors, 2007), http://www.fsg-impact.org/images/upload/From%20Insight%20to%20Action(3).pdf.

12. Bruce Sievers, "Philanthropy's Blindspots," in *Just Money: A Critique of Contemporary American Philanthropy*, ed. H. Peter Karoff (Boston: TPI Editions, 2004), 132.

13. Ibid.

Part II

Tools of the Trade

P art I had many examples of the ways that philanthropists, working in collaboration with their grantee organizations, can achieve their shared goals. The next three chapters categorize the various activities that not-for-profit organizations—and some businesses as well—engage in:

➤ Developing and disseminating knowledge (Chapter 11)
➤ Supporting the provision of goods and services (Chapter 12)
➤ Changing the behavior of individuals, governments, and businesses (Chapter 13)

These are the tools that you and your grantees can use to achieve your shared goals. Different strategies naturally require different mixes of means. Consider the approaches available to a philanthropist who is concerned with the plight of the poorest residents of her city. Depending on the situation and on her time horizons and interests, she might select these tools to accomplish the matching strategies:

➤ Providing direct services to meet immediate food, clothing, shelter, or health needs
➤ Supporting training to allow people to obtain jobs in the private sector
➤ Changing individual behaviors that keep people in poverty, as by reducing drug addiction or teen pregnancy
➤ Changing behavior of local government and industry by advocating systems for moving people out of poverty—for example, vouchers for housing, a higher minimum wage, or increased government expenditures or regulations that will improve the lives of the poor

Like a craftsman who has decided on a project, your selection of tools will be determined by your sense of which ones—alone or in combination—will best do the job. The goals lead to the selection of tools, not the other way around. With this in mind, the following chapters focus on the tools themselves. What is the array of tools available? What are the characteristics and limitations of different tools? Once a tool is chosen, how can you ensure that it is used well?

Following this survey, Chapter 14 examines the role of philanthropy in building fields and movements—an activity that typically calls for the use of a number of different tools.

Chapter 11 *Eleven*

Promoting Knowledge

T
HERE ARE AT least two fundamentally different forms of knowledge: knowledge that is basic and theoretical and has no immediate consequence but to satisfy our eternal curiosity; and practical knowledge that has useful applications. In his classic work entitled *Diffusion of Innovations*, Everett M. Rogers notes the relationship between these two:

> Most technological innovations are created by scientific research, although they often result from the interplay between scientific methodology and practical problems. The knowledge base for a technology usually derives from basic research, defined as original investigations for the advancement of scientific knowledge that do not have a specific objective of applying this knowledge to practical problems.[1]

Supporting the Institutions that Develop, Conserve, and Disseminate Knowledge and Culture

A toast of the Mathematical Society of England goes: "Pure mathematics; may it never be of use to any man!"[2] Philanthropy has played a key role in supporting universities, museums, and other institutions devoted to developing, conserving, disseminating, and teaching knowledge and culture without regard to their practical utility.

Progress in the arts and the social and natural sciences depends on the creativity of a diverse array of practitioners, scholars, artists, and thinkers. Creativity has been described as "recombinant growth" or "effective surprise"[3]—a process whereby existing knowledge is converted into something that had not been anticipated. Creating such knowledge is at the core of the missions of universities, arts organizations, and other learned and cultural institutions.

The continual fertilization and development of ideas cannot be accomplished by funding only specific projects with predetermined outcomes; it requires giving creative individuals the freedom to follow their own lights. To this end, philanthropists support artists, scholars, universities, and other institutions that foster and incubate creativity. By design, they produce diverse outcomes that are difficult to define in advance, let alone measure. There are inevitable efficiency losses in the short run. Not all artists and scholars will be industrious, not all of the industrious will be innovative, and not all innovative ideas will be worthwhile. But support for such open-ended creativity has paid off tremendously over time.[4]

Here are a few examples in which scholars' pursuit of their own interests eventually led to developments of tremendous practical significance— sometimes intended, sometimes serendipitous. The very infrastructure of the institutions on which their research depended was supported by gifts to universities or to schools and departments within them.[5]

➤ Claude Shannon's research on information theory at the University of Michigan and MIT was critical to all modern electronic technology.[6]
➤ As an immunologist at UCLA, Michael Gottlieb was on the lookout for "interesting teaching cases," which eventually led to the identification of the human immunodeficiency virus (HIV).[7]
➤ The 1995 Nobel Prize in Chemistry was awarded to Paul J. Crutzen and Mario J. Molina of MIT and F. Sherwood Rowland of the University of California, Irvine, for their pioneering work in atmospheric chemistry, which ultimately led to the Montreal Protocol on Substances That Deplete the Ozone Layer.
➤ Isidor Isaac Rabi's work at Columbia on the measurement of nuclear magnetic spin, for which he won the Nobel Prize in Physics in 1944, led to magnetic resonance imaging (MRI) and the atomic clock.

In addition to particular discoveries in the sciences and humanities, entire fields—ranging from conflict resolution to behavioral economics—have evolved in this way, starting with basic research that had no predefined or practical objective.

Philanthropy has supported not only science and technology but the production of art, music, and literature as well. Apart from various arts organizations, professorial positions often provide artists with the financial stability to pursue their passions. Writers and poets including Wallace Stegner, Toni Morrison, Joyce Carol Oates, and Seamus Heaney have held university positions. So too have composers, including Roger Sessions, Elliott Carter, Morton Feldman, John Harbison, and John Corigliano, and architects, such as Louis Kahn and I. M. Pei.[8]

In addition to large educational and cultural institutions, philanthropy also supports a broad range of other organizations—ranging from think tanks, such as the Brookings Institution and the American Enterprise Institute, to professional associations, such as the American Political Science Association, to communities of interest such as the Jane Austen Society of North America—that create and disseminate knowledge.

Philanthropy also supports the rapidly increasing number of organizations that deliver knowledge electronically through the Web—including universities, whose presence on the Web is expanding dramatically. MIT's OpenCourseWare project makes educational materials from all MIT courses available to the public;[9] the University of Texas at Austin's World Lecture Hall provides free materials from universities around the world;[10] and the University of California at Berkeley provides webcasts of courses and special events in streaming audio and video formats.[11] Philanthropy also supports the infrastructure for Web-based knowledge—for example, Creative Commons, which has developed alternatives to traditional copyrights under which the creators of music, art, educational content, and other copyrightable material make their works available to the public under generous licenses.

Supporting the Development of Applied Practical Knowledge: A Strategic Overview

Philanthropy also plays an important role in developing knowledge that, from the outset, is intended to have a practical application in solving a problem, whether poverty, poor health, the need for better education, or the deteriorating environment. Before investing in such knowledge, however, you need to know its place in an overall strategy. We suggest that you think through the following steps before making a commitment to research for a specific purpose:

1. Ensure that the research is on the critical path to solving the problem at hand.
2. Scope out the research and ensure that there is capacity to support it.
3. Be prepared for failure.
4. Be prepared for success.

Ensure That Research Is on the Critical Path

Sometimes more research is an essential component of the causal chain. But sometimes we know as much as is needed (or as much as it's worth the cost of learning) and the barriers to accomplishing your aim lie not in ignorance but in failed implementation. Although there are critical gaps in the knowledge necessary to prevent and cure many diseases, millions of African children die of intestinal diseases that we know how to prevent and treat, and that are not even particularly expensive to prevent and treat, because existing medicines are not distributed effectively. Although there are huge unknowns about the most effective pedagogical techniques of K–12 education, the absence of knowledge is not the primary barrier to providing adequate resources to inner-city schoolchildren. The science of global warming is by no means complete—and there is a great need for more practical technological solutions—but the most pressing need is to apply existing clean-energy technologies on a larger scale, and this is limited by political commitment, not by a lack of knowledge.

Scope Out the Research and the Capacity to Support it

If research is on the critical path to achieving your objectives, here are a few steps you can take to define its scope:

➤ Engage the opinions of experts in the field from the outset—not just the research community, but those on the frontlines who will ultimately make use of the research. For example, before funding development of a vaccine for use in developing countries, consult on-the-ground health professionals to understand the practical problems of storing and administering the vaccine. Before funding

Washington Think Tanks: Applied Research or Advocacy?

In an article entitled "Research Groups Boom in Washington," *New York Times* correspondent Elisabeth Bumiller describes the recent growth in the budgets of Washington D.C.'s policy-research organizations, or think tanks. The institutions range from the Center for American Progress on the left to the Cato Institute, the American Enterprise Institute, and the Heritage Foundation on the right, with others between including the Brookings Institution, the Carnegie Endowment for International Peace, the Center for Global Development, and the Center for Strategic and International Studies.

Much of this growth has been fueled by philanthropists' renewed conviction that politics, and foreign policy in particular, are important to the ends they seek. For example, Bumiller reports that the Bill & Melinda Gates Foundation "has committed more than $2 million to the Center for Strategic and International Studies . . . for a bipartisan H.I.V.-AIDS study group given the task of developing ideas for how to spend the billions the Bush administration has committed to fighting the disease." However, as Richard Haass, president of the New York–based Council on Foreign Relations, points out: "Institutions like this don't possess power. You're one of many voices in the political marketplace. It's up to those in the marketplace who possess power—congressmen, people in the executive branch—to run with one of your ideas."[12]

On a related point, in *The Rise of the Conservative Legal Movement*, Steven Teles notes that "the movement took ideas very seriously, and its patrons invested significant resources in serious, first-order discussion of the fundamental commitments with little if any short-term payoffs. While many contemporary liberals seem obsessed with creating their own think tanks to allow for 'instant response,' conservatives recognized the need to go back to 'first things.'"[13]

a database-management tool to give teachers continuous feedback on how their students are doing, consult teachers and principals to understand what hardware and software will actually be useful to them. Such consultation can help develop specifications to ensure that the product can be used under actual conditions.

➤ Subject the research design to an independent peer-review process—independent of the researchers you are likely to fund. Peer review need not be slow, overly formal, or bureaucratic. Sometimes a few phone calls to trusted experts will do the trick. Day-long workshops with experts from different realms can provide ideas for building strong programs and can serve as a vetting panel as well.[14]

➤ Medical and social science research projects regularly run into the millions of dollars, and can take many years to complete. A funder who initiates a research project should be prepared to see it through. Scope the entire project—costs, time, skills, and institutional support—and ensure that, whether alone or in collaboration with other funders, you will have the resources necessary to support both the research and its dissemination.

Prepare for Failure

It is difficult to push back the frontiers of human knowledge, and a single success usually requires many attempts. Most research projects fail, and for various reasons.

➤ The results are inconclusive. The effect (or the sample) may be too small to know whether a particular drug controls juvenile diabetes, or whether an early-childhood instructional approach contributes to a child's reading or social skills. Or even if the results are encouraging, there may be other possible explanations for them.

➤ The data may conclusively demonstrate that the intervention doesn't improve things. In this case, it's back to the drawing board, with the hope of finding another potential solution. This has recently been the case with a number of promising approaches to an AIDS vaccine.

➤ The intervention may actually be powerful and effective, but there may be economic, political, or practical barriers to implementing it in the field—for example, the educational intervention may require intensive one-on-one teacher attention, or the vaccine may have a short shelf life and require special care.

Failures in research outnumber successes by a considerable factor. But many people—possibly you as well as those you will support—tend to be overoptimistic. Plan for what will happen if the research fails in one or another way. Be prepared to regroup to find another route to solve a problem. And by all means, consider how failure can contribute to the knowledge base.

Prepare for Success: Adoption and Dissemination

Finally, the holy grail: success. The researchers discover, after considerable time and cost, that regular visits by a qualified nutritionist to Mexican-American immigrant families can significantly reduce teen obesity and the attendant costs of future medical care. Naturally, this finding will be immediately supported by legislative appropriations and will be incorporated into the work of state and local health agencies. Latino organizations will unify behind this concept, providing cultural support for the program. The Immigration and Naturalization Service will announce that no elements of this program will be used to find and deport people who do not have legal residence status. Your philanthropy was the necessary and sufficient cause for these results.

Right.

An important new discovery, even one that can save lives for pennies, is only the start down the road to success. Whatever knowledge is created from your research needs to find an avenue into society. Some new knowledge is commercially viable and will be quickly absorbed through the magic of the market. Other insights will require the enlightened action of policy makers to become relevant. And some discoveries require changes in individual behavior—for example, science finds that smoking causes cancer, but to give that research its full social value, hundreds of millions of people need to muster great willpower to stop smoking. Thus, preparing for success requires thinking in advance about next steps if the research establishes what you hope it will.

A demonstration project can be a useful way to test a concept. But you need to plan for what will happen next if it succeeds. Many demonstration projects seem premised on the hope that somehow they will speak for themselves and spread like wildfire. Although hope springs eternal, the chances of adoption are greatly increased by treating the demonstration project as only one stage in an overall strategy for impact. This will allow you to decide how to allocate the resources necessary for each stage, or to gain them from others, and how to engage people or institutions that may play a critical role in replication. The absence of a plausible path to widespread adoption should at least make you consider whether it's worth undertaking the project. If a model education program requires a teacher-student ratio twice that of current schools, replicating the program will require a huge increase in the district's education budget. Is this likely? If not, perhaps you should test another model.

Thus, before supporting a research or demonstration project, you should have satisfactory answers to these questions: Who is likely to adopt and disseminate it? Where will their funding come from? What can I do to encourage adoption if the demonstration is successful? The world is littered with demonstration projects that, though they arguably proved the concept, were never replicated, because no one prepared in advance for their replication.

Promoting the Development of Applied Knowledge: Tactics

Having decided that new knowledge of some sort could make the world a better place, how do you go about promoting its development? Consider a project to improve the lives of the inhabitants of a poor, rural region through an efficient low-fuel-use cookstove. You can think of this as happening in three stages—though the boundaries are not always distinct in practice:

1. *Develop the underlying idea or design.* After all, there are a number of possible models of an efficient cookstove.
2. *Test the design in the laboratory and in the field.* You would begin by building a prototype of the cookstove to test its efficiency and resilience, and then see how it fares in actual use—both technically and socially. The cookstove may indeed use fuel more economically than an open fire, but will it survive rough treatment? Is it portable? Can it hold traditional pots? Will it work for slow-cooked meals? Can it be made and repaired locally? Is it cost-effective? Does a distribution infrastructure exist, or can one be built? Is it consistent with the region's cooking traditions?
3. *Foster adoption.* What barriers lie in the path of making the cookstove available to people and having them use it?

A philanthropist may enter the scene at any of these phases. For example, an innovation may already have been developed and tested in the laboratory and now need support for field testing.

Developing the Underlying Idea or Design

The development of some kinds of solutions might be tasked to a specialist. For example, ApproTEC (now KickStart) noticed that many small-scale Kenyan farmers didn't irrigate their farms, because they couldn't afford irrigation pumps. After considerable investigation, ApproTEC determined that a useable water pump must

> ➤ use human power and accommodate barefoot users;
> ➤ cost less than $150;
> ➤ withstand harsh environments;
> ➤ be small and light enough to carry on a bicycle or public transportation;
> ➤ use materials, such as inconsistent sizes of milled and galvanized steel and plastic pipe, and manufacturing techniques, such as welding, that are common in Kenya; and
> ➤ be installable and run without special knowledge or tools, and require little to no maintenance.

To design such a device, ApproTEC partnered with IDEO, the product design firm that produced the computer mouse and the disposable insulin injector, among other things. IDEO was able to use its design expertise to work within these constraints to create the Super MoneyMaker pump, a deep lift pump that a farmer can operate with a motion similar to exercising on a stair-climbing machine.[15] The specially designed pumps have been a huge success and have generated over $37 million in revenues for farmers who use them.[16]

More recently, IDEO has been working with Acumen Fund on the problem of providing clean water to people in the developing world. The two organizations have brought together not-for-profit and for-profit experts on global water to develop working prototypes of products and services as well as business models that can be implemented by entrepreneurs in the developing world.

Stimulating Innovation Through Prizes

A number of foundations and other organizations support *inducement prizes* to encourage new contributions to a field or *recognition prizes* to honor those who have made past contributions. Our main interest in this section is inducing innovation, but we discuss recognition prizes as

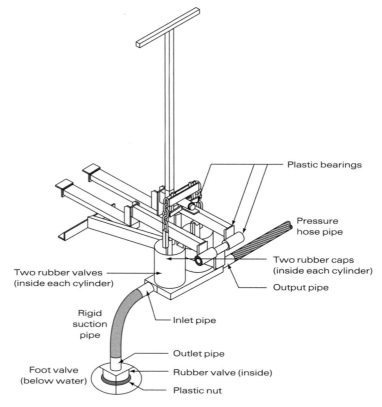

Plastic bearings

Pressure
hose pipe

Two rubber caps
(inside each cylinder)

Two rubber valves
(inside each cylinder)

Output pipe

Rigid
suction
pipe

Inlet pipe

Outlet pipe

Foot valve
(below water)

Rubber valve (inside)

Plastic nut

Reprinted with permission of KickStart

well. Recognition can be treated as an end in itself, and it can also be an indirect way of stimulating activities in the future.

Inducement prizes. An alternative to supporting research to produce a specified product or result is offering an inducement prize to anyone who does so. The logic behind inducement prizes is the same as that behind a tournament: instead of paying people to play, you pay them if they win. Under the right conditions, such competitions can stimulate new solutions to problems.

The British Parliament's 1714 prize for a practical method for determining a ship's longitude is an early example of an inducement prize.[17] The intervening centuries have seen thousands of prizes to stimulate technological advances, including transatlantic flight, human-powered flight, and nanotechnology.

The X PRIZE Foundation is devoted to using inducement prizes to stimulate innovative solutions in subjects ranging from genome sequencing to automotive efficiency.[18] The $30 million offered in 1992 by a consortium of U.S. utility companies for the most energy-efficient refrigerator that did not use a chlorofluorocarbon refrigerant (which destroys the ozone layer) provides a good news–bad news illustration.[19] To stimulate distribution as well as design, the consortium awarded the prize as a rebate for each energy-efficient refrigerator sold. Fourteen manufacturers submitted entries. The winning company, Whirlpool Corporation, devised a refrigerator that used 40 percent less energy than the federal energy-efficiency standard for new refrigerators. To pocket the prize, however, Whirlpool had to sell 250,000 superefficient fridges by July 1997; the money would be doled out as the special fridges were sold. But sales were low—reportedly 30 to 35 percent below the quarter-million target—and Whirlpool discontinued that model before the clock ran out on the program. At least at that time, consumers wouldn't pay extra for a highly efficient product.[20]

In recent years, inducement prizes have been used to stimulate solutions to social as well as technical problems. For example, with the support of the Robert Wood Johnson Foundation and others, Ashoka's Changemakers holds competitions to address problems ranging from domestic violence to improving health care and reducing corruption.[21] The MacArthur Foundation offers prizes of up to $250,000 for advances in new digital environments for learning.[22]

Inducement prizes offer a tool for encouraging thought and research in areas that the private sector might not otherwise address.[23] They can also encourage a diversity of research approaches. Unlike a grant, an induce-ment prize does not require the philanthropist to determine in advance who is best equipped to accomplish the goal or specify how a recipient should do so. But inducement prizes do require researchers to find support for their work from other sources, which makes prizes inappropriate as a tool for innovation in areas where the costs of R&D are prohibitively high—for example, creating a power source from high-altitude wind turbines. Prize money is a complement, not a substitute, for other forms of research fund-ing. In any event, before creating an inducement prize, you should think

A Different Sort of Prize: Advance Market Commitments for Vaccines

In 2007, as an incentive to develop vaccines against pneumo-coccal diseases for children in developing countries, the Bill & Melinda Gates Foundation and some developed countries committed $1.5 billion to purchase vaccines that met prede-termined standards of efficacy and safety for distribution in developing countries. Ruth Levine and Michael Kremer write:

> By promising in advance to pay for life-saving vaccines once they are produced, these countries [with the Gates Foundation's support] are creating incentives for biotech-nology and pharmaceutical companies to produce vac-cines appropriate for use in poor countries, and to sell them at affordable prices.
>
> Estimates from the World Bank and the Global Alliance for Vaccines and Immunizations (GAVI), which have worked closely with donor governments to hammer out the design of the innovative financing program, suggest this pneumococcal commitment could prevent an estimated 5.4 million childhood deaths by 2030.
>
> Why is an advance market commitment needed? An effective vaccine is currently available in the U.S. (under the Prevnar brand name), but at around $60 for each of the three doses required, it is too expensive for the poor-est countries, and it needs to be adapted to prevent the strains of disease that are common in developing countries but not the industrialized world. Normally it takes 10 to 15 years for a vaccine introduced in the U.S. to become widely available in the developing world. While maxi-mizing the benefits of the funding commitments depends on important contractual details, the 'pay for results' approach can shorten this lag and help to ensure that the vaccine will be adapted to suit the patterns of disease and health care systems of poor countries.[24]

about how the innovation will be disseminated or deployed, including who will hold the intellectual-property rights to any new technology.

Recognition prizes. The Nobel prizes, in fields ranging from physics to peace, are perhaps the best known of recognition prizes. Although their primary goal is to honor the recipients they can have more far-reaching consequences as well. For example, they may enable recipients to continue doing valuable work, and they can highlight the importance of an emerging field, encouraging others to pursue work in it.

Doubtless, the hope of winning a Nobel prize has added to some scientists' motivation to break new ground. Perhaps the Pulitzer Prize has similar effects. The Goldman Environmental Prize[25] not only enables its recipients to continue their good work, but, complemented by strong public-relations outreach, it also focuses attention on environmental leaders operating under challenging or oppressive conditions across the globe. In addition to giving heart to others working in similar circumstances, it may encourage other philanthropists to support environmental causes.

There are hundreds of thousands of other recognition prizes— national, local, and in your child's fifth-grade class. Their main value is not in the cash delivered but in the recognition conferred. The fifth-grade award aside, this requires that the prize itself be recognized by the general public or within a field. And this in turn requires continuity and publicity in the relevant communities, which takes time, focus, and money in addition to the prize funds. As a result, the costs of administering and publicizing the prize are often considerably greater than the award itself—by no means a negative if they amplify its benefits, but something that should be taken into account.[26]

Although prizes have a role in strategic philanthropy, the benefits are not assured, and other tools often have a greater impact. Prizes involve a one-time injection of funds into a project or individual's work. Social impact typically requires the patient commitment to support ongoing activities. The alternative to stimulating creativity through a prize is to seek it out and reward it with steady, ongoing support—to support the work of particular individuals or research institutions doing the best work in that field. Although prizes are appropriately included in a strategic philanthropist's toolbox, the question, as always, is whether a prize is likely to have at least as large an effect in achieving your philanthropic goals as an alternative use of your funds.

Testing the Design in the Laboratory and in the Field

Wherever an idea originated, it will likely need testing, whether through the formal means of randomized controlled experiments discussed in Chapter 9, through trial and error on someone's workbench, or through demonstration projects to see if the implementation of a particular idea actually works. Whereas a product like the cookstove is relatively easy to test, it is notoriously difficult to assess the success of many interventions in health, education, and other fields.

Suppose that you want to learn

➤ whether a particular drug-prevention program actually keeps kids out of trouble;

➤ whether providing bed nets to small African villages reduces malaria;

➤ whether longer school hours improve student performance;

➤ whether sex education reduces teen pregnancy; or

➤ whether public service announcements reduce obesity.

Demonstration programs can help answer these questions—but only if the programs are designed from the outset to test whether the intervention actually made a difference. If an evaluation can demonstrate that the theory of change is valid and generalizable—meaning that it can be applied to other populations and locations—then the theory can be implemented with confidence. If not, then it's back to the drawing board.

Fostering Adoption

There are several different avenues for fostering the adoption of an innovative idea or technology by its intended beneficiaries.

Markets

Just as commercial markets were the vehicle for spreading innovations such as the fax machine, the computer, and the cell phone, so, too, can they spread innovations supported by foundations and not-for-profits—contraceptives to prevent HIV/AIDS, bed nets to prevent malaria, and (if it proves successful) our low-fuel cookstove. Sometimes an innovation will be adopted by markets without further philanthropic intervention. In other situations, philanthropy must provide a continuing subsidy to get the innovation to the people who most need it.

Government Programs

Governments have funded charter schools to improve educational outcomes for inner-city kids, hospital protocols to reduce errors in prescribing drugs, and programs to reduce drug addiction and teen pregnancy. However, whereas markets tend to discard useless ideas, the same cannot be said for governments, which have sometimes persisted in supporting useless programs for preventing AIDS and unplanned pregnancies in the face of all the evidence.

Government Policies

Government policies and regulations affect private choices in complex and controversial ways.[27] They can also promote the diffusion of innovations and ideas—from photovoltaic cells to seat belts to healthy lifestyles.

THE REST OF Part II includes examples of all these methods for diffusing innovation.

Takeaway Points

➤ Philanthropy plays a valuable role in supporting knowledge for its own sake, as well as research to solve particular problems.
➤ Before supporting R&D,
   —ensure that the problem is a lack of knowledge rather than a failure to exploit existing knowledge;
   —ensure that, together with identified others, you have the resources to see the project through;
   —prepare for failure—for inconclusive or negative results; and
   —prepare for success—for how the fruits of the work can be adopted and used.

Chapter Notes

   1. Everett M. Rogers, *Diffusion of Innovations*, 5th ed. (New York: Free Press, 2003), 135.

   2. "Scientific Men and Their Duties," *Science*, December 10, 1886, 543; Fred M. Shapiro, ed., *The Yale Book of Quotations* (New Haven: Yale University Press, 2006), 715; Fred Shapiro, e-mail to the Math Forum @ Drexel mailing list, October 8, 2004, http://mathforum.org/kb/message.jspa?messageID=3226528&tstart=0.

3. Martin L. Weitzman, "Recombinant Growth." *Quarterly Journal of Economics* 113, no. 2 (1998): 331–360; and Jerome S. Bruner, *On Knowing: Essays for the Left Hand* (Cambridge, Mass.: Belknap Press, 1962), 18.

4. Note that indeterminate outcomes do not inevitably entail indeterminate strategies. For example, academia has a set of procedures—including academic freedom, sabbaticals, tenure, and peer review—designed to foster creativity and assess the value of its outcomes, even though no one can specify those outcomes in advance.

5. One could tell similar stories about universities outside the United States, which tend to rely more on government support than private philanthropy—for example, Amartya Sen's scholarship on development economics, see "Amartya Sen: Autobiography" in Tore Frangsmyr, ed., *Les Priz Nobel, The Nobel Prizes, 1998* (Stockholm: Nobel Foundation, 1999); Albert Fert's and Peter Gruenberg's Nobel Prize–winning independently researched work on giant magnetoresistance, which led to technologies for putting large amounts of information on the small hard drives used in laptops and iPods, see John Johnson Jr., "Two Europeans Share Nobel in Physics," *Los Angeles Times,* October 10, 2007, http://articles.latimes.com/2007/oct/10/science/sci-nobel10 (accessed July 2, 2008); and work leading up to the discovery of DNA. Most of the research conducted on DNA over the years occurred at universities, from the team of James Watson and Francis Crick and that of Rosalind Franklin and Maurice Wilkins at Cambridge University to Linus Pauling at the California Institute of Technology (Caltech). See Ralf Dahm, "Discovering DNA: Friedrich Miescher and the Early Years of Nucleic Acid Research," *Human Genetics* 122 (2008): 565–581, http://springerlink.com/content/8uuk483j11t513t6/fulltext.pdf.

6. "MIT Professor Claude Shannon Dies; Was Founder of Digital Communications," Massachusetts Institute of Technology News Office, February 27, 2001, http://web.mit.edu/newsoffice/2001/shannon.html.

7. Elizabeth Fee and Theodore M. Brown, "Michael S. Gottlieb and the Identification of AIDS," *American Journal of Public Health* 96 (2006): 982–983, http://www.ajph.org/cgi/content/extract/96/6/982.

8. Through at least the mid-nineteenth century, support came from the Church and from patrons (who did not get tax deductions—or, for that matter, pay taxes) ranging from the Medici family to Prince Esterhazy, in whose castle Franz Joseph Haydn composed. Although the artists had responsibilities to meet—Johann Sebastian Bach had to write a cantata for each Sunday's church service—and often had specific commissions, their patrons left them plenty of time to follow their own inspirations.

9. Massachusetts Institute of Technology, MIT OpenCourseWare, http://ocw .mit.edu (accessed June 30, 2008).

10. World Lecture Hall, http://web.austin.utexas.edu/wlh (accessed June 30, 2008).

11. See Adam Hochman, "Webcast.Berkeley Is Growing," iNews, September 13, 2007, http://istpub.berkeley.edu:4201/bcc/Fall2007/1114.html. Over ten million users downloaded content from the site in 2006, making it the most visited education site on the Web.

12. Elisabeth Bumiller, "Research Groups Boom in Washington," *New York Times*, January 30, 2008, http://www.nytimes.com/2008/01/30/washington/30tank.html?_r=2&ref=us&oref=slogin&oref=slogin.

13. Steven M. Teles, *The Rise of the Conservative Legal Movement: The Battle for Control of the Law* (Princeton, N.J.: Princeton University Press, 2008), 279.

14. A philanthropist interested in making a smaller investment in research will do well to align herself with a larger funder who has a peer-review process in place. If the larger funder has already made the investment to understand critical-path research requirements, that funder can share that information at little or no cost and with great benefit.

15. IDEO, "MoneyMaker Deep Lift Pump," http://www.ideo.com/portfolio/re.asp?x=50167 (accessed June 30, 2008).

16. KickStart, "Micro-Irrigation Technologies," http://www.kickstart.org/tech/technologies/micro-irrigation.html (accessed June 30, 2008).

17. See Dava Sobel, *Longitude: The True Story of a Lone Genius Who Solved the Greatest Scientific Problem of His Time* (New York: Penguin, 1996).

18. See X PRIZE Foundation, http://www.xprize.org (accessed June 30, 2008).

19. Foresight Nanotech Institute, "Feyman Grand Prize," http://www.foresight.org/GrandPrize.1.html (accessed June 30, 2008) (see section entitled "Super Efficient Refrigerator Prize").

20. See EcoMall, "The New Wave of Energy Efficient Refrigerators," http://www.ecomall.com/greenshopping/icebox2.htm (accessed June 30, 2008).

21. Robert Wood Johnson Foundation, "New Competition to Showcase World's Most Innovative Domestic Violence Prevention Programs," news release, January 17, 2007, http://www.rwjf.org/newsroom/newsreleasesdetail.jsp?productid=21933; and Changemakers, "Welcome Letter from Robert Wood Johnson Foundation," http://www.changemakers.net/competition/endabuse/framework (accessed June 30, 2008).

22. http://www.macfound.org/site/c.lkLXJ8MQKrH/b.1053853/apps/nl/content2.asp?content_id=%7BCB00292A-1602-403E-9FE9-5F392B5274F4%7D&notoc=1.

23. Much of this discussion is drawn from Thomas Kalil, "Prizes for Technological Innovation" (Hamilton Project Discussion Paper 2006-08, Brookings Institution, 2006), http://www.brookings.edu/~/media/Files/rc/papers/2006/12healthcare_kalil/200612kalil.pdf.

24. Ruth Levine and Michael Kremer, "Incentives for Better Health Around the World," posted to the Global Health Policy blog (of the Center for Global

Development) on February 12, 2007, http://blogs.cgdev.org/globalhealth/2007/02/incentives_for.php.

25. Goldman Environmental Prize, http://www.goldmanprize.org (accessed June 30, 2008).

26. If a prize is administered through a foundation, the procedure must be approved in advance by the Treasury Department as meeting the IRS requirements for making grants to individuals, which include running objective nominations and selections processes. See Instructions for Guide Sheet for Advance Approval of Individual Grant Procedures, http://www.irs.gov/pub/irs-tege/4945_g__guide_sheet_instructions.pdf (accessed June 30, 2008).

27. Richard H. Thaler and Cass R. Sunstein, *Nudge: Improving Decisions About Health, Wealth, and Happiness* (New Haven, Conn.: Yale University Press, 2008).

Chapter Twelve

Providing Goods and Services

S O YOU HAVE tested the low-fuel-use cookstove in the field and determined that it has the potential to improve the lives of tens of thousands of rural Africans. How do you get it to them? Two fundamentally different approaches define the ends of a spectrum.

At one end lie *private markets*. Most goods and services—from clothing to food, from healthcare to automobile repairs—are sold by for-profit companies through private markets.

At the other end lies the provision of free goods and services by *charities and governments*. The vast majority of not-for-profit organizations in the United States and across the globe provide goods and services, with missions ranging from feeding and sheltering the homeless to caring for preschoolers to saving people's souls. Some organizations, like churches, provide services that are unavailable in the private sector, whereas others, like health clinics, have for-profit alternatives. Some work in collaboration with, or as agents of, government; for example, many traditional charities provide welfare under government contracts. And governments themselves provide many essential goods and services such as public education, public libraries, fire and police protection, and national defense.

Between these ends of the spectrum lie varying degrees of subsidization as well as efforts to redress market failures caused, for example, by unclear property rights, high or asymmetrical information costs, high transaction costs, or cases where participants in markets impose significant costs on others, or are not able to capture the benefits of their activities.

To illustrate the very last of these, let's consider some examples in which not-for-profit organizations have assisted business in adopting technologies that have external benefits but for which the financial return alone might not have warranted investment of the company's own resources:

➤ In the late 1980s, amid concerns that landfills were overflowing with trash, the Environmental Defense Fund assisted McDonald's Corp. in phasing out its polystyrene "clamshell" containers and replacing them with more-environmentally-friendly packaging, such as paper bags, boxes, and napkins made from recycled fiber.[1] McDonald's new paper wraps represented a 70 to 90 percent reduction in packaging volume, resulting in significantly less space consumed in landfills. Compared with the polystyrene foam clamshell containers they replaced, the new wraps also offered substantial savings in energy used and reductions in pollutant releases measured over the full life-cycle of the package.[2] Many other fast-food chains ended up copying this industry leader.

➤ Benetech's Bookshare.org program has helped publishing companies deliver books to people who are blind or visually impaired. Using a Web-based library of digitally scanned books, the Bookshare program has given visually disabled individuals access to newspapers and popular book titles.

Sometimes a philanthropic investment is necessary to get a product into the for-profit marketplace. The use of philanthropic funds to foster innovation, discussed in the preceding chapter, is typical of such investments. Why is philanthropy necessary? Usually because markets for some products for the poor are too speculative and risky to justify private investments until someone else has proven the concept. Thus, the Bill & Melinda Gates Foundation has supported the Institute for OneWorld Health, a not-for-profit pharmaceutical company, in developing and testing a cost-effective treatment for visceral leishmaniasis (VL), the world's second most deadly parasitic disease after malaria. As OneWorld Health's founder, Dr. Victoria Hale, explained:

> Research and development costs for new medicines are in the tens of millions of dollars. The traditional sources of funding that would lead to

a for-profit entity—venture capital—just didn't work. We couldn't even get two minutes in front of a venture capitalist. Therefore, going forward with philanthropy first was the way to do it. Now, is it necessary to remain simply a not-for-profit pharmaceutical company? The answer is, we don't know. Because we have proven that we can develop a drug and bring it to market, we now have potential investors stepping forward to ask us to consider other models that are not not-for-profit. So would we be willing to open up to other possibilities? Absolutely."[3]

Ideally, once the concept has been proven, it can be sustained by markets. But sometimes its beneficiaries are so poor that continued use of the product or service requires ongoing philanthropic or government support. For example, access to low-cost antiretroviral drugs to treat AIDS in many developing countries still depends on philanthropic or government subsidization, as will efforts to put low-cost computers into the hands of the world's poorest children through the One Laptop per Child Foundation.[4]

The remainder of this chapter surveys different organizational approaches. Although some philanthropists and commentators have asserted that certain approaches are intrinsically superior to others, we believe that all of them can have value; as always, our view is that you must evaluate any approach in terms of its potential for achieving impact in light of your particular goals.

Market-Based vs. Non-Market-Based Solutions

All things being equal, it is preferable to provide goods and services through market mechanisms because of their built-in systems for seeking efficient distribution paths and for equilibrating supply and demand. But the decision needs to be based on the realities of the particular situation, not a preconceived ideology.

Some organizations that supply goods and services for the poor, such as soup kitchens and homeless shelters, provide their services free of charge because their clients cannot afford to pay anything. Others, like the HealthStore Foundation's Child and Family Wellness Shops (CFWshops), use market mechanisms to distribute goods and services, and typically subsidize a portion of the cost. Combining microfinance with established franchising practices, the CFWshops provide healthcare products in remote communities of Kenya.

Ashoka: Innovators for the Public is supporting innovative collabora-
tions between businesses and not-for-profit organizations through what
it calls Hybrid Value Chains,[5] to enable businesses to sell useful products
in very-low-income markets. Access to these markets is often constrained
by the purchasing power of potential customers, the complexities of a
high volume business based on small individual transactions, and the
businesses' poor understanding of the human and social capital of low-
income communities. However, citizen sector organizations—Ashoka's
term for nongovernmental or not-for-profit organizations—can help
businesses tap into these markets to the benefit of everyone involved. In
one project, two Ashoka Fellows, Arturo Garcia and Juan José Consejo,
are helping Amanco, a leading Latin American water-systems company,
develop markets that distribute products and services like irrigation
pumps and technical assistance to small farmers. Through a network
of farmer-owned and managed cooperatives in the state of Guerrero,
Mexico, run by Garcia and an environmental conservation organization
run by Consejo, the fellows use their connections with farmers on the
demand side and vendors on the supply side to help both parties recognize new, sustainable business opportunities. Amanco gains a profitable
line of business, the farmers produce greater crop yields and ultimately
earn more for their families, and the Ashoka Fellows advance their organizations' missions of improving irrigation and reducing environmental
damage.

Treated antimalaria bed nets provide an interesting example of
the alternatives of social marketing and free distribution in Africa.
Population Services International (PSI) and the Ifakara Health Research
and Development Centre have built distribution networks, including
wholesalers and retailers. But even with substantial government subsidies, less than one-third of the population of malaria-ridden Tanzania
uses them. In Kenya, 66 percent of the targeted population used the
nets when they were distributed free of charge, but only 7 percent
when they were sold even at subsidized prices. Given evidence of this
sort, the development economist Jeffrey Sachs argues strenuously for
free distribution. But Brian Trelstad, the chief investment officer of
Acumen Fund, argues for "complementary public free distribution and
stimulation of private channels." He states that free distribution is just
not an option in all African countries, and that "people will need to

have access to nets even when the wave of free distribution ends." Jane Miller of PSI expresses the similar concern that mass free distribution could undercut the commercial bed-net sector: "At the moment, the donors seem to be saying that money is no object. But it certainly will be in the future."[6]

And this brings us to a final thought on the subject—that you should also consider the possibility that subsidies can sometimes distort well-functioning markets and make the very people you want to help, or others similarly situated, worse off rather than better off. Subsidies originally designed to protect poor U.S. farmers from the vicissitudes of volatile crop prices have had the catastrophic unintended consequence of underpricing commodities on international markets, making it impossible for many developing-country farmers to earn a living. For example, U.S. subsidies to American corn farmers for ethanol, together with a fifty-four-cents-a-gallon tariff on imported ethanol, have prevented the entry of cleaner Brazilian ethanol, which is made from sugar rather than maize, and have contributed to the poverty of Brazilian farmers.[7]

Philanthropy vs. Charity

Because of our focus on impact, we also reject the facile distinction between "charity" and "philanthropy." Strategic philanthropy is about actual impact in achieving your goals, and this implies that you should consider any strategy in terms of its expected value. Suppose that you are concerned with the plight of the homeless in your community. The way the distinction is usually drawn suggests that a donation to a homeless shelter is charity, whereas a grant to an organization trying to eliminate the "root causes" of homelessness is (strategic) philanthropy.

But what if the impact of the donation is essentially a sure thing, and the effort to eliminate root causes is highly speculative, leading to a lower expected return? In our view, no approach is inherently strategic or nonstrategic; strategy lies in clarity about your goals and determining which approach best achieves them. That said, a high-quality strategy to change systems, although riskier than direct aid, often has the potential to produce much larger results.

Donated vs. Earned Revenues

Quite a few direct-service organizations depend on related earned income as well as philanthropic donations. The Salvation Army and Goodwill Industries International generate income through the sale of secondhand goods. The Girl Scouts sell cookies. Museums earn income from membership fees and gift shop proceeds. Rubicon Programs in the San Francisco Bay Area runs workforce-development programs for the physically and mentally disabled that provide goods and services—food, gardening services, and the like—to paying customers. Microfinance institutions support themselves through interest on loans. Self-Help and Habitat for Humanity—both of which provide affordable housing—have a built-in revenue stream from loan repayments and interest on loans. Universities, public and private, derive a substantial part of their budgets from tuition.

But there are many valuable service organizations that have little if any earned income—for example, America's Second Harvest, which relies on donated goods and services and individual and corporate financial contributions to feed 25 million Americans each year.[8]

By reducing an organization's dependency on donor funds, earned income may contribute to its impact, stability, and potential for growth. Whether it actually does so in any given case depends on factors such as the breadth of the organization's donor base and the relative costs of generating program-related income compared with fund raising. It is better to understand these factors in the context of the particular organization than to rely on earned income as a proxy for success.

Systemic Change vs. Yeoman Services

In *Capitalism, Socialism, and Democracy*, Joseph Schumpeter famously wrote about the rise and fall of business organizations, both new and established. Schumpeter noted the role of entrepreneurs in setting off "a chain reaction that encourages other entrepreneurs to iterate upon and ultimately to propagate the innovation to the point of 'creative destruction,' a state at which the new venture and all its related ventures effectively render existing products, services, and business models obsolete."[9] But although Schumpeter focused his analysis on traditional business enterprises, there are social entrepreneurs who play similar roles in promoting creative destruction in the not-for-profit sector.

In recent years, this idea of *social entrepreneurship* has captured the imagination—and the vocabulary—of these sectors, with particular emphasis on innovation in the provision of direct services.[10] Bill Drayton, the founder of Ashoka: Innovators for the Public, who coined the phrase,[11] says that social entrepreneurship involves large-scale, systemic social change:

> The job of the social entrepreneur is to recognize when a part of society is not working and to solve the problem by changing the system, spreading solutions, and persuading entire societies to take new leaps. Social entrepreneurs are not content to just give a fish or to teach how to fish. They will not rest until they have revolutionized the fishing industry. Identifying and solving large-scale social problems requires social entrepreneurs because only entrepreneurs have the committed vision and inexhaustible determination to persist until they have transformed an entire system.[12]

Along similar lines, Roger L. Martin and Sally Osberg describe social entrepreneurship as a successful effort to change the social equilibrium. Social entrepreneurship starts with "an unfortunate but stable equilibrium that causes the exclusion, neglect, marginalization, or suffering of a segment of humanity"; it involves an individual, "who brings to bear on this situation his or her inspiration, direct action, creativity, courage, and fortitude"; and ends with the ultimate "establishment of a new stable equilibrium that secures permanent benefits for the targeted group and society at large."[13]

Early examples of individuals now dubbed social entrepreneurs include Florence Nightingale, who founded the modern profession of nursing, and Maria Montessori, who developed a new approach to elementary-school teaching. The canonic contemporary example is Muhammad Yunus, who was awarded the 2006 Nobel Peace Prize. As head of the economics department at Chittagong University in Bangladesh, he established the prototype for Grameen Bank, which made "microfinance" loans to provide credit to the poorest of the poor in rural Bangladesh. Beyond growing to serve individuals throughout Bangladesh, Grameen Bank has been a model for similar institutions throughout the developing world, with even traditional banks getting into the microfinance business.

The work of social entrepreneurs varies widely. We already mentioned several examples, including the Super MoneyMaker pump, a product of Martin Fisher and Nick Moon's ApproTEC (now KickStart), which focuses on creating business opportunities in the developing world, and Wendy Kopp's Teach for America, a corps of outstanding recent college and professional-school graduates who teach in public schools and become advocates for education reform. David Green founded Project Impact, a not-for-profit organization that provides affordable medical technology and health-care services, with products including an inexpensive hearing aid and a foldable intraocular lens. Mark Freedman's Civic Ventures develops socially engaging alternatives to retirement for older Americans to "achieve the greatest return on experience."[14] Dr. Bernard Kouchner (now France's minister of foreign and European affairs) founded Doctors Without Borders, which delivers aid to people affected by armed conflict, epidemics, and natural and man-made disasters. Bunker Roy's Barefoot College teaches illiterate and semiliterate men and women skills ranging from installing and maintaining drinking-water systems and harvesting rainwater to creating affordable housing and solar power grids.

The precise definitions and characteristics of social entrepreneurship are hotly contested. For example, Bill Drayton asserts that only an individual, initially acting outside of any organization, can be a social entrepreneur, whereas an empirical study by Paul Light of New York University's Wagner School of Public Service finds that venerable organizations are capable of the same kind of innovation.[15] In any event, there are several reasons that you might support social entrepreneurs, as broadly defined, and several ways to do so.

1. You might support particular social entrepreneurs and their organizations because their activities further your objectives, say in health, education, or international development. You could provide support through ordinary grants or through the practices of venture philanthropy discussed below.

2. You might support as-of-yet unproved social entrepreneurs for much the same reason that you would support scholars at research universities and think tanks pursuing their own agendas—in the belief that, though not specifiable in advance, significant social value will emerge. This is the likely premise of the foundations and individual

philanthropists who give generously to Ashoka, and of the Skoll
Foundation and the Schwab Foundation for Social Entrepreneurship
in their support for the general field of social entrepreneurship.
3. You might be particularly enthusiastic about supporting ideas that
emerge from poor communities and developing countries, in the
belief that they are more likely to respond to the real needs of local
populations and to be implemented effectively in local conditions.
Here too Ashoka and the Skoll Foundation provide excellent examples. In addition, the Global Exchange for Social Investment helps
social entrepreneurs obtain support to scale up replicable enterprises
that provide basic goods and services such as water, electricity, communication, and health care in poor regions of the world.

Behind every organization that contributes value to society stands
an entrepreneur—perhaps more than one, because long-established
organizations sometimes "reinvent" themselves to meet changing
circumstances. But after the entrepreneur's innovation, whether in
business or in the not-for-profit sector, come consolidation, scaling up,
and replication that often call as much for good management as for
entrepreneurial skills. It may be appropriate to call the founder of the
Boy Scouts a social entrepreneur, but it is stretching matters to accord
that title to your local troop leader. Yet organizations that continue,
strengthen, and even copy the patterns set by social entrepreneurs add
tremendous value to society. All of which is to say that, although there's
great excitement in the best new thing, there also is great value in supporting the quotidian operations of stable institutions as well.

Service vs. Advocacy

For purposes of analysis, we have separated the activities that philanthropy can support into three categories: knowledge, services, and influence. But many organizations engage in activities that fit into more than
one category. To presage the next chapter, consider how one service
provider became an advocate for changes in government policy.[16]
Self-Help is a North Carolina–based not-for-profit community-
development lender and real estate developer that provides loans to people who are not able to borrow at market rates in conventional markets.
Self-Help began engaging in advocacy when it saw low-income North

Carolinians losing their homes in foreclosures by predatory lenders, who charged excessive fees and interest rates. After an unsuccessful effort to lobby Congress to change federal law, Self-Help mobilized a statewide coalition of seventy diverse allies (including churches, credit unions, and local AARP and NAACP affiliates), which led the North Carolina legislature to pass an anti-predatory-lending law in 1999.[17] In 2002, Self-Help launched the Center for Responsible Lending to conduct research and advocate for policy reform at the state and federal levels. Self-Help's direct programs continue to build home ownership—on the order of over $5 billion in loans to fifty-five thousand families and another three thousand loans to small businesses and community facilities nation-wide.[18] At the same time, Self-Help has become a formidable force for national policy reform, helping pass anti-predatory-lending laws in twenty-two states to protect the nation's most vulnerable citizens.[19]

Whereas Self-Help's advocacy grew out of its service mission, the National Council of La Raza (NCLR) began with a commitment both to being an advocacy organization and to providing grassroots services to achieve its goals. NCLR's mission is to improve opportunities for Latinos through civil rights advocacy and capacity-building help to a network of affiliated community-based organizations, as well as through its on-the-ground operations in education, health, housing, employment, and economic development.[20] For example, when NCLR's education-policy analysis shed light on deficiencies in Latinos' education, the organiza-tion started offering bilingual civics, math, and science curricula for after-school programs in Latino communities[21] and created a national charter-school network for Latino students.[22] In the words of NCLR's former president and CEO Raul Yzaguirre, "[Service] programs inform your public policy and give you the means to change it; and if you didn't have policy, you make your programs less potent."[23]

Strengthening and Scaling Up Organizations: Venture Philanthropy

Beyond making individual grants and gifts, some funders engage in the practice of *venture philanthropy*, which focuses on strengthening and scaling up organizations. Venture philanthropy involves *funding-plus*, where the "plus" includes strategic and management assistance. It also involves *general operating support-plus*, where general operating

support, though the primary mode of funding, is supplemented by project grants to assist the organization.

Although the practice is as old as the Rockefeller Foundation, the term
"venture philanthropy" is borrowed from the practices of the investors
who gave birth to companies like Yahoo!, Google, Amazon.com, and eBay.
These venture capitalists provided the early- and mid-stage risk capital,
organizational expertise, and access to networks that proved invaluable to
each company's growth and success. Unlike passive investors who monitor
a company's performance from a distance, venture capitalists often spend
significant amounts of time with their portfolio organizations to ensure
that their investments have the best possible chance of paying off.

Whereas most foundations make grants to maintain the programs of
existing organizations, venture philanthropists seek out high-potential
organizations with the goal of helping them scale up. As Peter Frumkin
writes, venture philanthropy is driven by the belief "that size matters in
the nonprofit sector, that achieving it is a sign of success and relevance,
and that creating organizations that go to scale is a legitimate and worthy
goal for philanthropy."[24]

Recall the Edna McConnell Clark Foundation's (EMCF's) support of
Harlem Children's Zone described in Chapter 1. EMCF tends to engage
high-potential organizations early in their life cycle. Its president, Nancy
Roob, explains EMCF's approach in this way:

> Rather than coming up with an idea yourself for how you think social
> outcomes should be achieved and funding people that do that, the Clark
> Foundation looks for the best organizations out there that are already
> doing it and asking how to help them do it better. . . . We are not at odds
> with the grantee. We are getting behind their plans and the set of results
> that their board is focused on to begin with. We provide the 'glue money'
> that is hard to raise and helps you build the capacity you need to grow and
> enhance your programs.[25]

EMCF's approach to funding youth-development organizations
is paradigmatic of venture philanthropy, whose elements include the
following:

➤ *Reliable money.* Though grants from venture philanthropists are not
  necessarily larger than grants from other funding sources, venture

philanthropists generally offer longer-term support and a greater proportion of general operating support, allowing organizations to hire staff and initiate planning without fearing that funding will be withdrawn unexpectedly.

➤ *Strategic and organizational coaching.* Venture philanthropists provide the technical assistance required at different stages of an organization's development. The intimacy and length of the relationship tends to promote trust and is conducive to collaborative troubleshooting.

➤ *Network effects.* Venture philanthropists are well connected in their field and provide their portfolio ventures access to networks of outside resources.

As is apparent from EMCF's support of Harlem Children's Zone, venture philanthropy employs many approaches to funding. But the venture-philanthropy philosophy is similar to that of providing general operating support: identifying promising organizations whose missions are aligned with the funder's and enabling their leaders to pursue those missions.

Consider the NewSchools Venture Fund, a venture-philanthropy firm in San Francisco committed to improving public education for low-income and minority children in urban communities.[26] Its portfolio includes charter-school management organizations, curriculum providers, and support organizations. NewSchools provides its grantees with financial and organizational assistance. Its practice of venture philanthropy, which is characteristic of the field, has five stages:

1. Adopting goals, a theory of change, and an overall strategy
2. Selecting an organization to fund
3. Designing a strategy and providing resources
4. Measuring performance
5. Finding an exit

1. Adopting goals, a theory of change, and an overall strategy. NewSchools' work arises from the beliefs that all children are entitled to a high-quality education and that education entrepreneurs can change large complex systems by seeking places in the system where philanthropic interventions can have high impact and leverage public dollars. Its investments are intended to influence other schools in the public education system to provide their students a quality education—a theory that, for the most part, has yet to be proven.

2. Selecting an organization to fund. As part of their due-diligence process, venture philanthropists typically ask these fundamental questions:

- ➤ Does the venture fit with the investment goals?
- ➤ Is the venture poised to have significant impact on the target populations?
- ➤ Is the venture's impact scalable? Does it have potential to grow?
- ➤ Can the venture's growth become financially sustainable so that its impact will increase over time?
- ➤ Do the venture's management team, market, and product indicate a high potential for success and impact?

These considerations were central in NewSchools' investment in New Schools for New Orleans. In the aftermath of Hurricane Katrina, that organization is creating a new type of public education system in which the choice among schools, including charter schools, plays a key role. The strategy involves strengthening and expanding charter schools while developing the infrastructure and human capital necessary to sustain improvements in both the charter and noncharter sectors. If successful, the New Orleans experiment could provide a powerful demonstration of system turnaround and transformation.

3. Designing a strategy and providing resources. Once an organization has been selected, the real work begins: bringing the organization to scale through the creation of a comprehensive business plan that clarifies the organization's mission, strategy, and tactics.

Venture philanthropists provide a mixture of project support and technical assistance in addition to core general operating support. As the business plan is implemented, they continue to serve as advisers to the organization with respect to issues of governance, planning, management, and fund raising. For example, the Robin Hood Foundation has in-house management experts that help programs with strategic and financial planning, recruiting, legal concerns, organizational issues, and capital needs. The NewSchools Venture Fund connects educational leaders in dialogue and collaborative projects to help move the field forward. Venture philanthropists will often formally cement their advisory role by putting a representative on a grantee's board of directors.

4. *Measuring performance.* Venture philanthropists have been in
the lead in measuring the impact of their philanthropic investments.
For example, NewSchools compares the performance of the schools it
supports with "control" schools serving the same populations. Its assessments indicate that NewSchools students outperform students at similar
schools by 23 percent in math and 44 percent in language arts at the
middle-school level and by 36 percent in math and 52 percent in reading
at the high-school level. New Profit Inc., a national venture-philanthropy
firm that supports social entrepreneurs, also measures the performance
of its portfolio organizations. For example, its grantee Upwardly Global,
which helps place highly skilled, underemployed foreign immigrants in
skilled jobs, has a 40 percent success rate with an average increase of
$15,650 in annual income.

5. *Finding an exit.* A venture capitalist who funds a for-profit enterprise has two possible exit strategies: take the business public through
an initial public offering (IPO) or have it acquired by a larger company
that views the business as a strategic asset.

For a venture philanthropist and its not-for-profit grantee, the exit
strategy is to find sources of funding that can help the organization
become sustainable and grow through some combination of earned
income, government subventions, and charitable donations. For example, Teach for America, one of NewSchools' portfolio organizations,
relies on contributions from corporations, foundations, and individuals,
as well as from federal and state governments and local school districts.
Revolution Foods, another NewSchools organization, relies on earned
income as a for-profit provider of healthy and organic school lunches.
Julie Petersen of NewSchools says that an exit can be the most difficult
part of a venture philanthropist's strategy:

> Exits are tricky. Exits are predicated on organizations, either finding a
> sustainable revenue stream—whether it's earned revenue, predictable con-
> tributions and philanthropy—or public funding, which is what we're often
> looking for in our charter management organizations, where we hope that
> they get to the point where they're raising enough public revenue based
> on their per-pupil funding that they get from the state. We'll exit when we
> see an organization is sustainable or when we see that there is someone
> else to take over the late-stage funding of these organizations. And what
> we're finding is that it's really hard for a lot of these organizations to raise

growth capital from foundations (foundations in a lot of cases are providing shorter-term project-based funding), and there's not a lot of growth capital out there to help these organizations grow to this bigger scale that we had once envisioned where we could simply pass them off to the next funder. In the venture capital realm, there's a whole host of mezzanine funders, private equity funders, investment banks, that are a part of a well-developed segmented capital market for entrepreneurs, but that just doesn't exist in the not-for-profit world. As a result, we haven't exited very many of our organizations.[27]

"Mezzanine" Financing in Venture Philanthropy

In the private sector, an initial venture capital round is often followed by so-called mezzanine funding to bring a company to the next stage. The not-for-profit sector has not seen much in the way of a parallel. As we write, however, the Edna McConnell Clark Foundation (EMCF) has announced a capital aggregation project to leverage its own grant-making budget to provide the capital to help successful ventures grow. Its pilot program involves the Nurse-Family Partnership, which provides nurse home-visiting programs for low-income first-time parents and their children; Youth Villages, which provides services for emotionally and behaviorally troubled children; and Citizen Schools, which finds adult volunteers who engage with middle-school students in after-school learning projects. So far, EMCF has brought in a number of other foundations, including The Atlantic Philanthropies, the Day Foundation, the Bill & Melinda Gates Foundation, the Robert Wood Johnson Foundation, and the Picower Foundation, as well as individual philanthropists, to support these organizations, investing $39 million of its own funds toward the $120 million goal for the entire fund; commitments of $88 million have been secured to date.[28]

For all the buzz about venture philanthropy, there are relatively few funders whose work encompasses most of these practices. At the turn of the twenty-first century, there were only about forty venture-philanthropy institutions, whose investments totaled about $60 million per year. This is a fairly small portion of overall giving in America (which in 2006 was about $295 billion annually). Whatever its future, however, venture philanthropy offers some valuable lessons for the broader field.

First is the value of supporting an organization as a whole rather than picking and choosing pieces of its activities—providing general operating support when possible, rather than funding discrete projects.

Second, although they have explicitly limited time horizons, venture philanthropists stay with an organization long enough to see it through success at a particular stage of development—something that contrasts favorably to the modus operandi of many foundations, which impose arbitrary and often counterproductive time limits on their support even for high-performing organizations, and often exit because of donor fatigue rather than as a result of any strategy.

And third, like their for-profit counterparts, many venture philanthropists are focused on particular fields—education for NewSchools, international development in the case of Acumen Fund—and are thus able to develop deep internal expertise and external networks to assist their grantees.

We end this section with a note of caution. Venture philanthropy is sometimes referred to as "engaged philanthropy."[29] As in the for-profit sector, engagement—whether through strategic coaching or serving on boards—certainly has the potential to add value to a not-for-profit organization. Because venture capitalists' time is in short supply, their engagement is almost inevitably designed to achieve impact. Although this is true of effective venture philanthropists, engagement may sometimes be a form of entertainment for a retired business executive turned philanthropist with time on his hands. Engagement for engagement's sake is not helpful. In the words of Shel Silverstein's children's song "Helping":[30]

> Some kind of help is the kind of help that helping's all about,
> And some kind of help is the kind of help
> We all can do without.

Organizational-Effectiveness Grants

A number of foundations award organizational-effectiveness grants—also called capacity-building or management-assistance grants—to selected grantees to strengthen their capacity to carry out their missions. Generally ranging from $10,000 to $50,000, organizational-effectiveness grants enable grantees to hire consultants to improve strategic planning, communications, evaluation, and fund raising to strengthen internal management, build boards, and address a host of other management and leadership challenges. As well as improving an organization's impact, organizational-effectiveness grants can reduce risks created by the sudden departure of an executive director or loss of a major funder, thereby helping ensure the organization's survival and giving donors the confidence to make longer-term investments in grantees.[31]

Takeaway Points

➤ Philanthropic support for goods and services takes place against the background of private markets and is designed to redistribute benefits to the poor or to correct for market imperfections.

➤ Philanthropists play a valuable role in ensuring reliable services year after year as well as promoting innovation.

➤ Philanthropists can fund the spectrum from individual social entrepreneurs to mature organizations. Venture philanthropists assist organizations that are poised for growth, through strategic and managerial assistance as well as funding.

Chapter Notes

1. Heather McLeod Grant and Leslie R. Crutchfield, "Creating High-Impact Nonprofits," *Stanford Social Innovation Review* Fall 2007, 37, http://www.ssireview.org/images/articles/2007FA_feature_mcleod_grant_crutchfield.pdf.

2. *McDonald's Corporation–Environmental Defense Waste Reduction Task Force Final Report* (1991), http://www.edf.org/documents/927_McDonaldsfinalreport.htm.

3. Eric Nee, "15 Minutes with Victoria Hale," *Stanford Social Innovation Review* Winter 2007, 22, http://www.ssireview.org/images/articles/2007WI_15minutes_hale.pdf.

4. David Pogue, "Laptop With a Mission Widens Its Audience," *New York Times*, October 4, 2007.

5. Ashoka: Innovators for the Public, "Hybrid Value Chain," http://www.ashoka.org/hvc (accessed June 30, 2008).

6. Eliza Barclay, "Charity vs. Capitalism in Africa," *BusinessWeek*, January 2, 2008.

7. Gerrit Buntrock, "Cheap No More," *Economist*, December 6, 2007.

8. Grant and Crutchfield, "Creating High-Impact Nonprofits," 36.

9. Joseph A. Schumpeter, *Capitalism, Socialism, and Democracy* (New York: Harper & Row, 1975), 82–85.

10. See Paul C. Light, *Searching for Social Entrepreneurship* (Washington, D.C.: Brookings Institution Press, 2008).

11. See David Bornstein, *How to Change the World: Social Entrepreneurs and the Power of New Ideas* (New York: Oxford University Press, 2004).

12. William Drayton, "Everyone a Changemaker," *Peer Review* 7 (2005): 8–12, quoted in Paul C. Light, *The Search for Social Entrepreneurship* (Washington, D.C.: Brookings Institution, 2008).

13. Roger L. Martin and Sally Osberg, "Social Entrepreneurship: The Case for Definition," *Stanford Social Innovation Review* Spring 2007, 29–39, http://www.ssireview.org/images/articles/2007SP_feature_martinosberg.pdf. Roger Martin is dean of the Joseph L. Rotman School of Management at the University of Toronto; Sally Osberg is president and CEO of the Skoll Foundation.

14. Civic Ventures, "Civic Ventures Overview," http://www.civicventures.org/overview.cfm (accessed June 30, 2008).

15. Light, *The Search for Social Entrepreneurship*.

16. Grant and Crutchfield, "Creating High-Impact Nonprofits."

17. Ibid.

18. Self-Help, http://www.self-help.org (accessed June 30, 2008).

19. Grant and Crutchfield, "Creating High-Impact Nonprofits."

20. Ibid.

21. Ibid., 35.

22. National Council of La Raza, "Charter School Development Initiative (CSDI)," http://www.nclr.org/section/charter_school (accessed June 30, 2008); and Crutchfield and McLeod Grant, 2008.

23. Quoted in Grant and Crutchfield, "Creating High-Impact Nonprofits," 44.

24. Peter Frumkin, "Inside Venture Philanthropy," *Society*, May/June 2002, 7–15.

25. Nancy Roob, "GEO Action Guide: Leading Change; Transforming Grantmaker Practices for Improved Nonprofit Results" (draft October 8, 2007).

26. We would like to thank Julie Petersen at NewSchools for her helpful comments on this section.

27. Julie Petersen, telephone conversation, January 23, 2008.

28. Nancy Roob, "President's Page," The Edna McConnell Clark Foundation, http://www.emcf.org/who/presidentspage/index.htm.

29. Christine W. Letts and William P. Ryan, "Filling the Performance Gap," *Stanford Social Innovation Review,* Spring 2003, 26–33.

30. Shel Silverstein, *Free to Be You and Me*, performed by Marlo Thomas and others, CDLS-2006 (compact disc).

31. See Paul Connolly and Carol Lukas, *Strengthening Nonprofit Performance: A Funder's Guide to Capacity Building* (St. Paul, Minn.: Amherst H. Wilder Foundation, 2002), 7.

Chapter *Thirteen*

Influencing Individuals, Policy Makers, and Businesses

S UPPOSE YOU ARE concerned about the rise in obesity among American youth—about both the health consequences and the economic burdens that will ultimately be imposed on society. Consider these various approaches for promoting healthy behaviors among your target population.

You might try to change the behavior of individuals by persuading them to eat more healthily. You could do this by informing them about the consequences of obesity and how to follow a healthy diet. These efforts might be aided by labeling foods according to their calories and fat content, but labeling usually requires legislation. You might try to inform parents in order to affect their behavior with respect to their kids' eating and exercise habits; for example, reducing the time spent in front of the television improves behavior in both dimensions.

You might also employ psychological techniques to influence behavior in ways that do not appeal solely to rational considerations—for example, by inducing fear of the consequences of obesity or by appealing, in a positive way, to feelings about being healthy or slim. These messages might be conveyed through various media, by school teachers, in homes and communities, or through counseling programs.

Using many of these same techniques, you might try to change the culture of the target population by making healthy lifestyles cool and obesity decidedly uncool. Although this seems more ambitious, it may be the most—perhaps the only—effective way to change individual behavior.

It often takes more than one tool to solve a problem. For example, external factors play a significant role in the obesity of poor children. Many children do not eat healthy foods at home because their neighborhoods lack supermarkets or because working (and often single) parents don't have time to cook. Many children get inadequate exercise because they don't have safe and convenient places to play. Thus, efforts to inform and influence behavior may need to be supplemented by creating actual alternatives for the children by changing the external environment, for example, by providing healthier food and more opportunities for exercise in schools, or supporting organizations such as the Boys & Girls Clubs that provide after-school activities, including sports.[1]

Some of your efforts may encounter not merely obstacles but opposition. For example, if schools have contracts with soft-drink companies to maintain vending machines on the premises, you may need to focus on obtaining a change in practices or policies. To do this, you will plan a strategy: whom to approach—the soft-drink company itself, a school principal, the district superintendent, or the school board—and which arguments and constituencies they will respond to. This requires understanding the countervailing pressures. For example, how important are the schools' economic concerns? Does the soft-drink company support the school football team? It also requires knowing who else might be mobilized (the PTA?) to influence the decision maker.

Before going any further, we should note that there are institutions that have great expertise and tremendous resources to influence the behavior of individuals and policy makers: the corporations that market products to consumers around the world. This is important for two reasons. First, philanthropists can learn a lot from corporate advertising, marketing, and policy campaigns. Second, philanthropists will sometimes find themselves addressing the same issues as corporations—sometimes on the same side and sometimes on the opposite side—on matters ranging from tobacco to guns to healthy foods. Understanding their interests is important to developing your own strategies and tactics.

Changing Individuals' Behavior

More often than not, cultural change lies beyond the purview of philanthropy. But when the conditions are ripe, practices and habits can be swayed. For example, in the "stop AIDS" campaign in the mid-1980s,

HIV-positive gay men conducted small group meetings in San Francisco's Castro neighborhood, teaching techniques of safe sex and asking participants who were willing to commit to practicing safer sex to hold such meetings themselves. Seeking out opinion leaders in the community, the campaign directly involved seven thousand men and indirectly reached another thirty thousand. The rate of unprotected sex and of AIDS declined.[2]

In another instance, a campaign to promote oral rehydration therapy for rural Egyptian children succeeded in reducing infant mortality from diarrhea by 70 percent, in the face of widespread illiteracy, cultural myths about the causes of diarrhea, and the absence of a word for "dehydration." One-minute television "dramas," coupled with cheap and readily available oral rehydration packets, made the difference.[3]

By the same token, a failure to tailor an intervention to deeply held cultural norms may doom the project. That was the case with an effort to induce rural Peruvian families to purify disease-ridden drinking water by boiling it, in a culture that associated warm foods with disease and illness.[4] An effort to provide rural Egyptians with purified tap water, in addition to having poor technology, failed to take account of the social reasons that women congregated on the banks of polluted canals to obtain their water.[5]

Philanthropists planning to operate in a sector where industry has strong interests should be aware of the magnitude of the resources that industry puts into creating demand for its products. Efforts to persuade drivers to purchase fuel-efficient vehicles must overcome hundreds of millions of dollars spent by car manufacturers to promote SUVs. Rather than fight fire with fire and waste your money on an advertising campaign, it's smarter to think of another approach to the problem. If you are on the same side as industry, realize that your power to promote the purchase of hybrids is minuscule compared with what Toyota spends on advertising the Prius. Again, use your philanthropic dollars where they can add the most value.

Sometimes the role of industry is less obvious. Efforts to promote breast feeding among American women—a practice that has great positive health outcomes for babies—face the challenge not only of advertisements for infant formula aimed at expectant mothers but also of free products offered to new mothers in hospitals. Just as tobacco products were marketed as symbols of sexual freedom and desirability, baby formula is marketed as a symbol of wealth, status, freedom, and modernity.

Efforts to promote breast feeding also illustrate the difficulties of changing cultural norms: women who breast-feed in public or in the workplace may face practical obstacles and even hostility. Best for Babes, a tiny not-for-profit organization, is trying to change views of breast feeding as embarrassing or offensive by promoting it as a chic, smart lifestyle choice for healthy, empowered women through celebrity endorsements, image campaigns, and the support of breast-feeding-friendly businesses and restaurants.[6]

Although the odds are often daunting, this does not mean that you cannot affect individual behavior or even contribute to cultural change. But you must pick your battles—and your weapons. Smoking has declined in the United States, through a mixture of public education, litigation, policy change, and factors beyond anyone's control. In recent decades, the United States has seen successful campaigns to reduce littering, drunk driving, teen pregnancy, and methamphetamine use, and to promote dental hygiene and recycling.

As you begin working with grantee organizations to develop and assess strategies for changing behavior, consider these factors:

> *Be clear about your ultimate goals.* "Raising awareness"—even raising awareness among a particular target population—is seldom a goal in itself but merely a possible means of achieving a goal. It may be necessary, but it is seldom sufficient.

> *Identify the target population.* Focus on the target population where you are likely to have the most impact. The messages of the National Campaign to Prevent Teen and Unplanned Pregnancy were directed at boys as well as girls, but the campaign focused particularly on girls because that's where it thought it could make the most difference. In the effort to reduce AIDS in San Francisco, different—and successful— communications strategies were designed for female Thai sex workers in massage parlors and for male Filipinos who hung out in rice bars.[7]

> *Script your message so that it matters to the target population.* In today's media scene, it is very hard to grab anyone's attention. This is especially true of the young audiences whose future patterns of behavior and consumption are being set—because every company in the world is trying to reach them. You need to ask, what messages appeal

to your target audience, and who can deliver them? Can the message be delivered in an essay or does it require a slogan? Should the message be delivered by an earnest-looking professional or a rock star? By the same token, make sure that the content of your message will resonate with your audience. In its effort to reduce teen pregnancy, the National Campaign to Prevent Teen and Unplanned Pregnancy both counseled abstinence and taught about contraception. More recently, the organization has turned its attention to reducing unwanted pregnancies among young adults. From the start, it realized that an abstinence message won't work for this group. Among other things, the campaign is trying to get information about contraception to women who have already had unplanned pregnancies and abortions. Failure to understand one's audience dooms a campaign. For instance, an effort to build support for the United Nations at the time of its founding by running hundreds of radio spot ads and speeches and distributing tens of thousands of pamphlets—all of a highly abstract nature ("The United Nations Begins with You")—had no effect on the Cincinnati, Ohio, residents to whom they were directed.[8]

➤ *Select the right media for your audience.* You won't reach teenagers through full-page ads in the *New York Times*. So perhaps you should try television ads, entertaining mini-dramas, or talk shows. Or perhaps the Internet. If so, where? Through websites laden with substantive information? On blogs? Online communities like MySpace and MoveOn.org? Do you try to get something rolling through viral marketing? Be prepared for some wild experimentation, failures along the way, and, with luck, a runaway success.

➤ *Look for free media.* It is prohibitively expensive to buy the attention of a large audience. You're usually better off trying to get free or so-called earned media in newspapers and journals, on radio and television news and talk shows, and on the Internet. The key to getting free media is having a message that is newsworthy, and then making sure that reporters and other media gatekeepers find the message compelling enough to use. There are firms and nongovernmental organizations that specialize in getting free media for causes. They will sometimes place paid advertisements, but usually only as a stimulus to further free media.

➤ *Co-opt others with similar values or related obligations.* Most important social problems affect a coterie of businesses, not-for-profit

organizations, and government agencies. Although the cigarette industry has been a relentless enemy of health, businesses as well as other
entities can be powerful allies in improving the world. Trojan Brand
Condoms is an ally of efforts to reduce unwanted pregnancy and HIV/
AIDS infections. A number of organic food companies and apparel
manufacturers, and even some hospitals—encouraged by the World
Health Organization and UNICEF's International Baby Friendly
Hospital Initiative[9]—are promoting breast feeding. On the other side,
the manufacturers of infant formula lobbied with some success against
a breast-feeding advertising campaign developed by the Department
of Health and Human Services (HHS). After HHS initiated a toned-
down campaign, the formula industry increased its own advertising
budget in order to counter the agency's "babies were born to be breast-
fed" message.[10]

➤ *Recognize the limits of media.* Everett Rogers notes that although
mass media allow you to reach a large audience rapidly and spread
information, mass media are only suitable for changing weakly held
beliefs. Changing strongly held beliefs or behaviors may require
interpersonal channels.[11] This technique was used with great success
in the efforts to reduce AIDS in San Francisco, as mentioned above.
The very successful Stanford Heart Disease Prevention Program in
the 1970s and 1980s used the mass media to recruit high-risk individuals into small group training sessions on aerobic exercise, nutrition, and smoking cessation.[12] The program tested its messages with
target audiences before implementing the massive program.

Efforts to influence behavior can benefit from the insights of social psychology and behavioral economics. Visit *www.smartphilanthropy.org*.

Changing Deeply Held Ideas

The discussion so far has focused on changing individual behavior and, more
ambitiously, changing cultural norms. Equally if not more ambitious are
efforts to change deeply held ideas and entrenched institutional practices.
The civil rights movement and the women's rights movement are examples
of doing this, with behavioral change significantly induced by legislation.

In Chapter 14, we recount one aspect of the thirty-year attempt by
conservative philanthropists to change Americans' view of the role of
government, a shift from the New Deal's view of government as a benign

Don't Mess with Texas

With the goal of reducing litter on its highways, the Texas Department of Transportation retained an advertising firm that did market research revealing that most Texans did not believe that littering did any harm and believed that the Department of Transportation would clean up after them. Rather than focus on the environment or the cost of cleanup, the firm developed a message that appealed to state pride: "Don't mess with Texas." As a result, litter decreased 72 percent.[13]

regulator and redistributor of entitlements to one that was hostile to government interventions and, to a large extent, hostile to government itself. More recently, we have seen ideological contests between interest groups, some of whose most powerful weapons are the names they give to their causes: the "estate" tax versus the "death" tax; "choice" versus the "right to life," "fetus" versus "unborn baby." The initial battleground for these ideas is the media—mainly unpaid. You will decide for yourself whether the conservatives have had the better ideas. But there is little doubt that they have built the better media machines—through policy think tanks, radio talk shows, speaker series, campus organizations such as the Federalist Society, and the like. This has required focus and patience—the willingness to stick with a set of long-term strategies year in and year out, sometimes with strong allies and sometimes with strong opponents in government office.

The Necessity of Evaluation

Everyone likes to hand out press clippings that show the attention paid to a group or a cause. Being part of the buzz is a thrill, especially for not-for-profit groups that labor in obscurity most of the time. But remember, media coverage is not an end in itself. The goal is to change the behavior of a targeted demographic—and that is fraught with difficulty.

So build evaluation into your outreach strategy. Specify what kind of behavior change you hope to achieve, and spend some time or money identifying clear benchmarks and a way to measure progress toward them. Then run the campaign, and check the numbers. If you get little return, the strategy may just need more time to prove itself. But don't be afraid to shut it down if all the signals are that it is not succeeding.

Changing Public Policy

In many cases, efforts to change individual behavior go hand in hand with efforts to change public policies. For example, a large increase in New York City cigarette taxes contributed to a huge decline in smoking, especially among teens.[14] And the increasingly common bans on smoking in public spaces and workplaces reduce the opportunities to consume. The history of seat belts in the United States is a mixture of education, persuasion, and regulation, with an initial strategy of preventing cars from starting unless the seat belt was buckled being withdrawn after a tremendous backlash, and replaced with annoying signals if the belt is not buckled.[15]

If you seek the adoption of government policies to achieve your ends, you should recognize that policies take many forms, including

- *labeling*, for example, requiring auto manufacturers to put actual miles per gallon on the stickers;
- *incentives*, such as rebates for purchasing hybrids or permitting hybrids in high-occupancy-vehicle (HOV) lanes;
- *government purchasing decisions*, for example, cities deciding to buy hybrids for their fleets; and
- *direct regulations*, such as the federal imposition of higher fleet fuel-economy (CAFE) standards.

The secretary of transportation, in consultation with the administrator of the Environmental Protection Agency (EPA) and the secretary of energy, must issue fuel-economy standards for cars and trucks under an energy law enacted by Congress in 2007. This law gives great flexibility to the transportation secretary on many crucial issues—such as labeling, testing procedures, formulas for fuel consumption, the definition of "non-passenger cars," and strategies for trucks.

Suppose that a philanthropically supported research program at a respectable laboratory demonstrates how fuel economy can be improved for trucks—without trade-offs in performance. In an ideal world, the researchers would brief the agencies' staff members and, after inviting other research studies, the agencies would adopt regulations that responded to the best available science. In our world, the research usually does not suffice. Here are some other factors:

Timing

Asking what makes an idea's time have come, the political scientist John Kingdon notes that for an item to get on a legislature's agenda it must be viewed as a problem, it must be amenable to some plausible policy solutions, and the political forces must be aligned.[16] The 2007 energy legislation was the result of decades of research, coalition building, and advocacy by environmental organizations—persistent and creative policy entrepreneurs, who both awaited and created windows of opportunity. The success of the conservative legal movement manifests these same characteristics.[17]

School vouchers are an example of an idea whose time has not come—at least not yet. From 2002 to 2006, twelve hundred national and regional foundations gave close to $400 million to over one hundred organizations concerned with school choice. The single largest funder was the Walton Family Foundation, whose strategy was to provide scholarships, vouchers, and tax credits to allow the families of poor children to vote with their feet between public and private schools. Its grantmaking included "funding public policy advocacy and parent organizing to build support for public policies that provide school choice; managing and strengthening publicly funded scholarship programs; providing families with clear and useful information about their traditional public, public charter and private school options; and evaluating the performance and effects of large school choice programs."[18] Despite widespread public concerns about the quality of public schools, however, these efforts so far have not produced the state or local funding necessary to bring the voucher movement to scale.

Venues

If it is possible to identify one or two decision makers—the EPA administrator or the transportation secretary—with the maximum influence on an issue, that is where you should focus your advocacy. But most policy decisions involve multiple decision makers, and even when the decision

is formally in the hands of a few people, there are others who can influence their decision one way or the other. Even if the agency heads were
persuaded by your research, they would be constrained by the chairman
of the House Committee on Energy and Commerce and the president,
who, in turn, heed the views of the United Auto Workers and the Big
Three auto manufacturers. So the ideal of the more or less unitary decision maker, guided by policy and informed by science, turns out to be a
cartoon of the more complicated reality.

In fact, achieving the 2007 increases in fuel-efficiency standards
depended on senior military officials worried about the dangers of too
much dependence on oil, religious leaders concerned about despoiling
God's creation, scientists who demonstrated that one could avoid trade-
offs between fuel economy and safety, pollsters who showed that United
Auto Workers' members favored higher standards even if their leadership was reluctant, and many others.

Whether you are aiming at a single administrative official or at members of Congress or a state legislature, here are some considerations to
keep in mind:

➤ *Legality.* The Internal Revenue Code and many state laws regulate
   the use of philanthropic dollars to influence government officials
   and voters. Although they do not prohibit all activities that a layper-
   son would call "lobbying," the regulations put some activities out of
   bounds. Private foundations are especially restricted in what they can
   do. Before proceeding in this realm, get good counsel and make sure
   that your grantees have good counsel as well.[19]

➤ *Clarity of your ask.* Is your message, or the policy "ask," clearly
   articulated and focused? It does no good to generate a huge political
   force for "better education." You need to advocate for (or against)
   specific measures: vouchers, teacher certification, statewide standards, longer school days, whatever.

➤ *Credibility and political weight.* The Hewlett Foundation once
   received a proposal to organize petition drives to ask the Bush
   administration to act seriously to reduce climate change. Apart
   from other problems, the applicant was going to work the campuses
   and streets in Madison, Wisconsin; Boulder, Colorado; and Boston,
   Massachusetts. Not to put too fine a point on it, these were not
   the centers of gravity of the Bush administration's constituencies.

Whether you're circulating petitions or buying a newspaper ad, the point is not that the source be credible to you, the funder, but that it be credible to the target audience.

This last point also suggests that you should consider funding across cultural or ideological boundaries. In designing an initiative to reduce unplanned pregnancies among young adults, the National Campaign to Prevent Teen and Unplanned Pregnancy has drawn on leaders from across the political spectrum, including people who disagree about the morality of abortion and of sex outside of marriage but are concerned about the very high abortion rate among women in their twenties. Look for odd bedfellows.

Related to credibility is whether the group has the political weight to make a difference. We recall one organization supporting renewable energy policy in the Northwest. The decision maker was a public utilities commission—the right choice, because it has a big role in determining the state's energy future and it is required to hear arguments on all sides of an issue and make decisions under clear procedures. Our grantee was sophisticated and technically capable. But when we privately asked some savvy observers of the commission whether the organization was effective, we got a resounding "no." The reasons? There were no political consequences to ignoring this group, but the political consequences of ignoring the utility companies were high. The solution was for our grantee to invite local businesses, academics, politicos, and others to testify alongside its experts, to get op-eds in the paper, to undertake polls showing public support, and to add political weight to its persuasive arguments on the merits of the cause.

Foundations themselves can be sources of credibility and political weight. Both of these factors depend on the foundation's reputation whether in its community or nationwide. Reputations can be built by good works, open-mindedness, and candor. In addition to whatever respect you have gained, political leaders want to meet with you for the same reason everyone else does: they want to influence your contributions. They are happy to offer advice on matters of mutual interest, and even to advise you what might work to influence them. Most foundations do not make the effort to build relations with politicians and policy makers. This is a mistake. You want them to know the foundation not as a lobbyist but as a potential source of impartial research and expert advice.

Your meetings should not be related to planned or pending legislation but concerned with general issues in which you both have an interest.

Grassroots Organizing

Much of the discussion so far has focused on what are called the "grasstops"—decision makers and opinion leaders composed of elected officials, community leaders, and well-organized citizens groups. But campaigns to change regulatory and legislative policy often involve grassroots organizing to reach residents who do not ordinarily participate in government decision making. This was an important aspect of the environmental-justice grantees' work in the Hewlett Foundation's New Constituencies for the Environment initiative described in Chapter 4.

The Association of Community Organizations for Reform Now (ACORN) and the PICO National Network are examples of major national organizations that organize low- and moderate-income families on social-justice issues. ACORN has neighborhood chapters throughout the United States. ACORN members work to improve housing conditions for the economically disadvantaged, secure living wages, and improve the quality of local schools.[20] PICO is a similar national network of faith-based community organizations, working to improve public schools, make neighborhoods safer, increase access to health care, build affordable housing, redevelop communities, and revitalize democracy.[21]

The Role of the Media

We discussed the role of the media earlier. The basic point is that media can affect public opinion and that politicians and administrative officials pay attention to public opinion.

A Campaign Strategy and a Campaign Mentality

A good policy advocacy strategy will be designed with all of this in mind. You and your grantees must have a comprehensive plan for real change, even if the different parts are outwardly unconnected with each other.

Consider a governor who is contemplating approving efficiency standards for home appliances. The strategy might start with a technical report on the energy that can be saved by the policy. It could be complemented by a financial impact report from an economist at the region's premier university. The governor may be prodded toward action by her most trusted colleagues. She will read a series of editorials endorsing the idea in her state's papers. A manufacturer or trade association, ideally in her own state, might express support. The state's senate majority leader will nudge her. Ultimately, the totality of forces will persuade her to adopt the policy.

Winning a major policy victory is not easy. Organizations that can do this are experts in their venues—the places where decisions are made. They understand the whole panoply of forces operating on the decision maker and know when and how to strike, and when to lay off. A philanthropist convinced that advocacy is the most appropriate tool for the task should be alert to these considerations and should look for grantees that show mastery of the venue in question. A campaign mentality and venue mastery—those are the keys.

A Sound Argument on the Merits

Most of the preceding paragraphs focus on wielding political influence, but it is important first to have a good argument on the merits of whatever position you advocate. Most of our political leaders want to do the right thing and—just like the rest of us—are willing to listen to arguments, at least within the bounds of their preexisting values. There are even moments when leaders will make the right decision at the cost of political expediency.

That said, we live in a democracy in which people on all sides of an issue believe their positions have merit. We are blessed with a mature independent sector, with every position fiercely defended by sophisticated advocates. Thus, although good arguments are necessary, they are rarely sufficient to advance your policy objectives. If you want to influence a decision maker, it is helpful also to influence him with potential political gains or losses.

Sausage Making

Politics isn't nice. It can involve nasty tactics, strange bedfellows, and compromises with opponents. Be ready to take heat from your friends when you make a pact with the devil. The prestigious Environmental Defense Fund roundly criticized the National Commission on Energy Policy (NCEP) for agreeing to a "safety valve" on carbon emissions, which NCEP regarded as essential to garnering sufficient support for a mandatory federal cap-and-trade law.[22] Opponents of junk food in public schools have attacked a leading ally, the Center for Science in the Public

Interest, for a compromise with the food industry that would ban selling candy, sugary soda, and salty, fatty food in school snack bars, vending machines, and cafeterias, but allow sales of chocolate milk, sports drinks, and diet soda.[23]

For the role of philanthropy in sponsoring commissions, visit *www .smartphilanthropy.org.*

Changing Corporate Behavior

Whatever issues concern you as a philanthropist, business probably plays a role in helping solve the problem—or sometimes in exacerbating it. If you care about the poor, it is businesses that provide individuals the jobs and opportunities to help escape from poverty. If you care about gun safety, then gun manufacturers can have a major effect—positive or negative—on achieving your goals. The key to stopping global warming ultimately lies in the myriad industries that make and consume energy.

The major tools discussed above—from developing knowledge to policy advocacy—are available to a philanthropist whose goals require changing the behavior of business, whether creating new employment opportunities, installing child-safety locks on firearms, or encouraging greener technologies. Earlier, we discussed the role of philanthropy in spurring innovation and creating new markets. Here we describe two more prescriptive approaches that philanthropists can use to influence business decisions: promoting corporate social responsibility and advocating for regulation.

Promoting Corporate Social Responsibility

The past few decades have seen the growth of the corporate social responsibility (CSR) movement—a capacious term that includes avoiding doing harm and doing affirmative good while simultaneously improving brand image. There are not-for-profit organizations dedicated to promoting CSR from the business school classroom to the corporate boardroom.

For example, the Aspen Institute Center for Business Education seeks to reshape MBA education to include the principles of corporate citizenship and sustainability through CasePlace.org, an online database of case studies, and Beyond Grey Pinstripes, a biennial ranking of business schools that highlights exemplary social and environmental curricula. And for the boardroom, AccountAbility and TransFair USA have developed certification procedures to identify and encourage good corporate behavior in sustainable development and fair trade practices, respectively.[24]

AccountAbility works to foster what it calls "responsible competitiveness," in which businesses adopt good health, safety, employment, social, and environmental practices as a result of market forces. Among its projects are the MFA Forum, which promotes responsible competitiveness in the apparel sector, and the AA1000 Framework, which sets standards for social and ethical accounting, auditing, and reporting. TransFair works with large well-known businesses from Starbucks and Tully's Coffee to Safeway and Trader Joe's. Through its unique brand and certification process, TransFair provides companies an opportunity to market and sell Fair Trade Certified products while ensuring that farmers get compensated reasonably.

Corporate Campaigns

Like much of human behavior, good corporate behavior reflects a mixture of voluntary decision making and external pressure.

Shareholders can attempt to influence corporate behavior through corporate campaigns and proxy voting. In Chapter 8, we discussed negative screens—disinvesting—as a means of influencing corporate behavior, expressing some skepticism about their value and suggesting that in any event they were unlikely to be effective apart from a concerted corporate campaign. Voting proxies, of course, requires that you not dispose of your entire holding. You must own shares of the company to vote for change.[25]

It is useful to distinguish between shareholder activism, which furthers shareholder value, and social activism, which furthers social or moral values (and which may correlate positively, negatively, or not at all with shareholder value).[26] The pursuit of corporate-governance reforms by the California Public Employees' Retirement System (CalPERS) exemplifies shareholder activism. Every year, CalPERS publishes a focus list that targets companies for corporate-governance reform,[27] and many listed companies adopt reforms such as separating the board chair and CEO positions, requiring that a majority of directors be independent, and performing annual evaluations of the CEO.[28] Some studies suggest that improved governance practices significantly improve shareholder returns.[29]

An increasing number of proposals go beyond corporate governance to encompass broader matters of corporate social responsibility. The As You Sow Foundation notes that investors "increasingly seek disclosure of a company's social and environmental practices in the belief that they impact shareholder value. Sustainability proposals are always among the highest vote getters of social issues."[30] These proposals often ask companies to report on the social, economic, and environmental impacts of their operations by adopting the Global Reporting Initiative standard developed by Ceres, an organization that integrates sustainable development into capital markets.

In other examples of social activism unrelated to, and sometimes in tension with, shareholder value, People for the Ethical Treatment of Animals (PETA) filed 24 proposals in 2007 pressing for more-humane slaughter methods and improved living conditions for animals used in laboratory testing.[31] The Interfaith Center on Corporate Responsibility filed 327 shareholder resolutions on such diverse issues as human rights in China and foreign sales of military equipment to Indonesia.[32]

Shareholder initiatives are sometimes connected to more aggressive corporate campaigns, like the decade-long successful effort to induce universities and other institutional investors to divest from companies doing business with the apartheid regime in South Africa. The energy provided by student protests was coordinated and channeled by several organizations, including the American Committee on Africa and the Interfaith Center on Corporate Responsibility.

A massive campaign was launched against Nike in the 1990s, focusing on poor working conditions in the manufacturing plants for its apparel. As the cost of the boycotts and protests became higher and higher, improving the working conditions in its factories became financially more attractive to the company. Hannah Jones, Nike's vice president of corporate responsibility, explained:

> We were one of the first brands to be targeted by NGOs in their effort to raise public awareness around these issues. It required us to focus on risk management and reputation management because that's what was under fire. It has been a huge change for Nike to go from that early era of firefighting to our current approach of engaging with external stakeholders in dialogue, consensus, and sometimes on-the-ground partnerships with even our harshest critics. It was through opening up the company and listening, learning, and engaging that we began to see how the social

and environmental issues involved challenges way beyond Nike. And it became clear that the only way to solve those problems was through multi-stakeholder partnerships.[33]

Of course, many efforts to change corporate practices do not succeed. The success of the antiapartheid movement is balanced by the failure of protests against the Dow Chemical Company to stop manufacturing napalm during the war in Vietnam. PETA has yet to succeed in its campaign to get Kentucky Fried Chicken to change its methods of chicken farming. The Southern Baptist Convention called off an eight-year boycott of the Walt Disney Company for providing health benefits to employees' same-sex partners. (Although Disney has not changed its policies, the convention announced that it had "communicated effectively our displeasure" and that a boycott "must be specifically targeted and of limited duration."[34]) Wal-Mart has been the target of a campaign with multiple demands, including establishing a living wage, providing affordable health care, and forbidding its suppliers in developing countries to employ child labor. The fact that the campaign has so many disparate goals and the fact that Wal-Mart customers, unlike the consumers of brand-name apparel, tend to be almost single-mindedly interested in value at low prices, may turn out to be barriers.

Boycotts are rarely a first option. As in most efforts to change other people's minds and actions, it usually pays to seek win-win solutions, and only turn to coercion when collaboration fails. A campaign to change corporate behavior requires the same strategic and tactical considerations as policy advocacy. This includes knowing the relevant venues and decision makers, enlisting the media, ensuring that your grantees have the skills to negotiate, having the power to turn up the heat if negotiation doesn't work, and deciding in advance under what circumstances to call off a boycott. Most corporations have a crisis-management group to handle the media when a refinery blows up or a product proves toxic or batteries melt in laptops. A boycott will get the attention of that group, so if you go down this road you should be prepared for a hard-hitting and sophisticated response.

Regulating Business

In a perfect world, the free market would produce everything that society wanted without harming anyone. But in the real world, markets are imperfect. Businesses that engage in free-market competition generate pollution, employ people in poor working conditions, and don't always make safe or reliable products. Thus, to correct what are considered "market failures," traditional political theory argues that the state should step in and change the behavior of business.

Governments play a large role in shaping business behavior. Regulations govern U.S. businesses' labor and employment practices, workplace and product safety, environmental impacts, and competitive practices, to name just a few areas. Philanthropy has supported organizations—from the Natural Resources Defense Council to the American Enterprise Institute and the Heritage Foundation to the Milken Institute—that promote or oppose governmental oversight in all of these realms.

IT IS WORTH emphasizing that there is nothing anticapitalist about advocating policies to improve business practices. Indeed, such advocacy is the corollary of the edict of the great free-market economist Milton Friedman that businesses should focus exclusively on increasing shareholder value.[35] Although not every business responds only to profit, when a business does, the only way to prevent that business from engaging in harmful behavior that is not already reflected in the bottom line is to create regulatory or other pressures to make it felt there.

For a case study of the Packard Foundation's Campaign to protect the world's ocean ecosystems, visit *www.smartphilanthropy.org*.

Ensuring That Laws Are Enforced: Watchdog Groups and Litigation

In a perfect world, enacted policies would be diligently pursued and their consequences tracked for future refinement. In our world, government agencies are often overwhelmed with other work and are sometimes even hostile to legislative directives. Not-for-profit groups play an important role not just in shaping policies but also in ensuring their implementation.

Watchdog Groups
The Office of Management and Budget (OMB) in the White House is among the most powerful agencies in the country. All major regulations

filter through this office, and it has oversight and influence over the entire federal budget. The OMB is where the president puts the detail into the operations of the government. For the most part, this powerful agency operates with little oversight. So in 1983, the not-for-profit organization OMB Watch was established to shed light on the OMB's veiled operations. OMB Watch analysts take apart the federal budget; its staff monitors the regulatory process, reviews the qualifications of appointees, and generally opens a window into this vital agency. The quality and focus of the work of OMB Watch has made it a must-have information source for Congress, especially for members of oversight committees.

The Center on Budget and Policy Priorities (CBPP) lies somewhere between a provider of applied knowledge and a watchdog group. Founded in 1981 with support from the Field Foundation,[36] the CBPP conducts and disseminates research and analysis to inform public debates over proposed budget and tax policies—with a particular concern to ensure that the needs of low-income Americans are considered in these debates.[37] The CBPP has been at the forefront of advancing fiscally responsible budget and tax policies at both the national and state levels and has contributed to important policy gains for low-income families in areas ranging from food stamps to health programs. As federal programs were devolved to the states in the 1990s, the CBPP's work expanded to include work at the state level.[38] It trains local partners to provide information and technical assistance to not-for-profit organizations and state government officials on issues ranging from state budget priorities and revenue structures to the design and implementation of low-income programs. The CBPP posts the results of its research on its website, which gets more than one million hits each month. It was recognized in a 1998 Aspen Institute survey of members of Congress and administration officials as the single most influential not-for-profit organization on federal budget policy.[39]

Litigation

Litigation is unpleasant, expensive, and time consuming. In most cases, it is a last resort. But the judiciary is part and parcel of the system of governance, and if agencies, individuals, or corporations are abusing the laws, then litigation—or the threat of it—may be the only recourse. Litigation is often used together with other tools. Although many of the gains of the civil rights movement were due to grassroots protests, direct action, and legislative advocacy, litigation, beginning even earlier than *Brown v. Board of Education*, was essential to the movement's victories, as it has been in establishing basic rights in other areas—gender equity, fair election practices, proper prison conditions, and so on.

Litigation has again proved invaluable in the contemporary environmental movement: consider the case against the U.S. Environmental Protection Agency to force it to regulate greenhouse-gas emissions, and the suit brought by automobile manufacturers to void California's car-emissions standards. In both cases, organizations including the Natural Resources Defense Council, the Environmental Defense Fund, and the Sierra Club played a key role in defending environmental standards.

Because the success of litigation depends on the law as well as the facts of particular cases, we make only a few general points here. Ensure that your grantees are qualified to take on the case and that they have the resources to do a first-rate job and see it through to the end—which may involve appeals and remands. Where possible, get pro bono assistance from the best law firms.

And don't forget that even when the court of law is the selected venue, the court of public opinion matters too. Filing the case is sometimes as productive as a decision or settlement. In the 1980s, a group of attorneys, appalled at the jailing of children together with adult prisoners in California county jails, filed a half-dozen lawsuits, all on the same day, in different urban and rural districts, with the different cases presenting dramatic examples of why these practices should be outlawed (for example, suicide, sodomy). The effort was carefully designed to create enormous media interest, with "cookie cutter" press kits. There were state and national news stories because of the breadth of the action, and local stories because of the local cases. The goal of the litigation was both to end unconscionable practices and to prompt the creation of new laws, courts, and separate penal facilities for children so that they would no longer be subject to the abuses of the adult system. In the end, the public-relations battle, which inspired a complete legislative reform in dealing with youthful offenders, was more important than the outcome of the litigation.

Pride and Prejudice: A Final Word on Tools

Many foundation guidelines proscribe support for certain tools. Trustees worry that research will result in tomes gathering dust in a distant library, or they are uncomfortable with legislative advocacy or litigation. Every possible tool has its adherents and its detractors.

No car mechanic would exclude a Phillips screwdriver from his tool chest. Nor should you handicap yourself by refusing to use the tools available to philanthropy.

Of course, some foundations may have both a preference for certain modes of action and the expertise to pursue them. This can work, as long as they collaborate with others that undertake related and complementary actions. Don't let internal guidelines keep you from achieving your goals. The world offers tough enough obstacles for reform—you don't need to add your own.

Takeaway Points

➤ When seeking to influence the behavior of individuals, identify the population where your message can have the greatest impact, design your message so that it speaks to that population, and use the media that will reach it.

➤ When seeking to influence the behavior of policy makers, identify the individuals who can change policy and script your message to them and to those who can influence them. Be aware that federal and state laws regulate foundations' and not-for-profit organizations' efforts to influence government officials and voters.

➤ You can influence the behavior of corporations through incentives and cooperation, by mobilizing consumers and investors, and by advocating for regulations.

Chapter Notes

1. See RWJF Healthy Schools Program.

2. Everett M. Rogers, *Diffusion of Innovations*, 4th ed. (New York: Free Press, 1995), 72–73.

3. Ibid., 380.

4. Ibid., 1–5.

5. Ibid., 107–109.

6. Best for Babes, http://www.bestforbabes.com (accessed June 30, 2008).

7. Rogers, *Diffusion of Innovations*, 366.

8. Also, it did not ask the recipients of the message to engage in any specific behavior. Ibid., 377–378.

9. Barbara L. Philipp et al., 2001. "Baby-Friendly Hospital Initiative Improves Breastfeeding Initiation Rates in a US Hospital Setting," *Pediatrics* 108, no. 3 (2001): 677–681, http://pediatrics.aappublications.org/cgi/reprint/108/3/677 .pdf; see also New York City Health and Hospitals Corporation, "NYC Public Hospitals Eliminate Baby Formula Giveaways, Ban Promo Materials in Labor Units to Encourage Breastfeeding," news release, July 31, 2007, http://www.nyc .gov/html/hhc/html/pressroom/press-release-20070731.shtml.

10. Mark Kaufmann and Christopher Lee, "HHS Toned Down Breast-Feeding Ads," *Washington Post*, August 31, 2007.

11. Rogers, *Diffusion of Innovations*, 205.

12. Ibid., 235–236.

13. *Wikipedia*, s.v. "Don't Mess with Texas," http://en.wikipedia.org/wiki/ Don%27t_Mess_with_Texas.

14. Joseph Califano, *High Society: How Substance Abuse Ravages America and What to Do About It* (New York: Public Affairs, 2007).

15. Even with all of this, and with penalties for not buckling up, a quarter of Americans drive without seat belts. Rogers, *Diffusion of Innovations*, 235.

16. John W. Kingdon, *Agendas, Alternatives, and Public Policies* (New York: Addison-Wesley, 2006).

17. Steven M. Teles, *The Rise of the Conservative Legal Movement: The Battle for Control of the Law* (Princeton, N.J.: Princeton University Press, 2008).

18. Rick Cohen, *Strategic Grantmaking: Foundations and the School Privatization Movement* (Washington, D.C.: National Committee for Responsive Philanthropy, 2007), http://www.ncrp.org/downloads/NCRP2007-StrategicGrantmaking-FINAL-LowRes.pdf.

19. There are both federal restrictions and state disclosure requirements on lobbying as variously defined. The restrictions depend on what type of organization is doing or funding the lobbying, and the disclosure requirements depend on the type of government agency that is being lobbied. Many of the kinds of activities you might want to engage in or fund—such as supporting impartial research distributed to the public and to decision makers, or working with administrative agencies to design the most effective regulations to carry out a legislative directive—are almost always permissible. Again, consult with your counsel. Although foundations cannot engage in direct lobbying and public charities may do so only to a limited extent, individual philanthropists who are willing to forgo tax deductions can put funds into 501(c)(4) and 527 organizations and political action committees.

20. ACORN, "About ACORN," http://www.acorn.org (accessed June 30, 2008).

21. PICO National Network, "About PICO," http://www.piconetwork.org/ aboutpico.html (accessed June 30, 2008).

22. Environmental Defense Fund, "Why Safety Valves Are Very Dangerous," http://www.environmentaldefense.org/page.cfm?tagID=1087 (accessed June 30, 2008).

23. Kim Severson, "Effort to Limit Junk Food in Schools Faces Hurdles," *New York Times*, December 2, 2007.

24. AccountAbility, http://www.accountability21.net (accessed June 30, 2008); TransFair USA, http://www.transfairusa.org (accessed June 30, 2008).

25. To file shareholder resolutions and other proposals on corporate governance and social and environmental issues, you must be a shareholder who owns at least $2,000 worth of company stock and must have held the stock for at least one year prior to the annual filing deadline. Rockefeller Philanthropy Advisors and As You Sow Foundation, *Unlocking the Power of Proxy: How Active Foundation Proxy Voting Can Protect Endowments and Boost Philanthropic Missions* (Rockefeller Philanthropy Advisors, 2004), 30, http://www.asyousow.org/publications/powerproxy.pdf.

26. Brad M. Barber, "Monitoring the Monitor: Evaluating CalPERS' Activism" (working paper, University of California, Davis, 2006), 10, http://papers.ssrn.com/sol3/papers.cfm?abstract_id=890321.

27. For example, in 2008, CalPERS included Cheesecake Factory Inc., Hilb Rogal & Hobbs Company, Invacare Corporation, La-Z-Boy, and Standard Pacific Corporation on its focus list.

28. CalPERS, "Reform Focus List Companies," http://www.calpers-governance.org/alert/focus (accessed July 1, 2008).

29. Barber, "Monitoring the Monitor," 10.

30. As You Sow Foundation, *Proxy Season Preview Spring 2007: Helping Foundations Align Mission and Investment,* http://rockpa.org/wp-content/uploads/2007/04/2007-proxy-season-preview.pdf, 10.

31. As You Sow Foundation and Rockefeller Philanthropy Advisors, *2007 Proxy Season Preview: Helping Foundations Align Mission and Investment* (San Francisco: As You Sow, 2007), http://www.asyousow.org/publications/2007_proxy_preview.pdf.

32. Interfaith Center on Corporate Responsibility, "ICCR Resolutions Filed Between Fall 2006 and Spring 2007," http://www.iccr.org/shareholder/proxy_book07/07statuschart.php (accessed June 30, 2008).

33. "15 Minutes with Hannah Jones," *Stanford Social Innovation Review*, Fall 2007, 29–31, http://www.ssireview.org/articles/entry/15_minutes_with_hannah_jones.

34. Alex Johnson, "Southern Baptists End 8-Year Disney Boycott," MSNBC, June 22, 2005, http://www.msnbc.msn.com/id/8318263.

35. Milton Friedman, "The Social Responsibility of Business Is to Increase Its Profits," *New York Times Magazine*, September 13, 1970.

36. The Field Foundation, which provided support to organizations promoting civil rights, civil liberties, and child welfare and to other groups and individuals working for social change, closed in 1998. For its archives, see http://www.lib .utexas.edu/taro/utcah/00091/cah-00091.html (accessed July 1, 2008).

37. Leslie R. Crutchfield and Heather McLeod Grant, *Forces for Good: The Six Practices of High-Impact Nonprofits* (San Francisco: Jossey-Bass, 2008): 257.

38. Ibid.

39. Center on Budget and Policy Priorities, "What Is the Center on Budget & Policy Priorities?" http://www.cbpp.org/info.html (accessed January 3, 2007).

Chapter *Fourteen*

Building Fields and Movements

I N CHAPTER 12, we discussed how philanthropists could help start, strengthen, and scale up particular organizations. Here we consider the role of philanthropy in building entire fields and supporting social movements—an undertaking that makes use of the various tools discussed in the preceding chapters. We use the term "field" to refer to a common set of issues, theories, and practices in which theorists and practitioners share a vocabulary, a set of norms, values, and basic texts. Fields range from medicine and law to education, human rights, and arguably philanthropy itself.[1]

Building fields and social movements may require supporting existing institutions or establishing new ones. It may, in fact, require creating organizations that will serve as the keelson of the field's or the movement's infrastructure. It may call for convening meetings, supporting research and communications, and engaging in policy advocacy.

The Innovation Curve: Goals, Grants, and Strategies in the Early and Later Stages of Fields and Movements

Field building and social change are difficult tasks and can take decades to accomplish. At the beginning, the theories and strategies may be unclear and untested; organizations' missions, and even their particular goals, may be fluid.

The trajectory of building fields and movements is captured by the "innovation curve," which was originally intended to describe the development

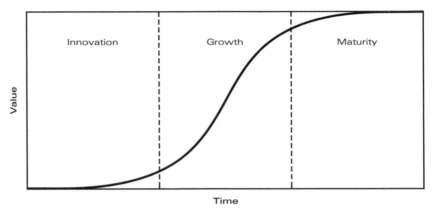

Innovation Curve

and diffusion of technological products.[2] This S-shaped curve is divided into three phases: innovation, growth, and maturity.

Most philanthropic programs tackling serious social or environmental problems aim toward maturity—to "go to scale"—whether the ultimate mechanism is market adoption, changing social mores, or changing policy. Thus, understanding where you are on the curve can help you think about how to direct money, what kind of results to expect, and what to do when a field or strategy matures.

1. *Innovation.* The innovation phase is a time for formulating goals, forming and testing hypotheses about social or scientific approaches to problems, and testing new strategies and policies. The innovation phase often calls for a broad set of grants, since many ideas must be tested to find some that work. It is crucial to look for limitations in the ideas that could inhibit later growth. Because testing is central to innovation, foundations should also be prepared to spend more on evaluation than in other phases.

2. *Growth and adoption.* In the growth phase, philanthropists want to "lock-in" successful strategies and look for ways to go to scale. Grants in this phase tend to be larger and more specific than in the innovation phase. Efforts to change social mores will target influential decision makers or grassroots populations. Efforts to promote changes in government or corporate policies might look more like campaigns—with message development, training of spokespeople,

venue analysis, elite education, and so on. Efforts to promote a market strategy might resemble a company's product rollout, with market assessments, advertisements, and the collection of customer acquisition and cost-of-sales data. Efforts to obtain philanthropic or government support tend to employ demonstration projects to show feasibility.

3. *Maturity.* At this point, an innovation takes hold and becomes sustainable without your support. This may happen through

   ➤ *changed social norms and mores*, for example, recycling waste becomes cool or teen pregnancy becomes uncool;
   ➤ *market adoption*, for example, contraceptives for family planning or preventing HIV/AIDS are distributed through markets in developing countries;
   ➤ *government policy and support*, for example, governments promote family planning or fund after-school programs;
   ➤ *sustainable philanthropic support*, for example, individual philanthropists subsidize after-school programs; or
   ➤ *corporate practices*, for example, businesses promote fair-trade coffee and wood products from sustainable forestry.

There may be many innovation cycles for each idea or policy that gets to the growth phase, and the growth phase itself may have a number of starts and stops, and may sometimes flatline early. What seemed like "maturity" may take a big dip, requiring a completely new cycle. Although reality is inevitably complicated, the innovation curve provides a valuable heuristic for thinking about philanthropic efforts to build fields and social movements.

Examples of Philanthropy's Role in Building Fields and Movements

Here are four examples where philanthropy has played an important role in developing fields and movements.

Care for the Dying

Modern efforts to care for the dying in the United States were initially supported by the Commonwealth Fund, a health-care foundation established in 1918. The roots of the movement lie in St. Christopher's

Hospice, founded by the English physician Cicely Saunders in 1967.[3] Offering both in-patient and home care for the dying and bereavement support for families, St. Christopher's core tenets included generous control of symptoms, attention to patients' psychological and spiritual needs, and care and support for patients' families.[4]

Florence Wald, dean of the Yale School of Nursing, learned of Dr. Saunders' pioneering work. Together with colleagues from the schools of medicine and divinity, she conducted a two-year study of American facilities that cared for the dying.[5] Wald resigned from the deanship in 1968 to support the growth of the hospice model nationwide.[6]

In 1973, the Commonwealth Fund made a small grant to Wald and her colleagues to study the feasibility of establishing the first modern hospice in the United States. With support from the Commonwealth Fund, the Ittleson Foundation, and the van Ameringen Foundation, Hospice Incorporated opened its doors one year later in Branford, Connecticut, both serving patients and acting as a clearinghouse for information on hospice care.[7] Program staff of the Commonwealth Fund also helped Hospice Inc. secure a $1.5 million grant from the National Cancer Institute.[8] Wald remains a leader in expanding the compassionate care of the dying, and has worked to bring hospice care to prison settings.[9]

The hospice-care movement has been complemented by other efforts to improve the quality of care for the dying. The Commonwealth Fund, in collaboration with the Nathan Cummings Foundation, has supported research on the "end of life."[10] Since 1989, the Robert Wood Johnson Foundation has given over $148 million to programs seeking to improve end-of-life and palliative care through professional education, institutional change, and public engagement. Among other things, it commissioned a PBS documentary series by Bill Moyers titled *On Our Own Terms*, that followed the stories of several people coping with impending death.[11] The Open Society Institute has funded medical-school faculty's research and training in end-of-life care.[12]

Though many Americans remain uncomfortable with their own mortality, the hospice movement has significantly altered the health-care landscape and provided comfort to many people in their last days and to their families. Although foundations continue to support research in this realm, it has largely reached the "maturity" stage of the innovation curve.

The foundations were agile in the forms of philanthropic support that were necessary to achieve their objectives—support for research, education, communication, organizations, and programs—and also used their networks and convening power to help build the field and movement. The story is one of funders' collaborating to support both social entrepreneurs and institutions.

The Women's Rights Movement

The foundations that supported the development of the end-of-life field typically made project-support grants to a relatively small number of grantees. By contrast, much of the support for the women's rights movement was in the form of general operating support grants to a broad array of organizations. As the Commonwealth Fund led the end-of-life work, so did the Ford Foundation play a major sustaining role in the women's movement, beginning in the 1970s. Susan Berresford, who retired as president of the Ford Foundation at the beginning of 2008, writes:

> In the early 1970's, representatives of the women's movement approached the Foundation's president, McGeorge Bundy, and the program vice presidents to argue that since Ford had been very supportive of the civil rights movement, it ought to be doing the same for women. Soon after, we began to explore what a women's program would look like.
>
> As the program gained momentum in the 1970's, it focused on promoting educational equity, supporting research in the new field called "women's studies" and increasing earning opportunities for women in the United States. We funded groups concerned with women's pay and entry into formerly all male jobs, girls' education and participation in sports, and women in the country's political life. We supported research, public discussion and litigation, some of which reached the Supreme Court. The Foundation made sizable, long-term commitments enabling a number of national and local organizations to challenge discrimination and to build a body of law, policy and practice to protect women's opportunities.[13]

As the movement developed, the Ford Foundation added grantmaking for women's reproductive health, work and family issues, and violence against women. Despite continuing challenges, the American women's movement has reached the maturity phase. In a sense, it reached maturity within the Ford Foundation itself when during a grant-review meeting a program officer raised an issue about women and a colleague responded by saying, "Well, that's taken care of in the women's program." Franklin Thomas, then president of the foundation, disagreed, saying, "We're *all* responsible for this." "From then on," Susan Berresford notes, "the message was clear: grantmaking officers would be expected to consider gender and ask whether it was an important factor in the problems each program addressed. With that decision, we moved beyond having a women-specific grant portfolio to placing a feminist lens over much of the Foundation's work."[14]

The Economic Analysis of Law and the Conservative Legal Movement

The rise of the modern conservative legal movement has achieved an almost mythical status, in no small part because progressive commentators have used the story to goad liberals to follow its example.[15] As we note later, the story involves less strategic planning than one might imagine.[16] First, though, we will recount one important aspect of the movement: the John M. Olin Foundation's contribution to building the field of economic analysis of the law.[17]

The law and economics movement built on the neoclassical economic tradition and on the work of scholars—most of them at the University of Chicago—such as Ronald Coase, Aaron Director, Guido Calabresi, and Richard Posner. Its main evangelist was Chicago-trained law professor Henry Manne, who had established a summer institute for law professors—colloquially named "Pareto in the Pines" for the Italian economist Vilfredo Pareto and the program's sylvan locale.

The Olin Foundation built a long-term relationship with Professor Manne. It supported the summer program, which expanded to include hundreds of state and federal judges. The foundation established the Law and Economics Center at the University of Miami, where Manne taught, and then a center at George Mason University School of Law when he moved there to become its dean.

By the end of the 1970s, the Olin Foundation's trustees recognized that, although the foundation was supporting "decent schools," the schools were "not academically respectable in terms of influence on public policy" and made "little or no difference in the hearts and minds of Americans as regards attitudes toward free enterprise."[18] Therefore, the foundation sought to establish programs at elite universities. The dean of Harvard Law School, which then was in a pitched battle between mainstream and left-leaning "critical legal" scholars, welcomed an Olin Foundation program in the mid-1980s. Within a decade, the foundation had established programs and named professorships at the University of Chicago, Georgetown University, Stanford University, the University of Virginia, and Yale University. Their faculty have written influential books and articles—often but not inevitably emphasizing the importance of property rights and the dangers of regulation. To facilitate the rising academic interest in the subject, the foundation funded the American Law and Economics Association.

Although the Olin Foundation would not have supported a program whose director was not generally sympathetic to its free-enterprise goals, it did not attempt to micromanage the programs and it provided them with sustained general support. Over a thirty-year period the foundation devoted $68 million to the promotion of law and economics. Not all the programs were successful, but the foundation stuck with those that were. When it closed its doors at the beginning of the twenty-first century, the foundation made $21 million in grants to its anchor institutions.

With the Olin Foundation's support, the economic analysis of law became a dominant paradigm in the legal academy and, to a considerable extent, in legal and policy communities beyond academia. In the words of the prominent liberal legal scholar Bruce Ackerman, law and economics was "the most important thing in legal education since the birth of the Harvard Law School."[19] And the conservative journalist John Miller wrote:

> As the law and economics movement matured, many of its adherents took positions in the government and won nominations to the federal bench. The notion that laws should be analyzed not just for their fairness but for their economic consequences began to spread. . . . Law and economics was also crucial in the drive for deregulation as well as the recent belief that new regulations should not be imposed without first considering a cost/benefit analysis.[20]

In recent years, the law and economics paradigm has been challenged by research in behavioral economics.[21] But for the foreseeable future, many federal judges and policy makers will reflect the values promoted by the John M. Olin Foundation.

In *The Rise of the Conservative Legal Movement*, Steven Teles puts the economic analysis of law in the broader context of the conservative legal movement, supported by a number of foundations besides the Olin

Foundation, as well as by individual philanthropists. He concludes with some observations relevant not only to field building but to the broader themes of this book:

> The lessons of the first generation of conservative public interest law show that the movement went through a very long period of almost complete organizational failure. . . . While the conservative movement has had its very considerable strengths, it was never a monolith, often made serious errors, and succeeded by shrewd adaptation rather than by the far-sighted pursuit of a grand plan.
>
> The history of the conservative legal movement suggests that successful political patrons engage in spread betting combined with feedback and learning, rather than expecting too much from grand planning. Conservatives' learning and feedback did not, however, involve using narrow, technical forms of evaluation. Conservative patrons were willing to accept fairly diffuse, hard-to-measure goals with long-term payoffs when they had faith in the new individuals behind the projects. . . . Conservative patrons were typically quite close to the entrepreneurs they funded and depended on their own subjective evaluation of both a given entrepreneur's effectiveness and the information that flowed through trusted movement networks—rather than on "objective" measures of outcomes.[22]

Teles notes that this approach went "against the grain of much of contemporary philanthropy, which emphasizes rigorous, usually quantitative, evaluative measurement."[23] This is an acute observation, but it is worth noting that different philanthropic objectives call for different approaches. Social movements are fundamentally different from, say, the provision of subsidized goods and services and targeted advocacy campaigns. Moreover, strategic flexibility and "spread-betting" (to use Teles' evocative term) are particularly appropriate in early phases of the innovation curve, which call for broadly exploratory grantmaking.

Teles makes another point about the conservative legal movement that is relevant to virtually all social movements:

> Legal conservatives became more effective by challenging, and ultimately changing, their ideas. Decades of debate in Federalist Society conferences and within the network of conservative scholars led to jettisoning the concepts

of judicial restraint and strict constructionism. . . . Conservatives . . . were willing to carve out enough space from the movement's old categories, commitments, and constituencies to allow serious intellectual discussion and argumentation, leading to a reconsideration of ideas, strategies, and alliances.[24]

To some extent this is an artifact of the central role of scholars in the movement. But it reflects something more fundamental. In discussing the goals of individual philanthropists in Chapter 2, we mentioned the "indeterminacy of aim" that is inevitable in all human affairs. The indeterminacy is all the greater when many actors are involved in a social movement. This was true in the women's rights movement and in the civil rights movement several decades earlier, where there was considerable fluidity and disagreement about whether the goal was equal treatment or equal outcomes, disparate treatment, disparate impact, or affirmative action as well. Goals were reassessed and clarified over time; organizations split, sometimes irreparably, over these issues.

The Population Field at the Beginning of the Twenty-First Century

Goals may be particularly fluid in the early stages of movements, but the "maturity" phase on the innovation curve may turn out to be the beginning of yet another cycle with revised goals. The population movement, to which philanthropy has contributed significantly, provides a good example.

After decades of family planning and the stabilization of global population growth in the second half of the twentieth century, a reaction against so-called population control—some aspects of which had been highly intrusive and coercive[25]—found its voice at the 1994 U.N. International Conference on Population and Development in Cairo. Even though sub-Saharan Africa and much of Asia were experiencing unsustainable growth, the agenda moved from curtailing population growth toward women's rights.

The Rockefeller and Ford foundations, which had been pioneers in the movement, abandoned the field or switched entirely to a rights focus. A few other foundations, including the Hewlett, MacArthur, and Packard foundations, continued to support family planning, though with muted articulation of the population rationale. Perhaps because of increasing evidence of the detrimental effects of overpopulation on economic growth and family income, population growth may again be emerging as a legitimate philanthropic concern—but with a pervasive concern for women's autonomy and health that was absent throughout much of the twentieth century. For an example of the Hewlett Foundation's efforts to build the field of conflict resolution, visit *www.smartphilanthropy.org.*

Takeaway Points

Building fields and movements follows the three stages of the innovation curve:

➤ The innovation phase often calls for many small grants to test new ideas and organizations.

➤ The growth-and-adoption phase calls for locking in successful strategies and looking for ways to go to scale.

➤ As a strategy reaches the maturity phase, be alert to whether it continues to have significant impact or whether the social returns have begun to decline.

Chapter Notes

1. See Phil Cubeta, "Philanthropy as a Field of Practice," posting to the blog Gift Hub: Blogging on Philanthropy, November 23, 2005, http://www.gifthub.org/2005/11/philanthropy_as.html; and Howard Gardner, Mihaly Csikszentmihalyi, and William Damon, *Good Work: When Excellence and Ethics Meet* (New York: Basic Books, 2001).

2. See Everett M. Rogers, *Diffusion of Innovations*, 5th ed. (New York: Free Press, 2003).

3. For more information on St. Christopher's Hospice, see its website, at http://www.stchristophers.org.uk/.

4. American RadioWorks, "The Hospice Experiment: A Revolution in Dying," http://americanradioworks.publicradio.org/features/hospice/a4.html (accessed June 30, 2008).

5. J. Scott Kohler, "Hospice Care Movement," in *Casebook for The Foundation: A Great American Secret*, by Joel L. Fleishman, J. Scott Kohler, and Steven Schindler (New York: Public Affairs, 2007), 126.

6. Harvey Cushing/John Hay Whitney Medical Library, Yale University School of Medicine, "End of Life Resource: Biographies of Florence Wald and Catherine Kennedy," http://www.med.yale.edu/library/reference/endoflife/biogs.html (accessed June 30, 2008).

7. Kohler, "Hospice Care Movement," 7.

8. Ibid.

9. Yale University School of Nursing, "Past Yale School of Nursing Dean and Leader in Research Awarded Title of 'Living Legend' by the American Academy of Nursing," news release, October 25, 2001, http://nursing.yale.edu/News/Press/72.

10. For more information, see the Commonwealth Fund website, at www.commonwealthfund.org.

11. J. Scott Kohler, "Care at the End of Life," in *Casebook for The Foundation* (see note 11), 199–200.

12. Ibid., 199.

13. Susan V. Berresford, "Women's Rights, Women's Lives," in "Now It's a Global Movement: A Special Issue on Women," Ford Foundation Report, Winter 2000, 4, http://www.fordfound.org/pdfs/impact/ford_reports_winter_2000.pdf.

14. Ibid., 4–5.

15. See Sally Covington, *Moving a Public Policy Agenda: The Strategic Philanthropy of Conservative Foundations* (Washington, D.C.: National Committee on Responsive Philanthropy, 1997).

16. Steven M. Teles, *The Rise of the Conservative Legal Movement: The Battle for Control of the Law* (Princeton, N.J.: Princeton University Press, 2008).

17. See generally ibid.; John J. Miller, *A Gift of Freedom: How the John M. Olin Foundation Changed America* (San Francisco: Encounter Books, 2006), chap. 4.

18. Miller, *A Gift of Freedom*, 74.

19. Ibid., 70 (quoting Bruce Ackerman).

20. Ibid., 71.

21. Paul Brest, "Amos Tversky's Contributions to Legal Scholarship: Remarks at the BDRM Session in Honor of Amos Tversky, June 16, 2006," *Judgment and Decision Making* 1 (2006): 174–178, http://journal.sjdm.org/jdm06125.pdf.

22. Teles, *The Rise of the Conservative Legal Movement*, 276–279.

23. Ibid., 297.

24. Ibid.

25. See Matthew Connelly, *Fatal Misconception: The Struggle to Control World Population* (Cambridge, Mass.: Harvard University Press, 2008).

Part III

Organizing Your Resources for Strategic Philanthropy

Having reviewed the core activities of strategic philanthropy, we now take a step back to examine some institutional questions. There is a variety of structures—from writing checks at your kitchen table to establishing a foundation staffed with program officers—through which you can practice philanthropy. If you are establishing a foundation, you may want to consider the much-mooted question of whether to preserve your endowment in perpetuity or spend it down during a finite period. The structure of your philanthropy can also bear on your relationships with grantees and collaboration with others in the field—relationships that can improve and complement your grantmaking or detract from it. We view these seemingly disparate issues from the perspective of what is likely to have the greatest philanthropic impact.

Chapter Fifteen

Choosing the Right Structure for Your Philanthropy

THIS CHAPTER CONSIDERS how the various organizational structures of philanthropy relate to goals and strategies and how they contribute to achieving impact. The structures through which you practice philanthropy will be determined by a number of considerations, including

➤ scale—how much money you want to spend;
➤ institutional form—whether you want to make your gifts as an individual or create an institution that will last for a while or in perpetuity;
➤ the level of engagement—how much time you and family members wish to devote to philanthropy;
➤ advice and staffing—how much advice you want from whom, and to whom you will entrust due diligence, implementation, and evaluation; and
➤ financial and tax considerations—how you want your assets managed and the tax consequences of different structures[1] (though we recognize that this last consideration bears importantly on the choice of philanthropic structures, we leave it to your financial and legal advisers).

We consider three broad categories of structure: (1) engaging in philanthropy more or less on your own, (2) delegating strategic planning, grantmaking, and other philanthropic activities to others, and (3) creating a staffed organization for these purposes. You needn't put all your golden eggs in one of these baskets, but can use a number of different structures for engaging in philanthropy.

On Your Own

Checkbook Philanthropy

Checkbook philanthropy is the most common form of philanthropy in America and around the globe—writing checks to charities you want to support, without any formal structure for your giving. It can occur on any scale, from $10 in the weekly church coffer to Bill Cosby's $20 million gift to Spelman College. It can be done strategically, making gifts to effective organizations that share your goals, or less so, giving just because you were asked by a friend. Whatever the case, checkbook philanthropy involves no administrative costs other than the time and energy you devote to researching organizations, making a decision, and keeping records of your donations.[2]

There are various sources of assistance available to checkbook philanthropists: donor education programs, philanthropic advisers who can help with planning, grantmaking, and evaluation, and online services that provide evaluative information about not-for-profit organizations. For more information on philanthropic advisers, visit *www.smartphilanthropy.org*.

Donor-Advised Funds

A donor-advised fund (DAF) is in effect a charitable bank account, in which a donor can set aside charitable funds while deciding on specific beneficiaries. DAFs are held by community foundations and other not-for-profit organizations and by for-profit financial services providers including Fidelity Management & Research Company, the Vanguard Group Inc., and Charles Schwab & Co. Depositing money in a DAF account represents an irrevocable donation to the entity that holds the account. The donation of money (or stock or property) is tax deductible when you put it into the account. Although the account holder has the legal right to use your funds for charitable purposes without your input, the funds are essentially always disbursed upon your recommendation—subject to a rudimentary due-diligence process and to meeting legal requirements and certain substantive criteria in the case of issue- or ideologically oriented DAF holders.[3] Many community foundations and some other DAF holders counsel donors on philanthropic missions and strategies and scout out grantmaking opportunities. For more information about donor-advised funds, visit *www.smartphilanthropy.org*.

Unstaffed Private Foundations

Private grant-making foundations are tax-exempt, not-for-profit organizations that "provide funds from the foundation's income or endowment to support not-for-profit organizations, charities, or other programs in accordance with the mission designated by the founder."[4]

Private foundations typically are established with substantial endowments of investment securities, although they can be set up with a steady stream of donations. Foundations must disburse at least 5 percent of their investments assets annually in "qualified distributions," which include payments for staff salaries and other administrative costs as well as grants. In addition to being subject to payout rules, investment requirements, and excise taxes, foundations are highly regulated by the Internal Revenue Code and by state laws with respect to political activities, compensation of employees, governance and self-dealing, and grants to organizations other than public charities.

Most of the nation's approximately eighty thousand private foundations—even those with millions of dollars of assets—do not have any professional staff. They reflect the visions, passions, values, and sometimes the quirks of the donors and their families. And they also often provide a place for learning about philanthropy, passing values on to one's children, and expressing one's views of the world.

A private foundation has a formal governance structure, with certain minimum obligations mandated by the government. As with other not-for-profit organizations, the responsibility for its governance falls to a board of directors or trustees. Many family foundations are essentially financial vehicles that exist as face-to-face organizations only on the days when the board meets to authorize grants.

The boards of unstaffed foundations can draw on outside advisers and can outsource most of their administrative work.[5] They can also learn from professionals and peers about substantive areas and the processes of grantmaking through the annual meetings of the Association of Small Foundations, the Council on Foundations, Grantmakers for Effective Organizations, the National Center for Family Philanthropy, and the Philanthropy Roundtable.

Giving Circles—Not Entirely on Your Own

The typical giving circle is an informal association of individuals who pool their philanthropic funds and then decide collectively how the funds will be donated. A cross between book clubs and investment clubs, giving circles offer a philanthropy-focused social environment for members and often help them learn about issues in specific areas of concern—from the needs of women in developing countries to particular populations in their own communities. Many are local, and some have national and international chapters. Social Venture Partners International (SVPI) is perhaps the best known of the formally organized giving circles, with over one thousand members in twenty-three affiliates.[6] SVPI requires a minimum annual donation of $5,000, and provides educational and networking opportunities. Like a private foundation, SVPI solicits formal grant applications and engages in multiyear relationships. SVPI takes a venture-philanthropy approach, engaging in long-term relationships with not-for-profits, funding capacity building and scaling up projects, and providing its members' professional expertise to the organizations it supports.

Giving circles can provide a good vehicle for learning about philanthropy, bouncing ideas off of peers, and gaining access to information about organizations. An astute commentator writes, "Through participation, members are more thoughtful, focused, and strategic in their giving inside and outside of the giving circle. Because they begin to see their giving in the context of issues and needs in the community, in which they want to have some impact, their donations are more targeted. For this reason, members say they have started giving fewer, but larger gifts."[7] For more information about giving circles, visit *www.smartphilanthropy.org*.

Giving to Other Foundations and to Intermediaries

If you want to achieve social impact but don't have the time or inclination to engage in philanthropy yourself, consider putting your funds in the hands of another foundation or a philanthropic intermediary. This requires ensuring that the organization is well aligned with your objectives and is pursuing them both strategically and effectively. Painstaking as this process may be, it will avoid your having to do due diligence grant by grant.

Giving to Other Foundations or Following Their Lead
When Warren Buffett, the chairman of Berkshire Hathaway Inc., announced his $31 billion pledge to the Bill & Melinda Gates Foundation, he acknowledged that he knew a lot more about making money than

about giving it away. So in deciding how to donate his enormous fortune, he approached the task like an investor. "When people are thinking about amassing wealth, they frequently go to someone else that they think knows more about it than they do. . . . Why not apply the same thinking when you're eventually dispersing wealth?"[8] he asked. Instead of creating his own foundation from scratch, Mr. Buffett decided to place his assets in an existing, proven institution.

Some commentators have wondered whether Mr. Buffett's gift imposed too great a burden on a young organization that was already on a challenging growth path, or whether it aggregates too much wealth in what was already one of the world's largest foundations. Be that as it may, Mr. Buffett understood that achieving social impact is difficult work and that the staff of the Gates Foundation has deep expertise in both the substance and procedures of philanthropy in shared areas of interest.

So one alternative to setting out on your own is to follow Mr. Buffett's example and place all or some of your philanthropic assets in an existing foundation that shares your goals and that has strong leadership and a track record of effective philanthropy. This is the philanthropic equivalent of investing your money in Berkshire Hathaway or in a good mutual fund. You could add to the foundation's endowment or, as Mr. Buffett did, supplement its annual grants budget. Although the Gates Foundation accepts only unrestricted contributions, another foundation might well allow you to invest more selectively in one of its program areas, say K–12 education.

As another alternative, without making any formal arrangement, you can follow another foundation's lead by putting your funds in the same organizations that it supports. Just as an individual investor might follow Berkshire Hathaway's lead and build a similar portfolio, let an experienced foundation do your due diligence for you.

Giving to Community Foundations

Community foundations are typically 501(c)(3) public charities, funded by individual and corporate donors, that make grants in a specific community or region. They may address the needs of a small city, such as Burlington, Vermont, a large metropolitan area like New York City or Boston, or an entire region, like far northern California or northwest Michigan.

Since their missions are generally oriented broadly toward improving quality of life in a particular locale, community foundations support

Online Microphilanthropy

There has been sizable growth in online microphilanthropy, a genre that facilitates small online donations for particular projects. A prominent example is Global Giving, which funds grassroots projects in social and economic development in developing countries. Individual donors have made grants of from $10 to $150,000 to projects. One can search the website by geographical region or cause—from AIDS relief to clean water—to find projects and their price tags. For example, $12 will fund a Uganda clinic's provision of HIV testing and counseling for three people; $50 will purchase twenty-five energy-efficient fluorescent light bulbs for low-income families.[9] As one of its cofounders sums it up, "Global Giving just enables small-scale grassroots projects to match up with relatively small donors all around the world, who want to help them make a difference."[10] Like Global Giving, Kiva supports entrepreneurs in the developing world, but through small loans rather than gifts.[11] You can lend—as did *New York Times* op-ed columnist Nicholas D. Kristof—$25 each to the owner of a television repair shop and a baker in Afghanistan

a wide range of programs and activities, promoting arts and culture, sustaining vulnerable populations, and broadly improving social and economic well-being. For example, the Chicago Community Trust's Chicago High School Redesign Initiative aims to create high-quality, autonomous small high schools throughout Chicago's neighborhoods.[12] The Oregon Community Foundation "awards grants to develop interpretive, educational, and economic projects to preserve and protect the cultural and natural resources of Oregon's historic trails."[13] The staff members of community foundations perform much the same roles as their counterparts in private foundations—though (as mentioned above) they also counsel individuals holding donor-advised funds, and it is quite typical for a single program officer to have a broad portfolio of grant-making areas. For more information about community foundations, visit *www.smartphilanthropy.org.*

and a single mother running a clothing shop in the Dominican Republic.[14] Kiva collaborates with microfinance institutions around the globe that recommend the borrowers and administer the loans.[15]

Online microphilanthropy has been described as what happens when "Facebook meets pocketbook."[16] It has the potential to draw individuals who are not wealthy into broader realms of philanthropy at the same time as it supports social entrepreneurship to benefit disadvantaged populations both in developing countries and at home.[17] However, the very attractions of online giving suggest its possible tension with strategic philanthropy. As one commentator observes: "People respond to compelling stories, not necessarily cold data and facts but personal stories about people. What [microphilanthropy] is doing is offering a potpourri of stories that affect our heartstrings, and we emotionally respond. And you're able to establish relationships with someone, which is what so many people want to do on the Internet."[18] The downside is that an estimation of impact may be replaced by the metric, "Whose posted photo has the cutest disadvantaged child?" For more information about microphilanthropy, visit *www.smartphilanthropy.org.*

Giving to Philanthropic Intermediaries or Funds

Philanthropic intermediaries have expertise in specific areas, such as education or international development. Examples of intermediaries, some of which have been mentioned in earlier chapters, include Acumen Fund, which supports projects in health, housing, and water in developing countries; the NewSchools Venture Fund, which focuses on education for disadvantaged children in urban communities; REDF, which supports market-oriented not-for-profit workforce-development organizations; and Local Initiatives Support Corporation (LISC), which is devoted to improving conditions for the rural and urban disadvantaged. These funds are expert in focused areas and provide ready vehicles for giving strategically on specific issues. For more information about philanthropic intermediaries, visit *www .smartphilanthropy.org.*

Staffed Foundations and Related Institutions

A staffed foundation has precisely the same legal structure as an unstaffed foundation, but having program officers uniquely positions the foundation to engage in strategic philanthropy. Employing even one or two program officers can enhance the resources provided by outside consultants—by establishing and maintaining relationships with grantee organizations, other funders, government officials, the media, and your board of trustees. The founder and board determine the foundation's mission and strategies, but the staff undertake research, design strategies, solicit and respond to applications, engage in due diligence, and monitor and evaluate grants and strategies. A glance back at Part I will remind you of these and other functions performed by program officers. In truth, it is difficult to undertake large-scale strategic philanthropy without the expertise that an internal professional staff can provide.

Most of the initiatives described in this book were supported by staffed private foundations, and we hope that you have gained a pretty good idea of their processes of grantmaking. To give you a sense of their internal operations, we describe a day in the life of the president of a hypothetical medium-sized staffed foundation. For more information about staffed foundations, visit *www.smartphilanthropy.org*.

A Day in the Life of the President of a Medium-Sized Staffed Foundation

Sally Holder is the president of the Larson Family Foundation (LFF), located in a southwestern city. Created by John Larson from his substantial real estate development fortune, the foundation has an endowment of about $600 million; it employs a half-dozen program officers, and makes annual grants of about $30 million in community revitalization, the environment, disadvantaged communities, and the arts. Most of the foundation's grants are focused in the city, though LFF has joined some other foundations in trying to reduce global warming. John Larson is chairman of the foundation's board of trustees, a majority of whom are family members. Before she came to the foundation, Sally worked in the corporate sector and in city government. These are highlights from Sally's appointment calendar for March 12, 2007:

8 a.m. Breakfast with the mayor and the other members of the city council, at a meeting to which city planners, developers, and

not-for-profits executives have also been invited, to discuss an urban planning initiative.

Because of its founder's belief that "smart growth" benefits everyone, the LFF has been concerned with this issue from the outset. Right now, the city council is considering a highly contested proposal that would create growth boundaries for the city, to encourage infill development and discourage new residential housing in some relatively undeveloped outskirts. Because of the foundation's expertise in this area, the city council had written to Sally requesting the foundation's technical advice and assistance on the proposal. Sally, John, and the cognizant LFF program officer believe that the proposal is essentially sound, and that with a bit of give and take on all sides, it could pass and would serve as a nationwide model. Given the foundation's reputation for impartiality and its benevolent concern for the community, the insights offered by Sally and the program officer are well received by the diverse group of interested parties at the table. The meeting surfaces several issues on which research and public-opinion polling would be useful to the city council. The foundation offers to help identify people to carry out this work and to pay for it.

10 a.m. Meeting with program officers and a consultant to review a study of LFF's after-school program grantees.

The foundation has a portfolio of four local organizations that run after-school programs for disadvantaged children. In addition to providing recreation and keeping them out of trouble, the programs are intended to provide academic support, especially for first-generation Latino children who cannot read English.

From the beginning, LFF worked with the program's managers and an evaluation expert to define outcomes in children's school attendance, literacy, and other factors, and to develop relatively inexpensive means of assessing progress. Two years into the programs, the consultant has delivered the first evaluation report. In preparation for meeting with the grantee organizations, LFF program officers meet with the consultant. Two of the sites show noticeable improvements in almost every respect. Although the numbers may not be statistically significant, the effects are large enough to be encouraging. The third site shows marginal improvements, and the fourth shows none at all—a surprise because during the program officer's site visits, the program always seemed well organized and the staff and kids seemed upbeat.

Sally and her colleagues pore over the data with the consultant, try-ing to understand the possible source of the differences among the programs. Does it lie in their different approaches? In the quality of the implementation? Or perhaps in differences in the populations served by the sites? In any event, they agree that after only two years of implementation, it would be premature to pull the plug on the low-performing sites. But they should not delay in meeting with the grantees to look at the data together. At those meetings, they remind themselves, it will be important to treat the disappointing outcomes as a shared problem of the foundation and the programs—a problem that they are hopeful has a solution.

11:30 a.m. Conference call with the presidents of three other foun-dations that are supporting efforts to reduce global warming.

Although global warming has been a growing concern of John Larson, this is not an area in which LFF has particular expertise. Several years ago, John asked Sally to identify major foundations that were working on the issue and, if she had confidence in them, to piggyback on their grantmaking. LFF is now part of a small collaborative group of funders concerned with climate change. Sally reviews reports from the grantees but relies mainly on other foundations' expertise. Over a period of several years, LFF's investment in this area has grown from $1 million to almost $5 million—about a sixth of its annual budget. John and Sally are pleased with the leverage of these grants, especially because, unlike LFF's other grantmaking, they require almost no staff time.

Noon. Lunch with the CEO and board chair of the city's United Campaign.

The United Campaign raises funds from businesses, individuals, and foundations to support charities serving disadvantaged groups, including the homeless, foster children, and drug addicts. The lunch has become an annual affair at which the United Campaign requests a large grant from LFF. The campaign's chair, an important businessman in the city, serves on the boards of several major not-for-profit organizations. He is used to getting his way.

Last year, Sally repeated her concern that the United Campaign had not developed measures of the effectiveness of the programs it supports. The campaign's CEO acknowledged the problem and requested a spe-cial grant to hire someone to begin to develop such metrics. It now turns out that the CEO dragged his feet in hiring someone and that the cam-paign has made no discernible progress toward this goal. Sally cannot help but express her frustration about the CEO and board chair's not "getting it" and their assumption that LFF would nonetheless continue to support the United Campaign. To the CEO's distress, Sally says she needs to think about whether the foundation will make a commitment for the coming year.

As Sally walks back to her office, she wonders whether, in view of the United Campaign's passive resistance, it is worth the effort to press for it to become more outcome oriented, and whether withholding an annual contribution would serve as a wake-up call. If she does withhold a contribution, the board chair will surely ask John Larson to override her decision, but she is equally certain that John will back her up.

3 p.m. All-staff meeting to discuss grantee perception report.

Some months ago, after consulting her board chair, Sally commissioned the Center for Effective Philanthropy to prepare a grantee perception report—a survey of grantees covering issues from the grant application process through awarding and monitoring the grant, including interactions between the grantee and foundation staff and the grantees' perceptions of the foundation's impact. With the report now completed, Sally convenes an all-staff meeting to discuss it.

She begins by noting that, although perceptions of the foundation are not the same as its actual impact, a grantee's sense of its relations with the foundation has some value as a proxy for impact. After all, grantees are a foundation's agents for change. All things considered, good relationships are conducive to impact.

On the whole, LFF has much to be pleased with. The foundation is regarded as a leader in education and arts funding in the city. It communicates its goals and grant guidelines clearly, and its application process is demanding but fair. Grantees appreciate the foundation's practice of making multiyear grants and its willingness to renew a grant on the basis of the organization's achievements in the previous period.

However, the survey raises some concerns as well. The foundation did not score high in its interactions with grantees, a few of whom used words like "imperious" and "curt" in referring to the program officers. More generally, although the program officers were helpful once one could get in touch with them, they were hard to reach, and they did not respond in a timely or helpful fashion to the reports required of grantees.

Sally says that the report raises some questions about LFF's general practices and ethos. This is a matter for foundation-wide analysis and problem solving, and she would like to get everyone's perspective on these issues. With this start, the meeting continues beyond its scheduled two hours. (In the days to come, Sally plans to schedule meetings with some individual staff members to discuss concerns that were raised about their interactions in particular.)

6 p.m. Arts Council dinner with founder John Larson.

Despite the foundation's active engagement in the city, John Larson does not like to be in the limelight. When the Arts Council announced its annual award to LFF, John asked Sally to accept it on the foundation's behalf, but she argued that his presence at the dinner would help the organization's fund-raising efforts. He agreed to attend if she and the program officer would accompany him.

On their way to the dinner, John mentions that he has become increasingly concerned with issues of international human rights and wonders whether the foundation shouldn't begin exploring grantmaking in that area. Sally says that she shares his concern and gives personally to this cause. But she says that there is considerably more that LFF could do within its existing program areas and that international human rights lies beyond the expertise of the foundation's program officers. If John wants the LFF to do some grantmaking in this area, perhaps he should follow the same path that the foundation has taken in climate change. Better yet, she adds, "Let's deepen our commitment to the areas in which we're already working."

"That's a good point, but—" he starts to reply, as they enter the Arts Council reception and are greeted by many admiring colleagues and citizens.

This vignette shows Sally in the role of grant maker, strategist, and evaluator of the foundation's work and that of its grantees. It shows her as convener, collaborator, political actor—always within the legal restrictions on lobbying—and shared recipient of the community's gratitude for the foundation's achievements. It does not include the many phone calls, e-mail exchanges, hallway meetings, or other tasks that consume her work day.

Operating Foundations

Operating foundations look like the public charities to which grant-making foundations make grants, except that they are mainly funded by their founding philanthropist through expendable contributions or an endowment.[19] It is their programmatic work that distinguishes operating from grant-making foundations, though some make substantial grants as well.

For example, the J. Paul Getty Trust maintains the two Getty museums in Los Angeles and manages art-conservation and research institutes. In 2004, the trust spent more than $375 million on its own programs and distributed $23 million in grants to other organizations.[20] The Stupski Foundation is a private operating foundation that supports systemic reforms in urban public-school districts to improve the quality of education for underserved students. In addition to making grants to enable the districts to obtain expert help from others, the foundation's own staff members provide on-site technical assistance and coaching and facilitate peer learning among grantee districts.

Hybrid Philanthropy

Hybrid approaches blend philanthropy with mission-related for-profit investments of the sort described in Chapter 8. Pierre Omidyar, one of the founders of eBay, was among the first to announce a hybrid approach when he decided in 2004 to begin supporting both not-for-profit *and* for-profit enterprises that promote his social goals. Through the Omidyar Network,[21] he now maintains a portfolio that includes social-entrepreneurship-minded companies and not-for-profit organizations. For example, the Omidyar Network has made grants to Grameen Foundation, the not-for-profit arm of the world's first microfinance bank, and also invested in BlueOrchard Finance S.A., a for-profit organization with portfolios of microfinance institutions. To complement these investments, when Mr. Omidyar gave $100 million to Tufts University's endowment, he required that they invest the funds in microfinance institutions.[22]

When Google announced the creation of its philanthropic arm, Google.org, it too decided that it would invest in both for-profit and not-for-profit organizations. Indeed, most of the money Google set aside was not put into the not-for-profit Google Foundation but into a fully taxable venture-capital fund. The money will be invested in for-profit firms doing research and development to improve energy efficiency, among other goals. The first head of Google.org, Dr. Larry Brilliant, explained that although the foundation hopes to turn a profit, "we're not doing this for the profit. And if we didn't get our capital back, so what? The emphasis is on social returns, not economic returns."[23] Google has announced its intention to make some bold investments in clean-technology ventures.

These new hybrid approaches have generated their share of criticism,[24] including skepticism about the conflict between achieving social and financial returns. Doubters wonder whether such approaches may be prone to the more self-serving practices and shorter time horizons of traditional corporate philanthropy, whether they will disadvantage not-for-profits that cannot provide financial returns, and more broadly, whether they have the capacity to foster real social change. As there is much more talk about hybrid philanthropy than actual practice now, it would seem premature to make generalized judgments about it.

Takeaway Points

> There are three general structures for engaging in philanthropy:
  —Doing it on your own, including writing checks to public charities, drawing on a donor-advised fund, participating in a giving circle, and setting up an unstaffed private foundation
  —Giving to other funders, including staffed foundations, community foundations, and philanthropic intermediaries
  —Creating a staffed private foundation
> Because of the effort involved in designing, implementing, and evaluating strategies, giving to others or creating a staffed foundation is more likely to have social impact than doing it on your own.

Chapter Notes

1. Though we recognize that this last consideration bears importantly on the choice of philanthropic structures, we leave it to your financial and legal advisers.

2. Donors are expected to have verified the charitable status of the organizations they donate to in order to take a tax deduction, and they cannot take a deduction to the extent that they receive something of value in exchange for it, like dinner at a charity benefit.

3. All DAF hosts must verify the charitable status of the recipient organizations to which you recommend a grant. This is because unless the donee organization has U.S. public charity status, the DAF host must either make a formal determination that it is a foreign organization that is "equivalent" to a U.S. public charity, or exercise "expenditure responsibility" over the grant to assure that it is spent only for charitable purposes. Many DAFs lack the capacity to make equivalency determinations or to engage in expenditure responsibility, and thus effectively limit the donor's choice to organizations registered with the IRS as public charities.

4. Joel L. Fleishman, *The Foundation: A Great American Secret* (New York: Public Affairs, 2007), 3.

5. Lauren Foster, "Support Upfront with Back-Office," *Financial Times*, March 9, 2007, http://us.ft.com/ftgateway/superpage.ft?news_id=fto0309200711 38557576.

6. Social Venture Partners International, "History," http://www.svpi.org/ about-us/history (accessed July 11, 2008).

7. Angela M. Eikenberry, "Giving Circles: Growing Grassroots Philanthropy," *Nonprofit and Voluntary Sector Quarterly* 35 (2006): 51.

8. Warren Buffett, interview by Charlie Rose, *The Charlie Rose Show*, PBS, July 12, 2006.

9. Larry Magid, "Tech File: Sites Help Small Investments Make Social Impact," *San Jose Mercury News*, October 29, 2007.

10. Marcia Sharp, "De Tocqueville Meets eBay: Giving, Volunteering, and Doing Good in the New Social Sector," *New Directions for Philanthropic Fundraising*, 2004, no. 45: 85–93.

11. Kiva, "What We Do," http://www.kiva.org/about (accessed July 11, 2008).

12. Chicago Community Trust, "Chicago High School Redesign Initiative," http://www.cct.org/page30306.cfm (accessed December 17, 2007).

13. Oregon Historic Trails Fund, http://www.oregonhistorictrailsfund.org (accessed December 17, 2007); see also Oregon Community Foundation, http:// www.ocf1.org/grant_programs/ohtf_rfp.html (accessed December 17, 2007).

14. Nicholas D. Kristof, "You, Too, Can Be a Banker to the Poor," *New York Times*, March 27, 2007. Kiva has attracted so many lenders that it has limited each participant to $25 per business so that everyone has a chance to make a Kiva loan. Cynthia Haven, "Small Change, Big Payoff," *Stanford Magazine* November/December 2007, http://www.stanfordalumni.org/news/ magazine/2007/novdec/features/kiva.html.

15. David Bonbright, Natalia Kiryttopoulou, and Lindsay Iversen, *Online Philanthropy Markets: From "Feel-Good" Giving to Effective Social Investing?* (Keystone Accountability, 2008), http://www.keystoneaccountability.org/files/ Keystone_Online%20Philanthropy%20Markets.pdf.

16. Joe Burris, "Safety 'Net,'" *Baltimore Sun*, May 9, 2007, business section.

17. Bonbright, Kiryttopoulou, and Iversen, *Online Philanthropy Markets*.

18. Burris, "Safety 'Net.'"

19. Council on Foundations, "What Is a Private Operating Foundation?" http:// www.cof.org/members/content.cfm?ItemNumber=551&navItemNumber= 2518 (accessed July 11, 2008).

20. Foundation Center's Statistical Information Service, "Ten Largest Grant-making Operating Foundations by Asset Size, 2004," http://foundationcenter .org/findfunders/statistics/pdf/11_topfdn_type/2004/top10_aa_op.pdf.

21. Omidyar Network, http://www.omidyar.net (accessed July 11, 2008).

22. Ben Gose, "The Big Promise of Small Loans," *Chronicle of Philanthropy*, July 20, 2006.

23. Katie Hafner, "Philanthropy Google's Way: Not the Usual," *New York Times*, September 13, 2006.

24. See Nicole Wallace, "Blending Business and Charity," *Chronicle of Philanthropy*, September 28, 2006, http://philanthropy.com/free/articles/v18/i24/24001401.htm; Hafner, "Philanthropy Google's Way," and Stephanie Strom, "A Fresh Approach: What's Wrong with Profit?" *New York Times*, November 13, 2006.

Chapter **16** *Sixteen*

Principal and Principle:
Foundation Spending Policies

PHILANTHROPISTS DEVOTE CONSIDERABLE effort to investing their endowments wisely, but they give little thought to how much of their assets or endowment should be conserved for the future and how much should be paid out now. Although, as the late Claude Rosenberg wrote in *Wealthy and Wise*,[1] this is a question for individual philanthropists as well as foundations, we focus on foundations.

The issue for philanthropists and their organizations is whether the foundation should exist in perpetuity or should pay down the endowment, eventually putting the foundation out of business. In particular, we consider the relation of payout to a foundation's mission. Many foundations pay out the minimum required by U.S. law—5 percent of their assets.[2] Assuming that its average investment returns are 8 percent, and assuming an inflation rate of about 3 percent, a foundation can maintain its inflation-adjusted payout forever. But unless the founding document indicates otherwise, nothing prevents foundations from spending more, or even spending all its assets in one year.

We described the fundamental question in binary terms: perpetuity or not. But there are actually many variations. You might spend down a portion of your endowment today and then maintain a payout that will keep the foundation going forever, albeit with a smaller budget. Or if you do spend down, you can do so over a longer or shorter period. You may choose to have your foundation's doors close soon after you enter the pearly gates, or allow your children or grandchildren to continue to make grants.

Two of the strongest statements against perpetuity come from extraordinarily successful businessmen who devoted much of their fortunes to philanthropy.

In 1929, the president of Sears, Roebuck & Co., Julius Rosenwald, whose philanthropy focused on educating African-American children, expressed in no uncertain terms his thoughts on this matter:

> I am opposed to the principle of storing up large sums of money for philanthropic uses centuries hence for two reasons. First, it directly implies a certain lack of confidence with regard to the future, which I do not share. I feel confident that the generations that will follow us will be every bit as humane and enlightened, energetic and able, as we are, and that the needs of the future can safely be left to be met by the generations of the future. Second, I am against any program that would inject the great fortunes of today into the affairs of the nation five hundred or a thousand years hence.[3]

About eighty years later, Warren Buffett noted: "There are certain dynamics that take over in terms of behavior, and one of those forces is usually the drive to perpetuate institutions. . . . That dynamic—though undoubtedly subconscious—sometimes takes precedence over considering what might be best for society."[4] Mr. Buffett gave much of his fortune to the Bill & Melinda Gates Foundation, which plans to spend down its assets within fifty years of the death of its last trustee—though given Bill's and Melinda's ages, this should be a very long time off.

On the other hand, Andrew Carnegie, John D. Rockefeller, Henry Ford, Robert Wood Johnson, Andrew Mellon, John MacArthur, David Packard, and William Hewlett created foundations designed to last in perpetuity. What considerations might have led to their decisions?

The Needs of the Present Versus Those of the Future

If you believe that the problems of the future will be greater than those today, or that there will be less flexible wealth to deal with tomorrow's problems than there is today, then it makes sense to husband resources to the greatest extent possible. This is an attitude that many of us have with respect to our personal finances: we like to put aside funds for a rainy day, or to give more options to our children and grandchildren. But does the same logic follow for a foundation?

Julius Rosenwald answered no. He thought that the world's economic growth would continue over time and that philanthropy would grow with it. Looking back over the last two hundred years, this seems right. And looking forward, the dollars devoted to philanthropy are predicted to increase tremendously with the coming generations of wealth transfers. Of course, you might worry that changes in culture, or in the tax laws, could change this path, but so could a meteor. (Actually, there are legislative and regulatory threats to the status quo for foundations and other charitable institutions, but these are likely to affect existing institutions as well as new ones.)

The Growth Rate of Your Assets Versus the Escalation of the Problem You Seek to Address

This is a question of expected return and particularly of the value of a dollar spent today compared with a dollar in the distant future. To some extent, but by no means perfectly, the answer relates to where your goals are located with respect to the small and big cubes described in Chapter 2.

On the one hand, there is no reason to think that the arts, culture, or higher education need your money more today than they will a century from now. On the other hand, if you are concerned about the effects of population growth on the development of certain sub-Saharan countries, meeting the demand for family planning to prevent unwanted pregnancies today has a far greater impact than doing so in another generation. Global warming presents a similar situation. In explaining why the Richard and Rhoda Goldman Fund pays out 10 percent of its assets each year, Mr. Goldman explained:

> For the environment and other charitable causes, the 'rainy day' is upon us. . . . I believe that now is the time to address the climate change issue head on, simply because the opportunity will never come again. If we do not act now, we will impose untold harm on future generations, and there will be nothing they can do to remedy the situation. This single issue has the potential to exacerbate nearly all other environmental and social problems.[5]

In other cases, the time value of your grants is not as starkly obvious. Do today's investments in sheltering homeless families, improving elementary and secondary education for inner-city children, or eradicating disease provide more value than tomorrow's? Your answer may depend on whether you believe that addressing the problems now will prevent their transmission across time or space.

All other things being equal, for most of the big problems that philanthropy seeks to address, our hunch is that a philanthropic dollar spent today is worth more than a dollar spent tomorrow. But let's look at some ways that other things may not be equal.

The Existence of a Strong Actionable Theory of Change Versus the Likelihood of a Better Strategy in the Future

In Chapter 3, we discussed the importance of having a strong and actionable theory of change. There are important cases—for example, in youth development and urban education—where present knowledge of what works is strong enough to justify scaling up a strategy through philanthropy or advocating for government support. But in many situations uncertainty dominates.

Take global development, which consumes billions of dollars annually—an increasing amount of it from private philanthropy—yet lacks well-tested actionable strategies. Some interventions have emphasized the need for basic infrastructure—roads, ports, power plants. Others have concentrated on good governance—transparency, democracy, taxation, and the like. Still others are designed to provide basic education, sanitation, health, and nutrition to the poor. Although all of these are legitimate goals, there is great uncertainty about where to invest philanthropic dollars most effectively. Perhaps this is an extreme example. But consider how little is known about how to alleviate poverty, especially among some minority communities, in the United States.

The lack of current firepower in these realms may be a reason to keep some of your powder dry for the future. However, philanthropy's most valuable role here is to support research, experimentation, and evaluation—and there are plenty of good projects to support. Indeed, given the toll of human suffering, you might want to increase grants beyond the 5 percent payout rate to increase the likelihood of finding a solution, investing in a series of well-managed experiments while saving the bulk of your fortune to roll out the one or two that work.

This was essentially the New York–based Aaron Diamond Foundation's approach when it tackled AIDS in 1985—except that it left the rollout to others. In the mid-1980s, knowledge about how to stop or control the virus was minimal. After considering alternative strategies, the foundation decided to jump-start basic research so that scientists could develop enough results to obtain federal funding. In 1989, the staff and board created an independent world-class laboratory with some of the most capable researchers in the land. By 1996, the Aaron Diamond AIDS Research Center led the field in the development of the antiviral "cocktail," which marked a turning point in the effort to control the virus. After ten years of action and $220 million in grants (40 percent for medical research) that helped make the AIDS cocktail possible, the foundation went out of business.

Jump-Starting Versus Sustaining Fields and Movements

In Chapter 14, we mentioned the John M. Olin Foundation, which supported the growth of the modern conservative movement as well as the development of the field of law and economics before closing its doors, as the founder stipulated, a generation after his death.

The Whitaker Foundation had supported biomedical engineering since its founding in 1975. In 1991, its governing committee recognized a crossroads, and concluded that the best use of the foundation's assets would be to establish and strengthen newly formed university biomedical engineering departments. The foundation decided to devote all its assets to this cause and to spend down the entire corpus in fifteen years.[6] By the time the Whitaker Foundation closed its doors in 2006, it had put over $800 million into biomedical engineering.[7] The money was used for research, education programs, fellowships, internships, curriculum development, conferences, leadership development, faculty hiring, building construction, collaborations with government and industry, support of professional societies, and international grants and scholarships.[8] The Whitaker Foundation's investment effectively jump-started the field, transforming biomedical engineering from a fledgling enterprise to a mature field with eighty departments in U.S. universities by 2006.[9]

It is reasonable to believe that the Olin and Whitaker foundations had more of an impact on their objectives through their concentrated infusion of grants than they would have had they spent 5 percent of their endowments annually in their pursuits. On the other hand, the Ford Foundation's endowment is large enough that it could both jump-start and sustain the women's movement and other progressive causes over a substantial period. The Packard and Hewlett foundations have sustained the population and environmental movements for many decades with an average payout of about 5 percent—and one cannot say that the needs are any less today than when the foundations entered these areas in the 1960s.

Perpetuating Institutional Knowledge, Culture, and Reputation Versus Fossilization

Granted that organizations rise and fall, and reemerge in different forms, imagine the loss of valuable organizational structure and knowledge if one were to arbitrarily shut down General Electric or Toyota, the Girl Scouts or CARE, Harvard or MIT.

Moreover, institutions that have indefinite time horizons tend to be concerned about the future and to engage in long-term projects. On the business side, consider some oil companies' research into renewable sources of energy. And with respect to philanthropy, consider the time horizons required for the Rockefeller Foundation's commitments to the Green Revolution, the Mellon Foundation's commitments to higher education and culture, and the Robert Wood Johnson Foundation's work in health.

It also takes time to build an institution's reputation, which can be a tremendous asset. When the Rockefeller Foundation makes a grant overseas, it not only sends money but credibility, because the Rockefeller name comes with a de facto mark of quality, and the project it supports thus receives a strong endorsement. So too for the MacArthur Foundation's grants in human rights.

The list could go on—but not indefinitely. Although reputations can be built on the local and regional level as well as nationally and internationally, many foundations that are intended to last forever have little institutional knowledge—or capacity, for that matter. For the most part, these demand the continuity that only an experienced and expert staff can bring. And even then, not everyone would agree on which of the long-lived big-name foundations have remained vital institutions.

This brings us to the question of accountability. Corporations, not-for-profits, and universities are accountable to investors, donors, students, and others. Joseph Schumpeter's "creative destruction" ensures the demise of businesses that have outlived their usefulness, and the process may apply—albeit to a lesser degree—to most organizations of civil society. But not to foundations, which are as unaccountable as they are susceptible to flattery. This should at least give one pause in making the case for perpetuity.

Trusting Future Generations Versus Binding Them to Your Views

This concept is a double-edged sword. You may believe that civilization is in constant danger of backsliding from hard-gained rights and liberties, whether individual economic autonomy or gay rights; or you may believe that cultural traditions, such as Western classical music, are in constant danger of extinction. A permanent foundation supported by a substantial endowment can act as a bulwark to protect these values.

But controlling, let alone predicting, the future is an impossible task. The more precisely you specify the foundation's mission, the more likely it is to be irrelevant in the future. Benjamin Franklin set up a loan fund in his will for married apprentices seeking to establish their own businesses. Girard College was founded in 1833 "for the education of poor white orphan boys." And a trust established in 1861 was intended "for the benefit of fugitive slaves" and to "put an end to negro slavery in this country."[10]

The more broadly you describe the mission, the more leeway future trustees will have to apply its principles in the light of their own time and not yours. The conservative commentator Heather Higgins observes that the trustees of a foundation committed to strengthening the United States might at one time believe that the mission was served by encouraging immigration and, at another, conclude that it was served by curtailing immigration.[11]

If you are willing to state a general intention and leave such decisions to the future, then you can rest easy. But the more precisely you want to specify your intentions, the better it may be for you to act within a foreseeable time horizon. If you care about the environment, then help the Nature Conservancy protect pristine lands and hold them in trust forever. If you wish to preserve cultural values, contribute the corpus of your foundation to the endowments of museums, universities, and similar institutions.[12]

Personal Concerns

The factors mentioned above all involve having an impact on society. But other factors may also weigh in your decision. Do you want to defer spending down your endowment to permit your children and grandchildren to enjoy the benefits of engaging in philanthropy—and perhaps to hold the family together? If so, for how many generations is this plausible? How do you balance the enjoyment of the act of giving and the attendant acclaim while you're alive against the hope of being remembered as generous and great when you're gone?

The answers to these questions depend on particular individuals, families, sizes of endowments, and other circumstances. Our main point in this short chapter is that spending decisions have strategic as well as personal consequences.

Finally, although we have focused on donors' decisions in establishing a foundation, the discussion also has implications for the trustees of a foundation whose lifespan was left undefined by its founders. The responsibilities of stewardship do not make perpetuity the default. Rather, a trustee's duty is to use the donor's resources wisely to achieve his or her philanthropic goals, and one can violate that duty as readily by failing to spend down the endowment as by protecting it for some future day.

Takeaway Points

The major considerations in determining whether to spend down your philanthropic assets or maintain an endowment in perpetuity are

- the needs of the present versus those of the future;
- the growth rate of your assets versus the escalation of the problem you seek to address;
- the existence of a strong actionable theory of change versus the likelihood of a better strategy in the future;
- jump-starting versus sustaining fields and movements;
- perpetuating institutional knowledge, culture, and reputation versus fossilization;
- trusting future generations versus binding them to your views; and
- personal concerns.

Chapter Notes

1. Claude N. Rosenberg, *Wealthy and Wise: How You and America Can Get the Most Out of Your Giving* (Boston: Little, Brown, 1994).

2. For the purposes of this conversation, we include administrative costs in the term "payout," as does the IRS.

3. Julius Rosenwald, "The Burden of Wealth," *Saturday Evening Post*, 1929, quoted in Diane Granat, "America's 'Give While You Live' Philanthropist," *APF Reporter* 21, no. 1 (2003) http://www.aliciapatterson.org/APF2101/Granat/Granat.html (accessed July 1, 2008). See generally Steven Schindler, "Building Schools for Rural African Americans" in *Casebook for The Foundation: A Great American Secret*, by Joel L. Fleishman, J. Scott Kohler, and Steven Schindler (New York: Public Affairs, 2007).

4. Stephanie Strom, "How Long Should Gifts Just Grow?" *New York Times*, November 12, 2007, http://www.nytimes.com/2007/11/12/giving/12money.html.

5. Michael Klausner, "When Time Isn't Money: Foundation Payouts and the Time Value of Money," *Stanford Social Innovation Review* 1, no. 1 (2003): 51–59.

6. Heidi Waleson, *Beyond Five Percent: The New Foundation Payout Menu* (Northern California Grantmakers, 2007), http://www.ncg.org/assets/beyond5/Beyond5_Report.pdf.

7. Ibid.

8. To learn more about the Whitaker Foundation's grantmaking in biomedical engineering, see the online archive of the foundation's work maintained by the Biomedical Engineering Society as a public resource, at http://bluestream.wustl.edu/WhitakerArchives.

9. Waleson, *Beyond Five Percent*.

10. Walter Isaacson, *Benjamin Franklin: An American Life* (New York, Simon & Schuster, 2003), 474; *Wikipedia*, s.v. "Girard College," http://en.wikipedia.org/wiki/Girard_College (accessed June 30, 2008); and Lawrence M. Friedman, "Dead Hands," forthcoming.

11. Heather R. Higgins, "The Case for Limiting the Lives of Foundations," in *Should Foundations Exist in Perpetuity?* (Indianapolis, Ind.: Philanthropy Roundtable, 2006), 9–31, http://www.philanthropyroundtable.org/files/Should%20Foundations%20Exist%20in%20Perpetuity.pdf.

12. "Universities as the guardians of culture?" you exclaim. "Just look at the postmodernist, deconstructionist academic movements of the late twentieth century!" Actually, we think that classical traditions remained alive and well even during this period and have survived well. But it is important to note that traditions inevitably change and are reinterpreted over time. What was canonic at Harvard in 1900 is different from the core curriculum in 1800.

A f t e r w o r d

The Challenges of Strategic Philanthropy

MUCH OF THIS book has examined the techniques and tools of strategic philanthropy and the opportunities it offers to make the world a better place. In closing, we examine the two fundamental challenges strategic philanthropy faces: the first concerns discipline more than strategy or technique; the second concerns the maxim "do no harm."

The Inevitability of Limited Resources and the Importance of Focus and Perseverance

You are more likely to have impact in achieving your philanthropic objectives—whatever they may be—if you focus on relatively few objectives. This follows simply from the fact that you have limited financial and human resources to devote to the enterprise.

Financial and Human Resources
The limitations of financial resources are self-evident—though it's important to remember that unless you are at the cutting (or trailing) edge of some cause, you are seldom alone.

The limitations of human resources are the consequences of the three sorts of expertise that strategic philanthropy requires:

➤ *Expertise in a particular subject area and in a field*—knowledge about promising approaches to improving educational outcomes for disadvantaged students, for example, and knowledge of the people, organizations, and networks concerned with research, practice, and evaluation in this area.

➤ *Expertise in analyzing problems and designing strategies, and in using tools to carry out those strategies*—although these skills must ultimately be applied to particular substantive areas, a good problem solver and strategist can be of tremendous help to colleagues in different areas.

➤ *Expertise in the processes of grantmaking*—that is, in selecting grantees, assessing their work, and engaging in the activities related to grantmaking discussed in Chapters 4 through 6.

Your grantees will surely have plenty of expertise in the substance and strategies relevant to their fields. Even so, you will need a degree of independent judgment to select them wisely, which calls for all three forms of expertise. Otherwise, you will have little but an applicant's reputation or blind faith to help decide which organizations to fund, and you will be poorly equipped to monitor their progress.

The importance of your own, or your foundation staff's, strategic and substantive expertise grows the more engaged you wish to be in your fields of interest. If, for example, you wish to develop strategies to solve environmental problems in the American West, you must have a deep understanding of the dynamics of the region and the decision-making processes that affect natural-resource choices. You cannot have a strong grantmaking program on water in the American West without understanding the history, constraints, and opportunities embedded in state water law. You cannot hope to protect roadless areas from new roads without understanding the economics of the timber and energy industries and the federal laws that govern management of national forests. Conversely, having depth in these realms gives you an important advantage: you can build grants packages that match and exploit key opportunities. In all these cases, you can engage with your grantees as a collaborator—to the extent that such engagement is helpful.

Focusing on a Limited Number of Problems at Any One Time

In Chapter 7, we discussed the hypothetical Pacific Spotlight and Floodlight foundations, which have narrow and broad interests, respectively. In this section we introduce two other hypothetical foundations whose breadths of interests differ even more radically. Each has an annual grants budget of $15 million, and each has three professional staff members. The Unity Foundation focuses exclusively on improving K–12 education in American schools. The Hundred Flowers Foundation's areas of interest include education, culture, the environment, immigration, gay and lesbian rights, and poverty. In addition, Hundred Flowers Foundation's living donor has a restless mind and an insatiable curiosity, and regularly brings the program staff new ideas and proposals from even more diverse areas.

Simply put, the Unity Foundation is likely to achieve more impact in its single area of interest than the Hundred Flowers Foundation is in all of its areas combined. The reason lies in the foundations' inevitably scarce human and financial resources. With respect to human resources, Unity's three program officers have concentrated expertise in education: one has a research background in the field, and the others have on-the-ground experience as teachers, principals, or superintendents. Their combined expertise enables them to maintain strong connections with key practitioners and researchers. They are aware of every school-reform initiative in the country and are involved in a number of them.

Hundred Flowers' three staff members span a variety of discrete grantmaking subjects. All of them came with expertise in some of the foundation's areas and have developed some knowledge of the other fields. But they are spread so thin that it's difficult for them to stay abreast of all the important developments in the fields. The staff members can discuss common issues of grantmaking, but because their domains of expertise don't overlap, they can't walk into the next office to get help on most substantive issues.

Unity is able to devote all of its $15 million to improving education. Its grants portfolio includes studies testing whether two particular interventions—providing immediate and continuous feedback on student performance, and having a longer than normal school day—improve student outcomes. Unity also makes large multiyear grants to some core national organizations devoted to school reform. Unity is considered a leader in the field of K–12 reform.

Hundred Flowers is the proverbial jack of all trades. Although the foundation is a noticeable presence in several of its fields, it is not a master of any of them. Hundred Flowers has the best chance of having impact by being a good follower—by following the lead of foundations like Unity, or by providing core operating support to high-performing organizations in its areas of interest. But even following another foundation's lead requires the knowledge to develop confidence in its work. Providing general operating support requires as much due diligence as any other kind of grant, and Hundred Flowers lacks the personnel to do this. Moreover, because its assets are diffused, it is not able to support those organizations through substantial multiyear commitments.

We do not mean to imply that a foundation with several programs inevitably has less impact than one that addresses a single problem. Like most other national foundations, our own employer is a conglomerate with several discrete areas of grantmaking: each of the Hewlett Foundation's six programs has two or more subprograms. In some areas, our staff and budget are just about the right size for the problems we're working on. In others, it is quite possible that devoting more money or staff to a particular issue would have a greater net impact on the foundation's goals. We can't say that being a conglomerate reduces impact as an a priori matter. But it is apparent that the more things you do, the more you diffuse your resources, and the greater the likelihood becomes that you will not deploy them in the most effective way.

In Chapter 1, we mentioned the Edna McConnell Clark Foundation's decision to focus its $25 million-plus annual grants budget on youth-development programs. This came about when Michael Bailin became its president in 1996 and wondered whether the foundation's resources were spread too thin. We don't know of any other transformations of a major foundation as dramatic as the Clark Foundation's, but we do know of many foundations whose concentrated focus has apparently served them well over the years.

Among the large foundations, for example, the Andrew W. Mellon Foundation focuses its programs on higher education, the arts, and culture, and this has led to some phenomenal contributions to these fields, including launching JSTOR, an online database that makes academic journals available to scholars throughout the world, and ARTstor, which is digitizing some of the world's great art treasures and making them available to scholars and teachers on the Internet. By the same token, the Commonwealth Fund and the Robert Wood Johnson Foundation have had great impact in their area of concern, health.

Many small foundations have distinguished themselves through clarity and focus and have become leaders in their respective fields. The Ploughshares Fund, which raises and spends some $5 million per year, is an expert in the complex subject of nuclear-weapons nonproliferation. Ploughshares became a leader in its field by building a smart staff, establishing a distinguished board of advisers, and consulting widely and wisely. With a somewhat larger budget, the Surdna Foundation became the leader in transportation reform. The Wallace Alexander Gerbode Foundation has extensive expertise in arts and culture in the Bay Area and Hawaii.

Perseverance and Follow-Through

Paralleling the value of focusing on a limited number of problems at any one time is sticking with those problems over time. Limited human and financial resources constrain an organization's effectiveness at any one moment. Fickleness and the absence of follow-through are constraints over a period of time.

Very few important social problems, whether local or global, can be solved with grants of a few years' duration. Conversely, some of the greatest successes of philanthropy have come from a foundation's willingness to stick with a problem for the long haul.[1]

➤ Work supported by the Packard and Hewlett foundations, and managed by the Energy Foundation, is helping build a sound set of environmental laws and practices in China. The results there are already dramatic, with new policies that will save billions of barrels of oil and hundreds of millions of tons of coal, and thus reduce both carbon dioxide emissions and unhealthy conventional pollutants. This would not have been possible with a short-term commitment.

➤ Inspired by the success of the Salk vaccine, the Edna McConnell Clark Foundation spent twenty years working to eradicate three horribly debilitating tropical diseases. Although its efforts to develop vaccines for schistosomiasis and onchocerciasis did not succeed—as we said at the start, strategic philanthropy is a risky enterprise—its trachoma program led to a collaboration with the World Health Organization, Pfizer Inc., and others, resulting in a multipronged strategy that greatly reduced the incidence of this blinding eye infection.

Many philanthropists like to provide seed funding for innovative work ranging from education to medical research. However, the value of pilot programs depends on whether there is anyone around to implement them—to bring them to scale. Although seeding is essential and exciting, it is useless unless the seedlings are watered, weeded, and nurtured until the crop can be harvested and baked. The foundation that is willing to stick with an idea from beginning to end can create lasting change. Those that only support a project while it is new and exciting are leaving their work to the whims of fate. In truth, many philanthropists don't even carry their projects through the seedling stage. The hypothetical Hundred Flowers Foundation is doubly disadvantaged in terms of having impact. Not only are its resources widely diffused at any one time, but its donor moves from one area to another without ever taking stock of who if anyone will continue the work she abandoned. A requisite for lasting change: don't start fixing the problem unless you are prepared to help see it through or at least identify others who will continue the effort.

Arbitrary limits on programs or grants, time horizons that are too short for the problem, and donor fatigue all militate against success. Your interests and objectives may change over time, but if you decide to exit a field where there are still vibrant organizations adding value, or when there are promising projects still in progress, plan for an exit strategy that doesn't leave the field reeling.

Of course, it is possible to march down the wrong path and continue a project or program far longer than desirable. But we think philanthropists fail much more often by being eager to try the new than by being committed too long to a dead issue. Foundations fail more by being too diverse than by being too deep, and by failing to build the expertise, relationships, and reputation to make grant dollars go as far as possible.

Special Opportunities and Opportunity Costs

Achieving impact calls for a disciplined approach to philanthropy. But what of requests that come to your attention that are too good to pass by, that tug at your heartstrings and that it would seem callous to turn down? An expected-return calculation may tell you that investing a dollar in agricultural infrastructure in Africa will have more impact than giving the dollar to a starving African child. But our brains are wired to respond to the personal plight of that one child.

A good way to accommodate present realities with the long-term advantages of discipline is to budget a modest portion of your philanthropic expenditures for special opportunities. The right portion will differ from one individual or foundation to another, and may vary over time as you develop strategies. But it is useful to think of special-opportunity grants in terms of opportunity costs—of what impact the same funds might have had in strategically designed programs.

The Responsibilities of Philanthropy

Our recommendations thus far have focused on attaining your own philanthropic goals, whatever they may be. In this closing section of the book, we discuss two ways that philanthropy can blunder: damaging the very field in which it operates and wreaking social havoc.

Responsibilities to the Field: Leaving Your Campsite Better Than You Found It

Here we suggest ways that you can improve the field of philanthropy, or at least not make it worse than you found it. Although most of these suggestions could be couched as enlightened self-interest, we think of them more normatively in terms of reciprocity or the Golden Rule.

Supporting the Organizations That Support the Field of Philanthropy
A number of so-called infrastructure organizations aid philanthropists and especially foundations in their work, including

- knowledge-building organizations like the Bridgespan Group, the Center for Effective Philanthropy, Grantmakers for Effective Organizations, and FSG Social Impact Advisors;
- membership organizations like the Association of Small Foundations, the Council on Foundations, Independent Sector, the National Center for Family Philanthropy, and the Philanthropy Roundtable; and
- regional associations of grant makers, such as the Donors Forum of Chicago, Northern California Grantmakers, and the Southeastern Council of Foundations.

In many cases, the membership or conference fees you pay do not cover the full costs of the benefits these organizations provide. To the extent that you benefit from their work, directly or indirectly, it makes sense to sustain and strengthen them through grants in addition to whatever fees they charge.

Acquiring and Disseminating Knowledge from Your Own Work

We have discussed philanthropy's support for knowledge and the important role of knowledge in philanthropy. Yet we know of few fields where knowledge is less systematically collected and disseminated—especially knowledge about the success (or not) of particular initiatives. We think this is less because philanthropists want to hide their failures than because they don't spend much time or money on evaluation. And this, in turn, is often because their goals are unclear.

Strategic philanthropy requires clear goals and constant feedback on progress in achieving them. Sharing evaluations with the field may well take more time and effort than just getting evaluations for your own use, but helping others learn from your experience can multiply the impact of your grantmaking.

Ethical Behavior and Good Governance

The increasing size of philanthropy is being accompanied by increasing interest and scrutiny by legislatures, regulatory agencies, and the press. One scandal can nullify hundreds of stories of the good that philanthropy does.

Philanthropy is already a privilege because of the tax breaks it offers. This privilege carries special responsibilities with respect to governance, among which is addressing conflicts of interest. So with the disclosure that one of the authors (Paul) was a member of the Panel on the Nonprofit Sector organized by Independent Sector, we strongly recommend that you and your trustees read its *Principles for Good Governance and Ethical Practice: A Guide for Charities and Foundations*[2] and consider how they apply to your own organization. (We should also inform you that the Philanthropy Roundtable, an organization of mostly conservative foundations, has voiced its disagreement with what it terms the panel's "one-size-fits-all" approach.[3])

Responsibilities to Society: First, Do No Harm[4]

Like a car repair manual, a guide to strategic philanthropy is essentially value neutral. The manual can be used equally to fine-tune an ambulance or the getaway car for a bank heist. By (almost) the same token, our book is useful for the pursuit of a wide variety of philanthropic goals, and some people, ourselves included, will regard certain of these goals as wrong-headed or even loathsome. When philanthropy addresses some of the hot-button issues that divide the citizens of our pluralistic society, it is inevitable that one person's ambulance is another's getaway car. Indeed, even when goals, such as poverty alleviation or improved education, are widely shared, there may be differences about the appropriate ways to achieve them—for example, voluntary private action versus government regulations.

Various justifications have been offered for the broad discretion enjoyed by philanthropy. For example, Kenneth Prewitt argues that philanthropy promotes polyarchy (government rule by many constituencies and interest groups), which is an important value in a pluralistic society.[5] In any event, the permissible breadth permitted to both ends and means is a fact of philanthropy in the United States. What does this entail for the strategic philanthropist?

It certainly doesn't mean giving up your values. Philanthropy has supported and opposed some of the nation's most important—and divisive—social changes, from the civil rights movement to the conservative anti-regulatory agenda of the Reagan and Bush years, from abortion rights to the right to bear arms. But we believe that this freedom imposes certain responsibilities on both philanthropists and their grantees:

> To base their strategies and activities on sound evidence
> To be fair and accurate in their public pronouncements
> To remain open to arguments about facts and perhaps even values.

If these are the responsibilities of policy makers and even ordinary citizens in a liberal democracy, they are especially strong for philanthropists because of the enormous power they wield: the power of the purse, which sometimes matches the resources of governments, but which is not subject to the constraints that make governments accountable.

We said at the start that strategic philanthropy is about making the world a better place. The intervening pages have included many examples of efforts to do this—some successful, some not. We hope that this book encourages you to be ambitious and willing to take risks. But your ambitions should be tempered by what is realistic to achieve, and the risks should be with your own capital and reputation, not with others' well-being.

The eighteenth-century English statesman and philosopher Edmund Burke cautioned that society consists of enormously complex networks of institutions, practices, and relationships beyond the grasp of politicians and policy makers, and that heroic efforts to improve matters can have disastrous, unanticipated consequences. Although you wouldn't expect the authors of a book on strategic philanthropy to be Burkean conservatives—and we're not—it would be an error to ignore his insights.

Strategic philanthropy is about improving the world, but it is not about heroic efforts. It is about intentionality and focus. Many of the examples in this book involve disseminating knowledge, supporting innovative technologies, building neighborhood and community organizations, helping individuals achieve their highest potential, and changing people's minds through education and argument. Smart strategies usually begin with pilot projects to test their actual effects.

But strategic philanthropy also includes efforts to change government policies in areas such as education, the environment and climate change, population, and international development. Many of these efforts might be characterized as "liberal" or "progressive" in conventional political terms because they seek to enlist government funding and regulatory power. Even advocacy for more autonomy from government, such as protecting civil liberties and promoting school voucher programs, seeks to affect social and economic systems in ways that defy Burkean conservatism.

Assessing the overall record of strategic philanthropy is a task for another book—someone else's, we hasten to say—and a Herculean task at that. In addition to the empirical challenges, there's an inevitable ideological component—inevitable because of philanthropy's diverse values and aims. It's striking that some of the outcomes that Joel Fleishman, a mainstream observer of the field, treats as positive philanthropic achievements are described by the conservative commentator Martin Morse Wooster as "great philanthropic mistakes." In Wooster's view, some not only wasted money but also caused affirmative harm in areas including school reform, medical education, and population.[6]

Citing what he believes to be the mistakes of ambitious strategic philanthropy, the conservative scholar William A. Schambra argues that philanthropy should eschew getting at "root causes" in favor of supporting grassroots community organizations—finding and funding the "unsung community leaders who have particular, concrete ideas about how the neighborhood can be improved, and who can do a great deal with a small grant at a particularly critical time and place."[7] If this "looks suspiciously like charity," Schambra says, that's as it should be: "Charity does indeed deal with 'mere symptoms' because they are what people themselves consider important."[8]

Our book has focused not on the distinction between root causes and charity but on impact. Does a vaccine against HIV/AIDS get at the root cause or a symptom? What about the distribution of condoms or antiretroviral drugs? Strategic philanthropy is about getting the job done effectively.

Listening to communities is extraordinarily important. One of our most hopeful case studies, the Edna McConnell Clark Foundation's support for Harlem Children's Zone, is a prime example of this. But our examples also include the Hewlett Foundation's disappointing efforts to listen to disadvantaged Bay Area communities—hardly the only failure of community-based philanthropy. "Community" is a facile concept that often masks different and even antagonistic interests. In any event, many pressing problems call for regional, national, or global strategies rather than community-based grantmaking.

So where does this leave matters? A wise critic of our manuscript with a Burkean cast of mind noted that strategic philanthropy has a bias in favor of action—of seeing the world in terms of problems to be fixed.[9] But to not act in the face of a perceived problem is also a decision. The best one can do, as we see it, is to heed Burke's cautions about the unanticipated complexities of social change, but not to adopt his bias in favor of the status quo. Those who seek change should bear the burden of proof, but this burden can be met with a sound, empirically based understanding of the situation and a carefully worked-out strategic plan with plenty of feedback at all stages of the process, from design to implementation. That is strategic philanthropy at its best.

Endnotes

1. Joel L. Fleishman, J. Scott Kohler, and Steven Schindler, *Casebook for The Foundation: A Great American Secret* (New York: Public Affairs, 2007).

2. The full report, with discussion, is available on the panel's website, at http://www.nonprofitpanel.org.

3. Adam Meyerson, "We're Not Signing It: Our Concerns About Independent Sector's 'Principles for Good Governance and Ethical Practice,'" *Philanthropy Magazine*, December 17, 2007, http://www.philanthropyroundtable.org/article .asp?article=1510&cat=1.

4. (Mis)attributed to the Hippocratic Oath.

5. Kenneth Prewitt, "The Importance of Foundations in an Open Society," in *The Future of Foundations in an Open Society*, ed. Dieter Feddersen and Bertelsmann Foundation (Gütersloh, Germany: Bertelsmann Foundation, 1999), 17–29; see also *Wikipedia*, s.v. "Polyarchy," http://en.wikipedia.org/wiki/ Polyarchy (accessed June 30, 2008).

6. Martin Morse Wooster, *Great Philanthropic Mistakes* (Washington, D.C.: Hudson Institute, 2006). Compare Wooster's and Fleishman's descriptions of the philanthropic contributions to public television and population control.

7. William A. Schambra, "The View from 1313: A Presentation to the Chicago Grantmakers for Effective Organizations," http://pcr.hudson.org/files/ publications/2008_07_01_Schambra_1313_Strategic_Philanthropy.pdf.

8. William A. Schambra, "The Ungodly Bright: Should They Lead Philanthropy into the Future?" in *Giving Well, Doing Good: Readings for Thoughtful Philanthropists*, ed. Amy A. Kass (Bloomington: Indiana University Press, 2008), 471–478. (The essay is also available online from the Hudson Institute, at http:// pcr.hudson.org/index.cfm?fuseaction=publication_details&id=5372&pubType= pcr_articles.)

9. James Piereson, who is currently a senior fellow and director of the Manhattan Institute's Center for the American University and president of the William E. Simon Foundation, and formerly executive director and trustee of the John M. Olin Foundation.

Index

About the Authors

PAUL BREST is the president of The William and Flora Hewlett Foundation. Before joining the Hewlett Foundation, he was a professor at Stanford Law School, serving as dean from 1987 to 1999. He teaches a course on judgment and decision making in the Public Policy Program at Stanford University and is coauthor of the forthcoming book *Problem Solving, Decision Making, and Professional Judgment.*

HAL HARVEY, a former director of The Hewlett Foundation's Environment Program, is now the president of ClimateWorks. He is also the president of the New-Land Foundation and has held positions at several different not-for-profit foundations, including the Mertz-Gilmore Foundation, the Heinz Endowments, and the Ploughshares Fund. He served on the energy panel of the President's Committee of Advisors on Science and Technology and chairs the MB Financial Corporation in Chicago.

About Bloomberg

BLOOMBERG L.P., founded in 1981, is a global information services, news, and media company. Headquartered in New York, Bloomberg has sales and news operations worldwide.

Serving customers on six continents, Bloomberg, through its wholly-owned subsidiary Bloomberg Finance L.P., holds a unique position within the financial services industry by providing an unparalleled range of features in a single package known as the Bloomberg Professional® service. By addressing the demand for investment performance and efficiency through an exceptional combination of information, analytic, electronic trading, and straight-through-processing tools, Bloomberg has built a worldwide customer base of corporations, issuers, financial intermediaries, and institutional investors.

Bloomberg News, founded in 1990, provides stories and columns on business, general news, politics, and sports to leading newspapers and magazines throughout the world. Bloomberg Television, a 24-hour business and financial news network, is produced and distributed globally in seven languages. Bloomberg Radio is an international radio network anchored by flagship station Bloomberg 1130 (WBBR-AM) in New York.

In addition to the Bloomberg Press line of books, Bloomberg publishes *Bloomberg Markets* magazine.

To learn more about Bloomberg, call a sales representative at:

London: +44-20-7330-7500
New York: +1-212-318-2000
Tokyo: +81-3-3201-8900